Sales and Operations Planning -

Best Practices

Sales and Operations Planning -

Best Practices

Lessons Learned From Worldwide Companies

AGFA US Healthcare
Division of AGFA

Amcor Flexible Packaging Group
Division of Amcor, Ltd.

Cast-Fab Technologies, Inc.

Coca-Cola Midi
Division of The Coca-Company

Danfoss Commercial Compressors
Division of The Danfoss Group

Eclipse, Inc.

Eli Lilly & Company

Engineered Materials Solutions, Inc.
(EMS)

Interbake Foods, LLC
Division of Weston Foods, USA

Norse Dairy Systems
Division of Interbake Foods, LLC

PYOSA S.A. de C.V.
Colors Division

The Scotts Company

Unicorn Medical Company (UMC)

John R. Dougherty and Christopher D. Gray

Partners for Excellence
2006

Note for Librarians: A cataloguing record for this book is available from
Library and Archives Canada at www.collectionscanada.ca/amicus/index-e.html
ISBN   1-4120-8210-2 (softcover)
          1-4122-0066-0 (hardcover)

First printing: May 2006

Partners for Excellence
100 Fox Hill Road
Belmont, NH 03220
1 603 528-0840

John Dougherty
Partners for Excellence
1 603 528-0840
jrd1@partnersforexcellence.com

Chris Gray
Gray Research
1 603 778-9211
cgray@grayresearch.com

Printed in Victoria, BC, Canada. Printed on paper with minimum 30% recycled fibre.
Trafford's print shop runs on "green energy" from solar, wind and other environmentally-friendly power sources.

Offices in Canada, USA, Ireland and UK

Book sales for North America and international:
Trafford Publishing, 6E–2333 Government St.,
Victoria, BC V8T 4P4 CANADA
phone 250 383 6864 (toll-free 1 888 232 4444)
fax 250 383 6804; email to orders@trafford.com
Book sales in Europe:
Trafford Publishing (UK) Limited, 9 Park End Street, 2nd Floor
Oxford, UK OX1 1HH UNITED KINGDOM
phone 44 (0)1865 722 113 (local rate 0845 230 9601)
facsimile 44 (0)1865 722 868; info.uk@trafford.com
Order online at:
trafford.com/05-3176

10 9 8 7 6 5 4 3 2 1

Table of Contents

How to Use This Book   *ix*

Acknowledgements   *xiii*

Introduction   *xvii*

Dedication   *xxiii*

Part I - The Companies, Sales and Operations Planning, and the Results

Chapter 1 - The Companies   *1*

Chapter 2 - Sales and Operations Planning: What and Why   *9*

What Is It and What Does It Do

Demand/Supply and Volume/Mix

Why Do Companies Use S&OP

Chapter 3 - The Monthly S&OP Process   *17*

Data Gathering

Demand Planning

Supply Planning

Partnership Meeting

Executive S&OP Meeting

Global S&OP Meeting

Chapter 4 - Benefits   *37*

    Hard Benefits (Quantified)

    Soft Benefits

Chapter 5 - Lessons Learned   *49*

Part II - Environments and Processes

Chapter 6 - Getting the Product to the Customers   *61*

    Make-to-Stock

    Seasonality

    Make-to-Order

    Finish-to-Order

    Engineer/Design-to-Order

    New Product Development

Chapter 7 - Tools for Linking Volume with Mix   *85*

    Resource Planning: ERP and MRPII

    Distribution Resource Planning: DRP

    APS

Chapter 8 - S&OP and Continuous Improvement through Lean Manufacturing and TQM/6 Sigma   *99*

    Lean Manufacturing

    6 Sigma/TQM

Chapter 9 - S&OP and the Extended Demand and Supply Chains   *113*

    Customer Linking

    Supply Chain Management

    Outsourcing

    Third Party Manufacturing

Chapter 10 - Organizational and Size Issues   *127*

    Small Companies

    Privately-held Companies

    Global Businesses

    Matrix Organizations

    Managing through Changes in Ownership

Chapter 11 - S&OP and Financial Planning   *147*

    Month-to-Month

    S&OP and Budget Preparation

    Planning for Capital Needs

    Managing Cash Flow

Chapter 12 - The Future of S&OP   *161*

Part III - Company Profiles

Chapter 13 - AGFA US Healthcare   *167*

Chapter 14 - Amcor   *179*

Chapter 15 - Cast-Fab   *189*

Chapter 16 - Coca-Cola Midi   *199*

Chapter 17 - Danfoss   *209*

Chapter 18 - Eclipse   *217*

Chapter 19 - Eli Lilly   *225*

Chapter 20 - EMS   *237*

Chapter 21 - Interbake Foods   *247*

Chapter 22 - Norse Dairy Systems   *259*

Chapter 23 - Pyosa   *269*

Chapter 24 - The Scotts Company   *279*

Chapter 25 - Unicorn Medical Company   *289*

Appendix A   *297*

Consultant Biographies

Index   *309*

About the Authors   *319*

How to Use This Book

This is a long book.

Inside you'll find facts and profiles on thirteen companies, descriptions of their processes, as well as the results that they have achieved and the lessons you can learn from their experiences. There are also explanations on how S&OP is used in many different companies, industries and environments, as well as how S&OP works in conjunction with other business processes. We've attempted to make the book as clear and concise as possible, but there is a lot of content.

But please don't be intimidated by the number of pages. It may look like *War and Peace,* but it's not a novel that needs to be read from front to back, unless you wish to. Think of it more as a series of short stories, combined with an encyclopedia. Once you've read the first five chapters in Part I, you can read any or all of the next twenty chapters in whatever sequence suits your interests.

What You'll Find Inside This Book

We've organized the book into three parts and twenty-five chapters to help you find familiar situations and problems, and then quickly identify the ways in which S&OP can work

> **Part I - The Companies, Sales and Operations Planning, and the Results** (chapters 1 through 5)
>
> **Part II - Environments and Processes** (chapters 6 through 12)
>
> **Part III - Company Profiles** (chapters 13 through 25)

Part III tells the stories of thirteen companies, some household names, some not, every one with outstanding experiences to share. We've devoted an entire chapter to each one. The information includes:

➢ A brief synopsis of the company

➢ What's unique about this particular company

➢ Company characteristics including:
   o Size
   o Products

- o Characteristics of the demand side of the business
- o Characteristics of the supply side of the business (plants, suppliers, co-producers)
- o Significant tools, methods, and systems employed to manage the business

➤ Characteristics of the S&OP Process including:
- o Demand planning
- o Supply planning
- o Partnership (middle management) communication and decision-making
- o Executive participation

➤ Hard benefits from implementing S&OP

➤ Soft benefits from implementing S&OP

➤ Lessons learned from implementing S&OP

➤ A consultant's summary - a brief commentary from the consultant who nominated the company and worked with them to implement a successful S&OP process

But the meat of the book is in chapters 3 thru 12 where we draw conclusions and describe the lessons we can learn from the various participating companies in the research. These chapters include:

➤ How the S&OP process works: Chapter 3

➤ Benefits: Chapter 4

➤ Lessons Learned: Chapter 5

➤ How S&OP interacts with different operating environments (in particular different fulfillment strategies, and various demand and supply strategies in the extended demand and supply chain): Chapters 6 and 9

➤ How S&OP affects or is affected by popular management improvement initiatives (ERP or MRPII, advanced planning systems, lean manufacturing and 6 Sigma): Chapters 7 and 8

➤ The effects of size, ownership, and management structure on S&OP: Chapter 10

➤ S&OP and Financial Planning: Chapter 11

➤ The Future of S&OP: Chapter 12

In each area we've interspersed commentary on the model companies, described what they've done and how, and the specific lessons they've learned, along with a few quotes from some of their key executives. And we've used cross-referencing extensively, to make it easy for you to navigate through the book and find what you're looking for.

How Can You Use This Book to Improve Your Own S&OP Process?

We do recommend that all readers take the time to **read all of Part I** (chapters 1 through 5), even those who consider themselves S&OP exerts. People have different views of exactly what is S&OP, and our view may differ from yours. Getting a common understanding and set of terminology will stand the reader in good stead as he or she moves through the book.

Plus, in Chapter 3 we begin to share some of the *notable best practices* of our thirteen model companies. And in chapters 4 and 5, we summarize and consolidate all of the benefits achieved and lessons learned by the companies.

After reading Part I, you can proceed in different ways:

> ➤ Read the rest of the book straight through, from **cover to cover**. This may appeal to people who have a real interest in the specific process definition and application of sales and operations planning: supply chain managers and specialists, software designers, consultants - both internal and external, students, and the like.

> ➤ Or **see how S&OP works differently in individual companies**, by reading the chapters in Part III (chapters 13 through 25) on individual company environments similar to yours - for example "seasonal products" or "sells to mass merchandisers" or "makes-to-order", etc. The tables contained in chapter 1 of the book will help you identify which companies share specific environments or characteristics. Here you can you can see how the different companies address the steps and mechanics of their S&OP processes, and what is similar and what is different from your organization.

> ➤ Or **address a specific situation or approach,** by reading the chapters in Part II (chapters 6 through 12) on different environments and processes that match your interests. These include lean manufacturing (chapter 8), supply chain management (chapter 9), global issues (chapter 10), and others. Each chapter contains the experiences and lessons from the applicable model companies.

Since every reader may not read the book from start to finish, we have intentionally repeated selected company references and quotes in the different parts of the book as described above.

The basic idea is to learn from the best and apply it to your own situation. You don't need to reinvent the wheel to implement a world class process. And while we'd love to provide you with consulting services to make S&OP work better at your company - it is the business we're in - many of you will be able to make an excellent start just by modeling the practices of our thirteen companies.

Acknowledgements

We'd like to thank the following professionals - clients, friends and business associates - who contributed both their time and energy to make this book possible. They provided the raw material for our research efforts and gave valuable suggestions and feedback during the writing. You'll find many of them again and again in the book - in comments and quotes about how S&OP works in the real world. They were critical to improving the quality of our work

Ray Baxter
President and CEO
Interbake Foods, LLC

Bill Belt
President
Bill Belt Excellence

Michel Blanchard
General Manager
Coca-Cola Midi

Ron Bohl
Global Supply Chain Advisor
Eli Lilly & Company

Denise Bullock
Vice President and General Manager Front Royal Plant
Interbake Foods, LLC

Ross Bushman
President and COO
Cast-Fab Technologies Inc.

Marilee Cameron
Former Director, Ortho/RoundUp Planning
The Scotts Company

John Civerolo
Senior Partner
Partners for Excellence

Scott Fullbright
Senior Executive Vice President
Norse Dairy Systems Norse Dairy Systems

Hector Gil
Vice President, Finance, IT and HR
PYOSA S.A. DE C.V., Colors Division

Jack Gips
President
Jack Gips, Inc.

Graeme Hazeldine
General Manager, Flexible Division
Amcor Flexible Packaging Division

Phil Heenan
Managing Director
Phil Heenan Consulting

Malcolm Jaggard
Director Supply Chain Management
AGFA US Healthcare

Bill Kerber
Vice President of Consulting
Future State Solutions

Rémi Lafon
Plant Manager
Coca-Cola Midi

Richard Ling
President
Richard C. Ling, Inc.

Eric J. Olson
COO
Engineered Materials Solutions, Inc. (EMS)

Lach Perks
President
Eclipse, Inc.

Didier Pradeilles
Vice President Global Operations
Danfoss Commercial Compressors

Bob Pryor
President
AGFA Healthcare, Americas

Michel Rabhi
Planning Manager
Coca-Cola Midi

Ken Reiff
Vice President, Product Planning
The Scotts Company

Bob Stahl
President
R.A. Stahl Company

Kevin Stevick
CEO
Engineered Materials Solutions, Inc. (EMS)

Jeff Townsend
Director of Operations
Eclipse, Inc.

Tom Wallace
President
T. F. Wallace and Company

Peter Were
Supply Chain General Manager, Flexible Division
Amcor Flexible Packaging Division

Special thanks to Tom Wallace who kicked off this project and provided help in both the research and the writing. He was immensely helpful in making the book a reality. He is one of the top professionals in our field. Thank you!

Introduction

This is a book that needed to be written.

As one of the most important business processes of the last twenty years, "Sales and Operations Planning - S&OP" sounds like something every company is already doing - and probably doing well. Yet while it is certainly true that most manufacturing companies are doing something with S&OP, just what they **are doing** generally falls far short of what they **could be doing**, or what they thought they would be doing when they launched into it.

For some companies S&OP is mostly "forecasting", for others it's mainly production scheduling and monthly meetings. For some it's detail, for others, high level numbers for management. For those disappointed in the results from S&OP, some attribute it to S&OP being "just another layer of meetings, without any real decision-making." Others blame it on the lack of leading edge software tools.

At the start they're hopeful, but eventually they scoff at the possibility of an S&OP process that fosters cross-functional communication and consensus based decision-making. They no longer see it as the magical link between demand and supply, between the sales people and the manufacturing people, between strategy and tactics, between optimistic objectives and real business results.

As time goes by, the range of definitions and opinions grows. So too the need for a clear understanding of what S&OP is truly about.

Although there has been an increasing amount of material on the subject - books, articles, and instructional videos - there's a real shortage of information from, or about, the best users of this management communications and decision-making process. There are literally hundreds, if not thousands, of companies who have achieved ever increasing benefits from the use of S&OP. So the real challenge is to understand the keys to their success.

How We Got Started Telling Their Stories

Our colleague Tom Wallace saw it first. Having contributed several important texts to the field, including one of the most recent on this subject[1], he wanted to "hear more

---

[1] *Sales & Operations Planning: The How-To Handbook, 2ⁿᵈ Edition* by Thomas F. Wallace, T F Wallace Company

from the frontlines". We've always believed that the best way to guarantee success with any new process or method is to learn from those that have done it well. And for Tom and for us, that meant going back to the best practitioners to document their methods and practices.

People who know us won't really be surprised by the approach. We've been helping companies improve their performance - reduce inventory, increase productivity, reduce cost, improve cross-departmental communications and decision-making- for thirty years now, and our method has always been the same: learn from the best and pass it on. The real "state of the art" in our field, and we suspect others, is driven by practitioners, not by consultants, not by academics and not by software suppliers.

So in early in 2004 Tom recruited one of the authors (John) to organize the effort and do the bulk of the work in organizing the research and writing the book itself. At John's request, Tom agreed to help with the writing, in addition to contributing two model companies for the case studies.

Later, because of shifting priorities, Tom had to drop off the writing team, and was replaced by the other author (Chris). We owe Tom a debt of great gratitude for his overall contribution to this book: helping launch it, contributing two significant case studies to the content, as well as the writing that he did to help us move the manuscript along towards publication.

How We Arrived At These Model Companies

It all seemed pretty simple at the beginning. Identify ten or fifteen of the "best" S&OP users in the world. Send them a questionnaire. Get it back. Write a chapter for each company and then a couple of chapters with "Lessons Learned". Done in a couple of months - a year on the outside. Sit back and wait for the applause.

Needless to say, there was a lot more work than anticipated - and all of it took significantly longer than expected.

First was the problem of identifying the best practice companies. Our strategy was to ask our most trusted colleagues for their clients who did the best job with S&OP. These are all leading consultants in the field - people we have worked with and who have established credentials in getting S&OP successfully operating in companies around the world. We contacted over twenty different individuals, asking each of them to nominate one or more model companies. In the end, about a dozen consultants contacted nearly twenty different companies about the project.

As you might expect, the next problem was to get the companies to participate in the project. For several, the problem was that some of the information was perceived to be confidential. In other cases, it was even worse (or better) - those companies felt that

S&OP was one of their key competitive advantages. Not wanting to give away the corporate "jewels", they bowed out before we ever got started. A few were just too new to the process and felt uncomfortable that it had not yet been sufficiently institutionalized. In a couple of cases, once excellent S&OP users had slipped in performance, recognized it, and chose not to pretend that they were operating at a "best practice" level of performance.

But we did end up with thirteen excellent examples of how S&OP should work. These unselfish companies felt that they had benefited from the experiences of companies before them, and now wished to "pay it back" to other companies. (But to be honest, we think they were all justifiably proud of what they'd done and wanted to show it off a bit!)

How We Got Their Stories

Generally speaking, the information that the companies provided is not publicly published anywhere else - the only place you will find it is in this book But nothing falls into the category of "highly confidential" - you'll find no secret formulas, detailed business strategies, organizational charts, or other company confidential information.

What you will find is an explanation of how S&OP and supporting business processes work at each of the companies - information provided by them, reviewed by them and then validated by them. It isn't just our idea of how it *should* work; it's their description of how S&OP *actually does* work for them.

Initially we sent a detailed questionnaire to each of the thirteen companies, gathering information in the categories listed on page xi and xii above.

The initial responses from the model companies were reviewed and critiqued by the consultants who nominated them. Each of them played a major role in collecting the company information and, even more importantly, making sure we understood it properly. They were the primary point of contact with the model companies, and they provided color commentary on the most interesting aspects of the company and how it uses S&OP.

When one of them would say "you really need to check this out" or "you need to get more detail in this area because what the company is doing is really different", it was a major advantage in getting the full story. We certainly owe them a debt of gratitude for the work they put into this book.

As a final step in this process, each of the thirteen companies reviewed the appropriate sections of the final manuscript to ensure that all the facts were accurate, and that their story was clearly told.[2]

What Can The Best Practice Companies Teach You?

This is really the point of the book - how can your process be improved based on the experiences of these model companies. Here are a few of the things that you may find in this book that will help you:

> How to describe the benefits of the process to help enlist the participation of executive management, as well as key players from sales and marketing, engineering, finance, manufacturing, materials and logistics.

> How to ensure decisions are made at the appropriate organizational level

> Strategies for integrating S&OP with supporting, detailed processes like MPS and forecasting

> The proper approach for using S&OP in make-to-stock, make-to-order, finished-to-order and design-to-order environments

> The best way to integrate new product development processes with S&OP

> How to deal with various configurations of downstream, demand-side sales and distribution channels, and various upstream, supply-side configurations of plants, suppliers, co-producers, etc.

> How S&OP works best with lean manufacturing and/or TQM/6 Sigma

> How you can structure a process that is truly global, one that works well in the often complex, sometimes matrix organizations of global companies

> In general, how to make the S&OP process more effective and more efficient

---

[2] One company, Unicorn Medical Products is a real corporation, but this is not their real name. They were a full participant in this project, provided us with all the necessary data, and were kind enough to review and verify the information being published about them. However, they have also asked that their real name not be used in the book. Respecting their wish to remain anonymous, some of the descriptive data about the company - annual sales dollars, number of employees, number of plants and locations - has been somewhat changed to disguise their identity. However, none of the information about their basic business processes has been modified.

Your Job Versus Ours

We put a lot of work into this book. But in the end our job was easy - we asked questions, we listened, we assimilated and organized the answers, and then we wrote it down and passed it on.

Your job is significantly more difficult.

You must listen and interpret - without getting confused by the differences between companies - taking advantage of the similarities to see how these concepts apply to your situation. Then you have to convince your colleagues and management to implement the concepts in a way that may be different from what they were originally thinking. Having done that you reach the really critical part -making the changes to actually improve how you manage your business through S&OP, with significant benefits the result.

We believe this book can be a valuable tool to assist you in this difficult work ahead and we send you our sincerest wishes that you too will join the ranks of the sales and operations planning best practice companies.

John Dougherty
Partners for Excellence
Belmont NH

Chris Gray
Gray Research
Stratham NH

Dedication

We are grateful to our "professional teachers": our mentors, our colleagues, our clients, and now these thirteen model companies. Not everyone realizes that consultants learn as much from their clients as they teach them. To all these people who have helped us along the way, we dedicate this book.

Part I

The Companies, Sales and Operations Planning and the Results

Chapter 1

The Companies

Who are these companies and why should I care?

Within this book, you'll be able to "go inside" a baker's dozen companies and learn how they use sales and operations planning to run their businesses better. You'll meet large companies and smaller ones, household names and names not widely known, companies whose products you use and companies whose products you've never heard of. You'll also hear from the consultant who helped them implement S&OP.[3]

AGFA US Healthcare
Division of *AGFA*
Greenville, South Carolina, USA
Medical imaging products (Chapter 13)
Consultant: John Dougherty

Amcor Flexibles Packaging Group
Division of *Amcor Ltd.*
Moorabbin, Victoria, Australia
Packaging for consumer packaged goods (Chapter 14)
Consultant: Phil Heenan

Cast-Fab Technologies, Inc.
Cincinnati, Ohio, USA
Castings and metal fabrications (Chapter 15)
Consultant: Tom Wallace

Coca-Cola Midi
Division of *The Coca-Cola Company*
Toulon, France
Beverage and juice products (Chapter 16)
Consultant: Chris Gray

---

[3] There is a commentary from each consultant at the end of each company's chapter in Part III of this book. Each consultant's biography and contact information is in the Appendix

Danfoss Commercial Compressors
Division of *The Danfoss Group*
Trevoux, France
Air-conditioning and refrigeration compressors (Chapter 17)
Consultant: Bill Belt

Eclipse, Inc.
Rockford, Illinois, USA
Industrial process heating equipment (Chapter 18)
Consultant: Bob Stahl

Eli Lilly & Company
Indianapolis, Indiana, USA
Pharmaceutical and animal health products (Chapter 19)
Consultant: Jack Gips

Engineered Materials Solutions, Inc. (EMS)
Attleboro, Massachusetts, USA
Clad metal components for industrial equipment (Chapter 20)
Consultant: Bill Kerber

Interbake Foods, LLC
Division of *Weston Foods, USA*
Richmond, Virginia, USA
Cookies, crackers, and ice cream wafers (Chapter 21)
Consultant: John Civerolo

Norse Dairy Systems
Division of *Interbake Foods, LLC*
Columbus, Ohio, USA
Filling and packaging equipment and baked products for the ice cream industry
(Chapter 22)
Consultant: John Civerolo

PYOSA S.A. de C.V.
Colors Division
Monterrey, Mexico
Industrial dyestuffs and pigments (Chapter 23)

Consultant: John Dougherty

The Scotts Company
Marysville, Ohio, USA
Lawn and garden products (Chapter 24)
Consultant: Tom Wallace

Unicorn Medical Company (UMC)[4]
Milwaukee, Wisconsin USA
Medical devices and supplies (Chapter 26)
Consultant: John Dougherty

A Word About *Best Practices*

The term *best practices* can be misleading. It's not always clear whether the term is used on an absolute basis, or a relative one.

So the question arises: are these companies the thirteen best users of sales and operations planning in the world? We can't say that with certainty. First, we don't know all of the excellent S&OP-using companies and, second, some of the companies we invited to participate in this book elected not to do so.

These may not be the absolute thirteen best, but they are most assuredly *thirteen of the best* - anywhere in the world.

Each of these companies is doing a superb job with sales and operations planning. If your company is new to S&OP, struggling with it, or simply curious as to how other companies use it, you can learn much from these best practice companies: their experiences and the benefits they've achieved. For instance:

➤ Customer service improvements between ten and 40%

➤ Improved market share of 9% (***Danfoss***)

---

[4] Unicorn Medical Products is a real corporation, but this is not their real name. They were a full participant in this project, provided us with all the necessary data, and were kind enough to review and verify the information being published about them. However, they have also asked that their real name not be used in the book. Respecting their wish to remain anonymous, some of the descriptive data about the company - annual sales dollars, number of employees, number of plants and locations - has been somewhat changed to disguise their identity. However, none of the information about their basic business processes has been modified.

➢ Average inventory reductions of about 40%, with some as high as 70% (**AGFA and Unicorn Medical Company**)

➢ Millions of dollars in various cost reductions, with one company totaling $41.3 million over the last few years (**Interbake Foods**)

➢ Data accuracy and performance to plans reaching 95% +

➢ Clarification of functional and personal accountabilities

➢ Improvements in cross-functional communication, and consensus based decision-making: better leadership and better teamwork

➢ For more detail on the benefits each company achieved with S&OP, go to Chapter 4, and to the individual company chapters in Part III of this book.

Another disclaimer we must make concerns timing: as these words are written, each of these companies is doing a first-rate job with S&OP. But that can change. Changes in ownership, changes in management, or other factors can sometimes result in a degradation of a company's performance in a number of areas. It's no different from the companies in Waterman and Peter's book *In Search of Excellence*. When it was written several decades ago, the companies contained in it were excellent; just several years later, a number of them had slipped.

The Companies' Environments and Processes

We've already seen that these thirteen companies differ in their products and in the countries where they're located. They also differ widely in ownership, organization, the challenges they face, and the business processes they employ.

The following pages show three tables categorizing the companies from different viewpoints.

We can see this in Figure 1-1, which shows the companies relative to their business processes and the tools they employ. Let's say that you have an interest in companies using S&OP on a global basis. Looking down the left column to *global S&OP* enables one to see that **AGFA, Danfoss, Eli Lilly** and **Unicorn Medical Company** are making use of that business process. The chapter number associated with each company is also shown so that you can turn right to it should you have interest.

Figure 1-1

THE COMPANIES AND THE BUSINESS PROCESSES THEY EMPLOY

	AGFA	Amcor	Cast-Fab	Coca-Cola Midi	Danfoss	Eclipse	Eli Lilly	EMS	Interbake	Norse	Pyosa	Scotts	Unicorn Medical
Chapter	13	14	15	16	17	18	19	20	21	22	23	24	25
Contract Manufacturing	X			X			X		X	X	X		X
Global S&OP	X				X		X						X
Lean Manufacturing			X		X	X	X	X	X	X			X
Matrix Management	X			X	X		X		X	X		X	X
Order Fulfillment Strategies:													
Design or Engineer-to-Order	X		X		X	X		X		X			
Finish-to-Order	X				X	X		X		X			X
Make-to-Order	X	X	X		X	X	X	X	X	X			X
Make-to-Stock	X	X		X	X	X	X	X	X	X	X	X	X
Supply Chain Management	X			X	X		X	X			X	X	
Total Quality/Six Sigma				X	X		X	X	X	X	X	X	X

Figure 1-2 relates the companies to their operating environment. We can see, for example, that companies *Selling to Mass Merchandisers* include **Coca-Cola, Interbake, Norse**, and **Scotts**. Companies using *Offshore Sourcing* are **AGFA, Coca-Cola Midi, Danfoss, Eclipse, Eli Lilly, EMS, Pyosa** and **Unicorn Medical Company.**

Figure 1-3 relates the companies to the type of manufacturing they perform, breaking down the broader categories from Figure 1-2 into greater detail. For example, in this table we can see companies with sites doing pure assembly operations (**AGFA, Danfoss, Eclipse, Norse** and **Unicorn Medical Company**), those involved in chemical manufacturing (**Pyosa**), consumer products (**Coca-Cola Midi, Interbake, Norse, and Scotts**), etc.

One final observation about the companies - they represent fine examples of manufacturing from all four corners of the world. Among the thirteen companies are major manufacturers in Asia, Australia, Europe, North America and Latin America. Many market and sell their products on every continent except Antarctica.

Coming up in the next chapter: Just what is S&OP and why do companies do it?

Figure 1-2

THE COMPANIES AND THEIR OPERATING ENVIRONMENTS

	AGFA	Amcor	Cast-Fab	Coca-Cola Midi	Danfoss	Eclipse	Eli Lilly	EMS	Interbake	Norse	Pyosa	Scotts	Unicorn Medical
Chapter	13	14	15	16	17	18	19	20	21	22	23	24	25
Annual Sales: S < $100MM, L> $1 Billion [3]	L	S	S	M	M	S	L	S	M	M	S	L	L
Changes in Ownership[4]	X		X		X	X		X	X	X		X	X
Closely Held			X		X	X		X			X		
High Growth[5]	X			X	X	X	X					X	X
Offshore Sourcing	X			X	X	X	X	X			X		X
Primary Manufacturing Type:													
Process	X	X		X			X	X	X	X	X	X	X
Fabrication & Assembly	X		X		X	X		X		X			X
Seasonal and/or Cyclical	X	X	X	X	X			X	X	X		X	
Sell to Mass Merchandisers				X					X	X		X	
Sell to Other Manufacturers	X	X	X	X	X	X		X	X	X	X	X	
Shrinking Markets/Products	X		X		X		X	X					X

[3] These sales volumes refer only to the business unit itself, not the larger corporation. For example, the Coca-Cola division in France is a small percentage of the total sales of The Coca-Cola Company.

[4] These companies were either acquired, spun off, combined with others, or acquired others, or were subject of a merger, LBO or IPO

[5] High Growth can refer either to the total business or to a product line or region.

Figure 1-3

THE COMPANIES AND THEIR INDUSTRIES

	AGFA	Amcor	Cast-Fab	Coca-Cola Midi	Danfoss	Eclipse	Eli Lilly	EMS	Interbake	Norse	Pyosa	Scotts	Unicorn Medical
Chapter	13	14	15	16	17	18	19	20	21	22	23	24	25
Assembly	X				X	X				X			X
Chemicals											X		
Consumer Goods				X					X	X		X	
Food and Beverage				X					X	X			
Foundries and Metal Working			X					X					
OEM and Component Manufacturing			X		X	X		X					
Packaging Material		X								X			
Pharmaceuticals and Medical Products	X						X						X
Software	X												X

Chapter 2

Sales and Operations Planning: What and Why

What is this thing called S&OP and why do successful companies use it?

Let's tackle the second question first: why do so many companies use sales and operations planning (S&OP)? Here are some reasons why, as stated by people from companies featured in this book:

> A CEO said S&OP's capacity to anticipate changes in market demand, coupled with lean manufacturing, has enabled the company to become an industry leader in customer service while cutting inventories by over half.

> A company that has introduced *five times* as many new products as its industry average attributes much of its ability in this arena to its global sales and operations planning process.

> A division president of a consumer goods company claimed that S&OP has had enormous impact in balancing cash flow, cost, and customer service levels.

> The vice president/general manager of a company using lean manufacturing praised S&OP's contribution in integrating value-streams on the supply side with customer groupings in the demand area leading to increased growth and profitability.

> The chief operating officer of a supplier to original equipment manufacturers (OEM's) stated that S&OP provides substantial visibility into future shifts in demand.

> A senior executive vice president pointed out that S&OP is the company's best communication tool.

> Referring to S&OP's use as a tool to monitor business improvements, a vice president of manufacturing stated that the company would not have achieved such a high level of results without it.

> A Sales Vice President referred to S&OP's ability to keep everyone on the same

page and to provide a forum to keep on task.

> Lastly, addressing S&OP's role in enhancing teamwork, a vice president of product planning cited S&OP as a primary catalyst for reaching consensus.

You'll be seeing these and similar views, with names and companies attached, in the pages that follow.

It's obvious that these users of the process are enthusiastic about it. But what actually **is** the process? What's S&OP all about? To get us started, let's look at this definition:

> **Sales and operations planning is a communication and decision-making process:**
> - **to balance demand and supply**
> - **to set plans for volume that will guide the detailed mix, and**
> - **to integrate financial, product development and operating plans**

The first two bullets identify what we call the "four fundamentals": demand and supply, volume and mix. Let's look at the first pair.

Demand and Supply

Figure 2-1

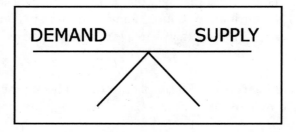

What happens when demand and supply aren't in balance? Well, if demand greatly exceeds supply, bad things happen: customer service suffers, sometimes leading to lost business; costs increase with overtime and premium freight; and quality sometimes "gets lost in the shuffle" as the company strives mightily to get product shipped.

But when supply substantially exceeds demand, other bad things happen: as inventories increase cash flow can become a problem; production rates may be lowered causing underutilization of resources (people and equipment); and/or prices could be cut in an attempt to increase sales, resulting in profit margins getting squeezed.

Not a pretty picture: bad customer service, lost business, higher costs, lower quality and margins, a cash crunch, and the possibility of layoffs.

Is it always bad if demand and supply aren't in balance? No, sometimes it can be a good thing. It all depends on where the imbalance lies. For example, if projected demand ten months in the future exceeds current supply, and if the company can economically add more capacity sooner than that, that's fine. Demand is growing; business is good. Being able to see the projected imbalances soon enough is what's needed, so that *potential* imbalance problems can be eliminated before they become real ones.

So the name of the game is to get demand and supply *in balance over time* and to keep them there. Put processes in place to do it. Have early warning capabilities to alert people that imbalances may occur. Make the adjustments early (and in some cases gradually) so that they can be manageable, as opposed to making large, radical corrections later.

Volume and Mix

The other two fundamentals are volume and mix. If volume is handled effectively, it's much less difficult to deal with mix problems as they arise. Many companies get themselves in trouble because they can't distinguish volume-related problems from those of mix. In the figure below, we can see the difference between the two: volume is the big picture, and mix is the details.

Figure 2-2

Volume versus Mix

Volume	=	The Big Picture:	How Much?
			Rates
			Product Families
Mix	=	The Details:	Which Ones?
			Timing/Sequence
			Individual Products
			and
			Customer Orders

Unfortunately many companies spend almost all of their time on mix. Why is that? It's simple: mix - individual products - is what companies ship to their customers. That's where the pressure is. Mix in the near term is pressing and time-consuming. The effective planning of future volumes may be seen as important, but it carries less urgency.

As a result, many companies set their volumes - sales rates and production rates by product line or family - no more than once per year, when they do their annual business plan. But how often during an average year do volume levels actually need to change? It's almost always more often than once a year. For most companies, it's more than once per quarter.

We submit that many companies don't work hard enough at planning their demand and supply volumes and spend too much time on mix. They overwork the details and don't focus enough on the big picture. Smart companies plan their volumes first, and spend enough time and effort to do it well. They find that doing so makes mix problems much less difficult.

The four fundamentals: demand and supply, volume and mix. Shipping product to customers with world-class reliability and speed requires that all four of these elements be well managed and controlled.

And S&OP is the management process that addresses the balancing of demand and supply volumes, in a way that can guide the detailed mix forecasting, customer order management and supply scheduling. And it does it in a forward-looking way, helping management to identify imbalances (which may be problems or opportunities in disguise). S&OP won't uncover any volume problems that wouldn't be confronted eventually, but it will highlight them *sooner*, when they can be more effectively managed.

A Look Back

Sales and operations planning, the management process that addresses volume, actually evolved from methodologies mostly oriented to managing mix. Back in the 1950's and early 1960's, some leading manufacturing companies developed a new method for managing inventories and making scheduling decisions. This method, material requirements planning (MRP) was then, as it is now, about managing mix - calculating requirements and need dates for manufactured and purchased items.

But MRP's early adopters soon realized that trying to effectively manage the supply mix in the absence of demand visibility didn't really work very well. It needed better integration with all the sources of demand - real customer orders, forecasted future sales, distribution requirements, interplant demands, etc.

And as MRP evolved, it became something more than just a manufacturing system - now linking to strategic and tactical planning in the areas of sales, marketing, new product development, supplier development, resource planning, financial and capital planning, and human resources. It had grown into a management tool: manufacturing resource planning (MRPII) - a company-wide, cross-functional resource planning process - that addressed both volume and mix.

The part of MRPII that looked at volume was originally called "Production Planning", since it tended to focus more on the supply and resource side. But companies came to realize that volume could not be well managed without equal attention being paid to demand. When our consulting colleague Dick Ling proposed renaming the process: "sales and operations planning - S&OP" in 1987, the name change was immediately and widely accepted, since it much better described what made the process successful.

Thus S&OP emerged as a critical part of an overall approach to managing supply and demand: MRPII.

Over the years, companies worked at linking their MRPII process, and the supporting software tools, with their other business processes and software tools. The challenge of accomplishing this in an accurate, timely and repeatable fashion caused problems for many companies. So the software vendors who supplied MRPII packages began to develop or interface other modules or packages that supported functions such as general ledger, accounts payable, accounts receivable, fixed asset management, maintenance and repair, new product development, etc.

Eventually a new term emerged - enterprise resource planning (ERP) - which encompassed all (or most) of the business processes required to run a business, as well as all (or most) of the software tools to support them. In the 1990's, the term ERP not only replaced MRPII, it was extended to encompass non-manufacturing companies and non-manufacturing business processes.

To this day, the term ERP can be used as a synonym for the resource management and planning process previously called MRPII, or it can refer to all the connected business processes of a company, or it can refer to a suite of connected software tools to support these processes.

For simplicity's sake, in this book we will generally use the generic term "resource planning" as a synonym for what used to be called MRPII, and is now often called ERP. And this term does include sales and operations planning (S&OP) as a critical component.

A Word about Terminology

As in any field, over time, the use of terms and acronyms gets sloppy. Some expand the term to include meanings that are important to the user, but which were beyond the scope of the original concept. Others use a term to focus on one particular aspect of its meaning. For example, the broad and narrow uses of the term ERP described above. Or the way some people use the term continuous improvement to mean just lean manufacturing, while others would say it encompasses total quality management and 6 Sigma.

S&OP has not been immune to this practice. Especially today, many people use the term to mean many different things. Some see it is primarily focused on maintaining and improving forecast accuracy. Others use it to mean a process whose primary focus is producing an aggregate supply or production plan (similar to the older term "production planning").

Still others use it in an expanded sense to include the managing of both volume and mix, so that the processes of weekly, item level forecasting, customer order management, and master scheduling, are part of S&OP. Some postulate that we're not very far away from using the term S&OP as a synonym for resource planning, MRPII or ERP.

And there are others who would include all the tactical activities to manage demand and supply in the definition of S&OP, if they are triggered by the S&OP decision-making process. So for example, S&OP by this definition might include elements of sales management, customer management, marketing promotion and pricing, supply chain management, and other similar activities.

The only thing that everyone seems to agree on, is that there is no one single, accepted definition. Some consultants have coined new terms to cover the standard, historical definition of S&OP that we have explained here. These include "Sales, Inventory, and Operations Planning (SIOP)", "Executive S&OP", "Enterprise S&OP", and "Integrated Business Management". There are probably others, and doubtless more will be added to the list in the future. We're sympathetic to the intention of these consultants, since we agree that the terminology waters have been muddied.

However, after careful consideration, we believe these new terms, in fact any new term, will only add to the confusion, rather than clarify the situation. The fact that none of our thirteen best practice companies have adopted these new terms (in fact they generally use the standard terminology that has been around for years), was the clinching argument for us.

Therefore, throughout this book, we will continue to use the term "sales and operations planning - S&OP" to describe this communication and decision-making process focusing on *volume* issues.

We will continue to use the standard historical terms of sales forecasting, demand management, customer order management, master scheduling and capacity planning to reference the related detail-level tools for the managing of mix. See Figure 2-3.

Figure 2-3
Balancing: The Four Fundamentals

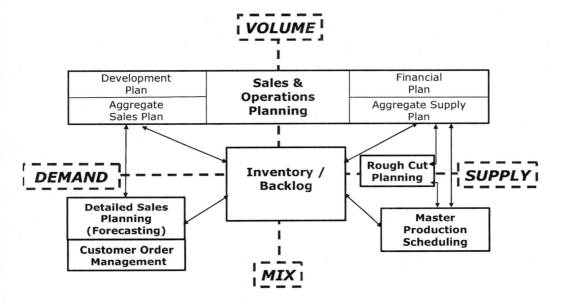

This book focuses on S&OP. But as the thirteen model companies demonstrate, we believe that:

Best practices in sales and operations planning require that the related mix management processes be integrated to S&OP, and be executed very well.

Coming up in the next chapter: how S&OP works.

Chapter 3

The Monthly Sales and Operations Planning Process[5]

What's involved in S&OP, what are the steps, and how does it work?

The essence of S&OP is decision-making. For each product family, and for the business overall, decisions are made on the basis of recent history; analysis, experience and recommendations from middle management; and the knowledge of business conditions and objectives of the executive team. The decisions can be:

➤   Changes to the sales plans (forecasts)

➤   Changes to the supply plans

➤   Changes to the inventory or customer order backlog targets and plans

➤   None of the above, that is, the current plans are okay

These decisions form the authorized plans representing the commitments of all the participants in the process. Therefore it's essential that communication processes work both ways - up to the executive staff for final approval or adjustment, and down to middle and lower management for execution. In other words, once the plans are approved, they must be documented and disseminated throughout the organization.

The approved plans are the overall game plan for sales, operations, finance, and product development. (In fact there's hardly a group within the company that operates independently of the sales and operations plans - HR does hiring and training within the boundaries of the S&OP, the plant engineering and maintenance departments plan equipment maintenance and overhaul schedules around plant shutdowns and shift schedules set by S&OP, quality people may specifically focus improvement initiatives on products with scrap or profitability issues as directed by sales and operations planning, etc.) These functional groups insure that the aggregate plans from S&OP are reconciled to all detailed forecasts and schedules for individual products, customers, regions, plants, and materials.

*"Sales and operations planning is not just a set of meetings - it's the way we run our business."*Graeme Hazeldine, General Manager ***Amcor Flexible Packaging Division***

---

[5] This chapter, with permission, has used extensive material from *Sales & Operations Planning: The How-To Handbook, 2nd Edition.* by Thomas F. Wallace, T. F. Wallace & Co.

Sales and operations planning, as Mr. Hazeldine points out, is not a single event that occurs in a two-hour executive meeting each month. Preliminary work begins shortly after month end (in some of our companies even before that, as we'll see shortly) and continues for a number of days. The steps involve middle management and others throughout the company who impact or are impacted by demand and supply plans. Examples of specific job titles involved in the S&OP process are listed in each company chapter in part III of this book.

The S&OP process typically encompasses:

> collecting data on actual performance - sales against the forecast, production against the supply plan, actual inventory against the inventory plan, current backlog against backlog plan, as well as other business measurements or key performance indicators (KPI's)

> updating the sales forecast

> reviewing the impact of required changes in the supply plans, and determining whether adequate critical resources will be available to support them

> identifying alternative solutions where problems exist

> identifying variances to the business plan (budget) and potential solutions

> formulating agreed-upon recommendations to top management regarding critical changes to the plans, and identifying areas of disagreement where consensus has not been reached

> communicating this information to top management with sufficient time for them to review it prior to the executive meeting

> communicating this information to appropriate people throughout the organization - and sometimes to key suppliers, manufacturing partners and customers (this is done at prescribed times throughout the S&OP cycle of activities, depending on each company's policy regarding approvals for change)

"It is difficult to imagine running our business today without the SOP process. It has become the way we plan and run the business. SOP is the key process for ensuring accurate, honest, and timely internal communications between all functional areas on what we are going to do and how we are going to do it to meet the needs of our customers." Ray Baxter, President and CEO ***Interbake Foods, LLC***

Thanks to the work that's gone before, the monthly executive S&OP Meeting should not take a long time - for eight of our model companies this ranges between thirty and one hundred twenty minutes, the other 5 companies spend between ninety and one hundred eighty minutes. The net result for the top management group should be less total time in meetings (many "ad hoc" meetings may be eliminated), more productivity in their decision-making, and a higher quality of work life. And most of the middle-management people involved in the earlier processes will experience the same benefits.

Another point about timing concerns elapsed time: How long should it take to complete the entire cycle from start to finish (the executive meeting)? All thirteen of our best practice companies have cycles lasting about three to four weeks. Size, geography, and organizational complexity are among the factors contributing to this.

So the month is nearly over. Isn't this a problem? No, it need not be. And the reason why gets at what the S&OP process is all about. It's not a detailed scheduling meeting; it's not a shortage meeting; it's not a meeting to decide which customer orders are going to ship next Tuesday. Rather, it's a medium- to long term planning process, focusing primarily on months two through six and the end of the fiscal year. Planners and schedulers are free to change the mix - the individual products in a family - within the current month, limited by the volume boundaries authorized in the S&OP process, and short term material and capacity availability.

If volume changes are sometimes needed within the current month, one of three approaches can be helpful:

1. Push the authority (within some prescribed limits) to make these decisions down lower in the organization, so that the changes can be made and implemented earlier in the month and in the S&OP cycle, as is done at *AGFA.*
2. Move up the finish date for the S&OP process by compressing the whole cycle (*Cast-Fab*)
3. Start the cycle before month end so the finish date is earlier in the next month (see the "Starting Point" paragraph below).

Let's now take a look at each of the steps in the S&OP process shown in Figure 3-1.

Figure 3-1

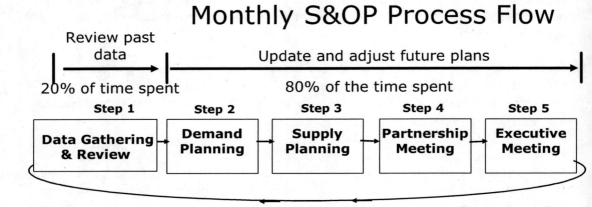

Step 1 - Data Gathering and Review

Much of this activity occurs within the information systems department, and it happens shortly after the end of the month. It consists of four elements:

1. Updating the files with data from the month just ended - actual sales, production, inventories, and so on.

2. Generating information for sales and marketing people to use in developing the new forecast. This could include sales analysis data, statistical forecast reports, key performance indicators (KPI's) on demand, service level data, inventory levels and worksheets for field sales people.

3. Generating information for supply chain, planning and manufacturing people to use in reviewing and updating supply plans. This could include actual production and purchasing data, KPI's with respect to supply, capacity information and inventory numbers.

4. Disseminating this information to the appropriate people.

Notable Practices of Our Model Companies:

➢ **Starting Point:** To make S&OP a timely process overall, it's important that this step be completed within a very few days after the end of the month at the very latest. Some companies, where demand is relatively stable or where there is a significant backlog of unshipped customer orders, start Step 1 before month end.

o   ***Pyosa*** begins this step during the last week of the month.

o   At ***Coca-Cola Midi***, it starts two weeks prior to the end of the month, with preliminary results used to project performance over the balance of the month. These numbers are used up to the end of the month, at which point the process switches to actual results.

o   This provides both companies the ability to make do-able changes to near term plans.

➢ **Families:** All companies maintain and use item (SKU) level data. But since S&OP is about managing volume, this data is presented in a smaller number of S&OP families, since the item-level mix will be managed by the detailed forecasting and master scheduling processes.

Occasionally, sales and marketing people may wish to define families in one way - say by region, or market or type of customer, while people from operations may wish to look at families based on manufacturing technology employed, or plant locations. The item level data can be rolled up to both of these groupings for the appropriate review. However, once the demand and supply data is combined for each family for review at the partnership, and sometimes executive meetings, an official "S&OP Family" grouping must be used. Often this is the sales family. Sometimes a third (often higher level grouping) is used, like that described for ***Unicorn Medical*** Company below.

o   Six of our companies use between four and seven families

o   Seven companies use between twenty and thirty

o   Three companies consider "major" products with multiple sizes or packages as families. ***Eli Lilly*** looks at forty-five "minor" products only in the earlier stages of the S&OP process, with the twenty-five "major" products the focus of attention through the whole process

o   Two companies use "subfamilies" to review and develop forecasts and supply plans. They then aggregate these into families. For example, at ***AGFA***: one hundred subfamilies aggregate to five families. At ***EMS***, twenty-three subfamilies become seven families

o   ***Amcor*** and ***Cast-Fab*** look at major customers

o   Three companies look at "major" SKU's as well as families (***Interbake, Norse Dairy Systems*** and ***Scotts)***

- o ***Unicorn Medical Company*** also aggregates their twenty-seven families into five business lines and ten product categories

- ➤ **Planning Horizon:** S&OP is a medium- to long- term planning process. S&OP plans should be compared to the annual business plans, and is often the starting point for developing these annual plans and budgets. Therefore it should encompass rolling monthly (or quarterly further out) demand and supply plans at least twelve to eighteen months into the future.

  All of our thirteen companies maintain horizons between twelve and twenty-four months

  - o Seven companies focus on the next six to eight months, but extend or expand the data to twelve to twenty months when needed

  - o Six companies maintain a minimum of eighteen months, expanding to eighteen to thirty-six months when needed

  - o ***Eli Lilly*** maintains an additional 5 years of planning data, updated quarterly, to encompass new product planning, and manufacturing sourcing and facility planning

Step 2 - The Demand Planning Phase

"S&OP allows us - and forces us - to lift our heads up and look out into the future." Ross Bushman, President and COO, ***Cast-Fab Technologies***

The demand planning phase is where people review the information (actual sales performance data and KPI's), they received from Step 1. They analyze and discuss it, and generate the new management forecast for the next twelve or more months (including both existing products *and* new products).

It's the job of people in sales and marketing management to use their knowledge of the products, the customers and the marketplace to come up with the *management* forecast (as opposed to the statistical forecast, usually generated by a forecasting software package, which often is used as a starting point). That is their responsibility. And, actually, it's also in their best interest, since the computer can't be held accountable for errors in the statistical forecast, but these people should be responsible for planning and executing their management forecast.

In many companies the management forecast is more accurate than any statistically generated projection. Why? Because the statistical forecast is based heavily on past history. As long as the future is going to be much like the past, then everything works well. But usually changes in the product line, the customer base, the competition, promotion plans, the economy, and so on, can make the future quite different from the past. It's the job of *people,* using their innate intelligence and their knowledge of current conditions and the expected future outlook, to adjust the statistics and establish the best forecast possible.

Involving the folks in new product development is important here. They often have the best handle on the latest *timing* of new product launches. Sales and marketing should have already developed forecasts, and these should be periodically reviewed for possible changes. The current expected new product demand must be included here so that the Supply people can make appropriate plans. This should include new product launches currently underway plus others expected to be launched within the S&OP planning horizon.

The forecasts of future demand are usually best made in units and then translated into dollars. This can be used as a "sanity check" of the updated forecast before it goes further. It also can provide early warning for revenue, profitability or budget problems. This can give sales and marketing an opportunity to adjust their plans (and sometimes the supporting activities) to better meet the business objectives, rather than experiencing an unpleasant surprise later on. People from finance should be involved in this to help the responsible managers compare, validate and reconcile the latest forecasts to the company's financial targets and plans.

Since the output from this demand planning phase is the management-approved forecast, it's often worthwhile to get the senior sales and marketing executive into the loop earlier rather than later. In some companies, the forecasters make a brief presentation of the updated forecast to the Vice President of Sales and Marketing. Bringing the senior executive into the process at this point does several things:

> It allows him or her to ask questions, challenge the numbers, challenge the assumptions, and if need be, change some of them.

> It avoids surprises at the executive meeting.

> It results in a truly "management-approved forecast," one that all of the key players have bought into. This forecast then represents sales and marketing's best estimate of future demand.

Notable Practices of Our Model Companies:

> **Demand Planning Review Meetings:** Do our best practice companies have formal demand review meetings? Some do and some don't. In general, the larger companies tend to hold a formal meeting to get the management forecast nailed down, while frequently the smaller companies have a series of smaller, somewhat less formal face-to-face sessions.

o Nine of our companies have one to ten meetings each, with between three and ten attendees

o *Amcor, Coca-Cola* and *Scotts* have specific meetings with major customers

o *Scotts* has ten monthly meetings: six with major customers, then four by major brand or product line, each of which lasts four to six hours, since individual SKU's are reviewed

o *Eli Lilly* has 130 sales affiliates (internal country or region specific sales departments within the company) each of which has a monthly meeting with three to eight attendees

➤ **Level of Detail Forecasted**:

o Eight companies generated at least some of their forecasts at the item (SKU) level, then aggregated these into family totals. These companies had mostly make-to-stock products.

o Three of the companies generated family forecasts for make-to-stock products for a future part of the horizon. Using typical mix percentages, these family #'s were then disaggregated into SKU level forecasts.

o Three companies generated at least some of their forecasts at the family or model level. Generally, these were for design-, make- and finish-to-order products

o *AGFA* and *Eclipse* generated all their forecasts at the subfamily level, then aggregated them into family totals.

Step 3 - The Supply (Capacity) Planning Phase

Coupled with the effectiveness of lean manufacturing, S&OP has transformed our job shop, customer order-by-order approach to one where we anticipate changes in market dynamics, with the production ability to respond. As a result, we've become the service leader in many of our markets, even though inventories (which many of our competitors view is the only way to service the market) have been reduced by over 60%." Kevin Stevick, CEO, **Engineered Materials Solutions (EMS)**

The supply planning phase is the responsibility of people in operations (or manufacturing and/or supply chain management) responsibility. Their first step is to modify the supply plans for any families or sub-families that require it based on changes in the size of the customer order backlog, the sales forecast, inventory levels, or material and capacity availability. Also, poor past performance in any single area, or performance that is slightly off target in several different areas (like actual production slightly low and sales slightly high) may force adjustments to the supply plan.

Outputs from the supply planning step include information on future capacity issues, including any impact of new product development trials, testing or sample production, on standard manufacturing resources. Any supply problems that cannot be resolved or that require decisions further up the organizational ladder, must be identified.

In some cases, demand (as expressed by the customer order backlog plus the forecast) simply exceeds supply by too great a margin: the constraints cannot be overcome within the time allowable. Sometimes these constraints are in the company's internal resources, at other times they may exist elsewhere in the supply chain, i.e., at outside suppliers. Occasionally, acquiring the resources necessary to meet the demand may be feasible, but will require spending that can be authorized only by top management. These are the kinds of issues that the supply folks carry into the partnership meeting.

Notable Practices of Our Model Companies:

➤ **Supply Planning Review Meetings:** As with demand planning, some companies will conduct a formal meeting for this supply planning step, while others find it more effective to simply work the process informally one on one.

  o Four companies have between one and three meetings each, with between four and ten attendees in each

  o *Norse Dairy Systems* has four plant-based, product line specific "Demand and Operations Planning -D&OP" meetings focusing mainly on production issues

  o *Coca-Cola Midi* holds a "Monthly Operational Meetings with Suppliers" *after* the final Executive S&OP meeting, covering four suppliers representing 71% of their total juice product volume.

  o *Lilly* has a monthly meeting at each of their twenty-four plants, plus two "Hub" meetings that review groups of major third-party manufacturers

➤ **Level of Detail Planned:**

  o At least nine of the companies first develop their supply plans at an item (SKU or module) level, and then aggregate them up to family totals.

  o Six companies with design-to-order, make-to-order and finish-to-order products establish supply plans at a model or family level, and then use "planning bills of material" to drive their detailed material planning.

o **Interbake Foods** and **Norse Dairy Systems** plan their make-to-stock items at the item level for their eight to twelve week master scheduling horizon. Beyond that, they use family production plans and "planning bills of material" to drive their detailed material planning.

Steps 1 through 3: Managing Volume or Mix?

Both!

Data gathering and review, by its very nature, starts at the item (SKU) level and is aggregated into family totals. As we highlighted in the "Notable Practices" sections above, more than half of our companies start their demand and supply planning at the detail level, then summarize it by family. Those that forecast and plan at a more aggregate level, use those numbers in conjunction with "planning bills of material" to drive their detailed planning.
So you can see that Steps 1 through 3 drive not only the S&OP process, but the detailed forecasting and master scheduling processes as well. This overlap probably helps explain some of the confusion around terminology (the scope of S&OP), that we addressed in chapter 2.

Step 4 - The Partnership Meeting

Objectives of this meeting include:

➢ discussing, challenging, and validating the demand and supply plans, and the assumptions that underlie them

➢ making decisions regarding the balancing of demand and supply

➢ reviewing progress on action items assigned in the previous meeting

➢ resolving problems and differences so that, where possible, a single set of decisions or recommendations can be presented to the executive meeting

➢ identifying those areas where agreement cannot be reached and developing, where appropriate, scenarios showing alternate courses of action to solve a given problem (for example, sales wants an immediate supply plan adjustment requiring premium air freight and overtime expense to preserve service level, while operations wants to phase in a capacity increase to minimize costs, using up safety stocks to keep the service level high)

> ➤ setting the agenda for the executive meeting and determining how each issue will be presented

The key players in this meeting typically include several of the people from the demand planning phase, including someone from product development, operations people from the supply planning step, one or more representatives from finance, and It will also include the person with the overall responsibility for the maintenance and execution of the S&OP process (if not one of the above).

Their job is to do a family-by-family review of the updated S&OP spreadsheets[6] (including subfamilies where they exist), and to make adjustments where appropriate. They also check for resource constraints and, where found, establish demand priorities by product, market and/or customer (of course, this can only be done by sales and marketing people).

The outputs from the partnership meeting include:

> ➤ An updated financial view of the business, including matching the latest sales plan to the business plan for the total company. This is typically done on a rolled-up, dollarized display covering all families.

> ➤ Recommendations as to the future course of action for each product family, corresponding to the numbers on the updated spreadsheets:
>
> o Stay the course, no change
> o Increase/decrease the demand plan, and/or
> o Increase/decrease the supply plan.

> ➤ New product launch issues not covered within the product family review

> ➤ A recommendation for each resource requiring a major change: e.g., add people, add a shift, add equipment, offload work to a sister plant, outsource, or reduce the number of people or shifts

> ➤ Identified areas where a consensus decision could not be reached, possibly as a result of disagreement or where competing alternatives might be "too close to call." In such cases, it's often very helpful for alternative scenarios to be presented - Plan A, Plan B, Plan C - with dollarized data as well as units, to show the financial impact.

> ➤ Recommendations for changes to demand/supply strategies, inventory guidelines and/or lead times, where appropriate.

---

[6] Screens or documents that show actuals and future plans for demand, supply, inventory levels, customer order backlogs, for past and future months, for each family or subfamily. These can be presented in tabular (like an Excel spreadsheet) and/or graphical format. See chapter 6 for examples of spreadsheets for make-to-stock and make-to-order environments.

> ➤ A list of tabled issues that needs to be reviewed in the future for a decision. For example, a required capacity increase (like hiring and training additional people) that may be needed ten months in the future, where the lead time to do it is three to four months

> ➤ The agenda for the executive meeting.

To sum up, the partnership meeting is not just a "get-ready" session for the executive meeting. It's actually a lot more than that, because the partnership meeting is a *cross-functional communication* and *decision-making* session. The mindset that the partnership meeting participants should have is: "If this were our business, what would we decide to do?"

"*S&OP establishes base plans for production and sales to measure their performance. We put all of our energy into limiting problems, avoiding organizational arguments, and achieving these plans.*" Glen Melanson, Vice President, Reagent Manufacturing, **Unicorn Medical Company Corporation**

A Word About Terminology

In the early days of S&OP this meeting was called "The Pre-S&OP Meeting". In those days, the focus was often on just "preparing" the data so the executives could make all the decisions in the executive meeting. And in large, complex, and global companies, where multiple meetings were scheduled before the executive meeting, all of them were often referred to as "pre-S&OP meetings".

As the process evolved over time, and more decision-making occurred at this meeting, some began to call it the "partnership meeting".

Currently, different companies and different consultants use different terms including: "pre-S&OP meeting", "compromise meeting", "reconciliation meeting", and others. Regardless of the name, in companies successful with S&OP, the content of these meetings tends to consistently match what we described above.

We use the term "partnership meeting" with our clients, in all of our speeches and writings, and in this book, because we have found our clients respond well to this term that implies cross-functional, consensus-based teamwork. The companies in this book use varying terminology including: "partnership", "pre-S&OP" and "compromise" meetings.

Notable Practices of Our Model Companies:

➢ **Number of Meetings:**

  o *Amcor* and *Cast-Fab* have NO partnership meeting due to their size and compressed organization levels. *Amcor* and *Cast-Fab* executive meetings last two hours and one hour, respectively.

  o *Eclipse* originally had no partnership meeting, but recently has established one even though the attendance overlaps with the executive meeting.

  o *EMS* and *Pyosa* hold one meeting covering all their products.

  o *Coca-Cola Midi* has had two different meeting configurations - when they were smaller, there was no partnership meeting, but the executive meeting was followed with a communications meeting for other people affected by the S&OP decisions. Today, *CCM* has both a partnership and executive meeting, but follow that with an additional meeting with the outside suppliers of all their juice products (72% of their volume)

  o *Danfoss* has three, by region (continent)

  o *AGFA, Interbake Foods* and *Norse Dairy Systems* have multiple meetings by product line (2, four and 5, respectively)

  o *Lilly* has four quarterly, "global Compromise" S&OP meetings, focusing on their four global manufacturing networks.

  o *Unicorn Medical Company* has ten meetings, one for each product line

  o *Scotts* has ten, six by major customer, then four by brand

➢ **Length of Meetings:** they last between thirty minutes and three hours

  o Three last sixty minutes or less

  o Nine last between ninety and one hundred twenty minutes

  o Fifteen can last between three and six hours

➢ **Number of Attendees:** there are between four and twenty-five attendees in each meeting, most between eight and fifteen

- o Twenty-seven have between four and nine attendees

- o Ten have between ten and fifteen attendees

- o Four have about eighteen attendees

- o Two have twenty-five attendees

Other Evolutionary Changes are described in the "Making It Work" section of *Chapter 5 - Lessons Learned*

Step 5 - The Executive Meeting

This is the culminating event in the monthly cycle. Its objectives are:

➤ To approve or make decisions on each product family: accepting the recommendations from the partnership meeting team or choosing a different course of action

➤ To authorize changes in production or procurement rates, where significant costs or other consequences are involved

➤ To compare the dollarized version of this latest set of plans to the business plan and, where they deviate, decide to:

- o Initiate changes to sales, marketing, production, procurement or product development tactics and activities to bring the plans back in balance, and/or

- o Adjust the demand or supply plans, and/or

- o Adjust the business plan, as appropriate

➤ To "break the ties" for issues where the partnership meeting team was unable to reach consensus

➤ To review customer service performance, other critical KPI's, new product issues, special projects, and other issues - and make the necessary decisions

➤ Outputs from the executive meeting include the meeting minutes, which spell out the decisions that were made; modifications to the business plan, if any; and the final version of the S&OP planning numbers (including any changes) approved at the executive meeting

This group typically will include the president (general manager, COO, CEO) and vice presidents (directors) of most major functions, including sales, marketing, product development (design engineering), supply chain management (logistics, planning), manufacturing (operations), finance, and human resources. It will also include the person with the overall responsibility for the maintenance and execution of the S&OP process (if not one of the above).

Most executive teams for S&OP are include other people who can add value to the process, people with titles like demand manager, product manager, sales manager, customer service manager, supply chain manager, plant manager, materials manager, master scheduler, supply planner, controller, and new product coordinator.

"With the S&OP process we get to speak the same language and use the same numbers between all departments, helping us to make decisions more intelligently and effectively." Emilio Assam, President, **Pyosa**

Notable Practices of Our Model Companies:

➢ **Separate, Stand-alone Executive S&OP meeting** (rather than making S&OP a topic in an existing meeting)

For each of our thirteen companies, as well as for hundreds of others we've worked with over the years, S&OP was implemented with a new executive management meeting devoted to dealing with demand and supply issues.

Sometimes, in the interest of time management we see companies try to make S&OP an agenda topic in an executive review meeting that already exists. This approach is high risk, since at the start, S&OP deserves high priority and attention to get it focused, fine tuned and working effectively and efficiently. It may take between two and four months until the meeting evolves to this state.

Without the proper, focused executive attention, the meeting may never reach this level of effectiveness. In some cases, the process is either totally abandoned or lacks the proper executive participation.

Once the process, and especially the executive meeting, has matured, stabilized and been institutionalized as a key part of the communications structure of the company, the executive meeting is sometimes merged into a broader executive meeting, but with S&OP as a major segment (see **Interbake Foods** and **Unicorn Medical Company**).

> **Number of Meetings:**

- o *Unicorn Medical Company* has five separate meetings, for their five lines of business, with a designated meeting leader, who is not organizationally in charge of the attendees

- o *Lilly* has four quarterly, "global" Network S&OP meetings, one for each of their four global manufacturing networks, with major focus on capacity utilization, allocation of production responsibilities, and planning for introducing new products and outsourcing old products.

- o The other eleven companies have one meeting each

> **Length of Meetings:** the length of the meetings varies between thirty and one hundred eighty minutes

- o Four are between thirty and ninety minutes

- o Four are between sixty and one hundred twenty minutes

- o One is between ninety and one hundred eighty minutes

- o Seven (including the five at *Unicorn Medical Company*) are one hundred eighty minutes long

> **Attendees:**

- o Eleven include the chief executive in attendance, only *Lilly* and *Unicorn Medical Company* do not (in these larger, more complex organizations, the final responsibility and authority for detailed decision-making on supply, demand, inventory and related issues rests at a level below the CEO)

- o Five companies have between eight and twelve

- o Eight have between thirteen and eighteen

Other Evolutionary Changes are described in the "Making It Work" section of *Chapter 5 - Lessons Learned*

Figure 3-2 is an expanded version of Figure 3-1, showing the 5 Steps described above, along with a list of the detailed activities that occur at each step.

Figure 3-2

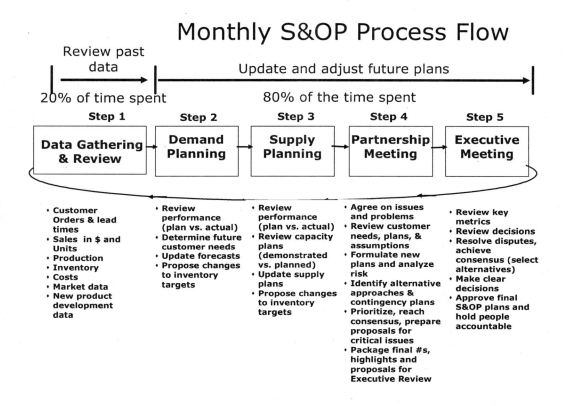

Global S&OP

A special problem exists for large multi-national corporations, operating around the world and wanting to achieve a high degree of coordination. In other words, coordinate globally; act locally.

Before we get into the nitty gritty of this, let's review some fundamentals. S&OP balances demand and supply, and it integrates operational plans and financial plans. So, with a business operating globally, these processes need to occur globally as well as locally.

In these kind of organizations, the sales (and occasionally marketing) responsibilities often reside in separate, regional organizations, sometimes called regional sales companies. Sometimes these regional sales companies are called business units (BU's). In other cases, the term BU can refer to global organizations focusing on certain product lines or markets. How sales and marketing responsibilities are organized and named can vary from company to company. For the example below we will use the term BU to mean a regional sales company.

The manufacturing and distribution responsibilities can also be divided by region, or in some cases, by product line, each of which may have multiple regional locations. The data gathering and review responsibilities are sometimes centralized, sometimes divided like the manufacturing side, and in other cases are integrated with the business units. Obviously, a company's particular organizational configuration may necessitate adjusting the generic steps described below.

Please refer to Figure 3-3, which shows the monthly process expanded to include the steps necessary for global coordination, in a company with business units made up of individual sales companies.

Figure 3-3

Multi-Site Global S&OP Time Line

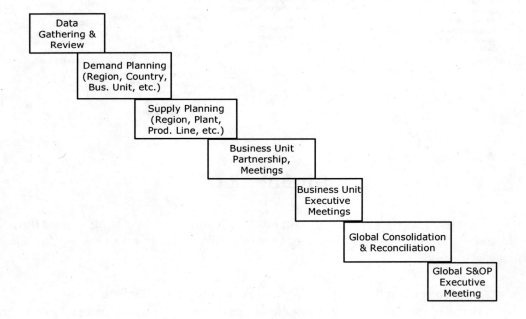

Step 1: Data gathering and review activities can be done centrally or within the business units (BU's) and manufacturing locations.

Step 2: Demand planning is done primarily within the business units. However, sometimes portions of the markets are managed globally, meaning that some central demand people could be involved with the BU's.

Step 3: Supply planning is sometimes done within the business units. Inter-unit demand is demand from one BU that is supplied from another, for example demand from South America supplied by North America. This is treated as a transfer of supply, with the demand showing both in the BU where it originates and the BU from which it will be supplied. Care must be taken in the global consolidation (see step 6) not to add this demand twice.

If manufacturing is not organized along business unit lines, then there must be a step that divides the specific demands from each BU and posts them to the manufacturing organization or location which is their prime supplier. The supply planning is then done by location, or groups of related locations, sometimes with global planning input.

As demand patterns and manufacturing capabilities change, periodic reviews are required to ensure the proper balance and resource utilization. Sometimes this results in changing the sourcing of a specific product for a specific BU to a different manufacturing location. This is often done annually, with quarterly reviews and smaller adjustments where necessary. The S&OP process is particularly critical to support this (see *Eli Lilly*).

Steps 4 and 5: The business unit partnership meetings and executive meetings are held within the BU's in much the normal fashion. These meetings often require representation from key manufacturing locations or organizations. Again, one difference might be the need, on occasion, to re-communicate across business unit boundaries in order to achieve a balance of demand and supply.

Steps 6 and 7: The global consolidation and reconciliation process and the global executive meeting are of course done centrally and attended (often electronically) by key players from the business units, manufacturing organizations, and any other functions not a part of the BU structure. This is where reviews and adjustments of the rolled-up financials take place, as well as any rebalancing of global demand and supply. Rebalancing at this level occurs rarely, because it's almost always handled among the BU's and their supplying manufacturing locations, during the earlier steps in the S&OP cycle.

Please note: the model described here is for an organization (an entire corporation or perhaps a division thereof) primarily in one line of business, operating globally. On the other hand, a true conglomerate would execute the process somewhat differently. The global model shown here could work nicely for each business, within the conglomerate. However, for a conglomerate, at the corporate level, the overall global process would consist almost exclusively of financial reviews, because balancing demand and supply across different businesses with widely different products and resources is rarely practical.

"S&OP is a universal business process at Lilly. It is hard to move throughout the company and not have a large contingent of people who understand it, support it and are responsible for some element of its success." Ron Bohl, Global Supply Chain Specialist, ***Eli Lilly and Company***

Notable Practices of Our Model Companies:

See Chapter 10 - *Organizational and Size Issues* for the experiences of a few of our model companies.

Coming up next: a review of the hard and soft benefits achieved by the thirteen model companies.

Chapter 4

BENEFITS

S&OP is like any other business process or approach - if it doesn't produce real business benefits it's not worth doing! Let's review the benefits gained by our thirteen model companies. All of these are described in greater detail in the individual company chapters.

Hard Benefits

Here were talking about benefits that are measurable and quantifiable. Typically they have a direct impact on a company's profit and loss or balance sheet.

An effective S&OP process, in every case, will produce hard benefits. In fact, it wouldn't be an effective S&OP process unless management focused the S&OP process on setting targets for improvements and monitoring selected KPI's to insure the improvements are achieved.

There are many other business processes and improvement initiatives that can achieve similar benefits. For example, a good lean manufacturing initiative will improve supply reliability and shorten lead times resulting in improved customer service. S&OP will inevitably improve customer service as well. And similar improvements could result from ERP, TQM or a formal new product development process.

So what?

Rarely does a company implement S&OP in an entirely static environment. Often they are concurrently pursuing improvements in other processes or launching other major initiatives such as those described in chapters 6 through 11. So how much of the hard benefits can be directly and solely attributed to S&OP, versus the other initiatives? That's a question that's almost impossible to answer exactly. However, managers from our model companies have estimated that without S&OP linked to, and guiding these other processes, improvements in any of the areas described below would've been reduced anywhere from 25 to 50%.

As Glen Melanson, **Unicorn Medical Company's** Vice President of Manufacturing said: *"Without such a good S&OP process, we would have still pursued the same business improvements. But I don't think we would've achieved the same level of results."*

The benefits fall into several categories:

The Customer

"Customer service never reached the level it has now with so little inventory." Guillermo Diaz Trillo, President, **Danfoss Commercial Compressors**

On-time delivery to customers improved between 10 and 40%:

> *Amcor* improved 10%, with a very high customer retention rate, a significant issue in their industry

> Both *Cast-Fab* and *Eclipse* held high customer service levels while sales increased about 40%

> *Coca-Cola Midi* reduced customer service defects by 41%

> *Danfoss* improved from 60% to 90% on one product line, while their market share grew 9%

> *Interbake* has improved from 90% to 98%, and held that level since 1993!

> *Pyosa* improved from 80% to 92%

> *Scotts* went from 91% to 97.8% on all products, with an order fill level to Lowe's at 99.4%, all this while reducing the number of finished goods warehouses by two thirds

> *"S&OP has been a cornerstone in our strategic plan. It has allowed us to provide world-class service on a global level."* Dom Archino, VP Business Development (until recently the VP of Sales and Marketing), one of the prime drivers of S&OP at *EMS*

Cash Flow - Inventory

Inventory levels were reduced by between 12% and 70%, most by 40% or greater over a two to three year time period. For some companies inventory turns increased as much as 300%:

> *The impact of S&OP in terms of balancing prudent cash flow management, cost, and Class A customer service levels has been enormous, as our metrics will attest."* Bob Pryor, President **AGFA Healthcare, Americas**

➢ At *AGFA* even while closing plants and transferring production:

   o customer service was continually improved

   o total inventory was reduced from one hundred twenty days to forty days over the last three years!

➢ *Amcor* cut inventory by 40%, with reduced obsolescence

➢ *Coca-Cola Midi* reduced inventory by 56%

➢ *EMS* reduced inventory by 62%, allowing for a significant improvement in cash flow to meet the tighter targets set to support the LBO, while still meeting customer on-time delivery expectations.

➢ *Norse Dairy Systems* reduced equipment service parts inventory by $600,000, improving turns by 22%

➢ *Pyosa* estimates that inventory is half of what it would have been without S&OP, ERP and TQM

➢ *Scotts* reduced total inventory by $100 million or 33%

➢ *Unicorn Medical Company* reduced inventory by $100 million over three years, which was key in supporting the cash flow requirements necessary to go public

Cost Reduction

➢ *"It is our belief that balancing supply with demand puts you at the point of least cost. This includes overtime, distribution, and factory efficiency. S&OP's main intention is to balance supply with demand and so is one very important variable in the total product cost."* Graeme Hazeldine, General Manager, *Amcor Flexibles Division*

➢ *Amcor* reduced total cost by 2%

➢ *Interbake Foods* achieved savings of $41.3 million over the years in which S&OP, along with their 6 Sigma program called IPM, directed their continuous improvement efforts

➢ Multiple companies achieved distribution and transportation savings of between 5% and 30%

➢ Manufacturing savings in several companies:

- o Downtime reduced by between 20% and 51%
- o Plant efficiency improved between 2% and 33%
- o *Amcor* experienced significant reductions in overtime
- o *Interbake Foods* reduced overfills from 7% to 1.5%, while improving output per man-hour by 33% since 1993
- o *Norse Dairy Systems* reduced scrap by 55%, and overfills of individual packages by 38%

➤ Purchase costs were reduced significantly at *Scotts*

➤ *"The value of S&OP at **Lilly** has been the ability to launch all of our products in a very complex environment without adding significant cost, resources or inventories. We have managed a strong customer service performance metric while controlling our growth in assets. The benefits are not cost reductions, but revenue generation at the most affordable and optimal cost!"* Ron Bohl, Global Supply Chain Advisor, *Eli Lilly*

Capacity Utilization

S&OP doesn't tell a company anything it wouldn't find out anyway! But with S&OP, the problems and opportunities will be identified much sooner, giving the company time to deal with them in a cost efficient and effective manner.

➤ *Cast-Fab* was able to bring back laid-off employees and add to the work force in a planned, orderly way because S&OP provided an "early warning" on the need to increase labor.

➤ *Eli Lilly* optimized the use of "network" capacity (their twenty-four plants plus multiple third-party manufacturers) while controlling risk, and avoiding costs, loss of sales, delays in new product launch and increases in inventory.

New Product Introduction

By linking the overall planning of S&OP to a formal, well managed new product development process, many of the benefits listed in this chapter are facilitated, while new products are launched more quickly, efficiently and in a timely fashion.

"In the past three years we have launched ten new products and met all demand despite two products that sold significantly above the high-side forecast. Without global sales and operations planning,, we would have been driven to reaction mode, which could have resulted in an increase in investment in new assets, a slow down in our launch plans, and/or missed demand opportunities." Dan Gehring, Supply Chain Steward for the *Eli Lilly* "DPN" Network

Cycle Time Reduction

When companies use S&OP to drive improvements in customer service and inventory turnover, they often target cycle time reductions as a means to those ends:

➤ *Coca-Cola Midi* points to reductions in purchasing and customer order processing cycle times

➤ both *Danfoss* and *EMS* used lean manufacturing initiatives guided by S&OP to reduce manufacturing cycle times

➤ the Equipment Group at *Norse Dairy Systems* reduced design time by 27% with a 30% improvement in efficiency, and shortened customer machine order configuration time from forty-five days to four days

Planning Performance

S&OP is where all demand, supply, new product and financial plans come together. It ensures that the detail and aggregate plans are reconciled. Targets won't be met, and decisions will be faulty unless all plans are valid and reliable. S&OP provides the visibility and the forum where management can monitor improvement in planning performance.

➤ Forecast accuracy improved at *Coca-Cola Midi* by 9.7%. Forecast errors fell 90% at *EMS*

➤ Production plan performance by family of at least 98% and Master Schedule performance of at least 95% was achieved by *AGFA, Amcor, Cast-Fab, Coca-Cola Midi, Danfoss, Interbake Foods, Norse Dairy Systems, Pyosa and Unicorn Medical Company,*

➤ Supplier delivery performance of at least 95% was achieved by *Amcor, Coca-Cola Midi, Interbake Foods, Norse Dairy Systems, Pyosa* and *Unicorn Medical Company,*

  o *Coca-Cola Midi* improved from 50% to 95%
  o *Norse Dairy Systems* enjoyed 98% on-time performance from their third party manufacturers

➤ On-time completion of engineering design documents (drawings, bills of material, and specifications) was improved to 98% at *Norse Dairy Systems*

Data Accuracy

With S&OP, every level of management uses the same set of numbers, at the appropriate level of detail. If the base data is not accurate, it quickly becomes obvious to everyone in the S&OP process, since targets will not be met and plans need to be continually altered.

> ➤ *AGFA, Amcor, Coca-Cola Midi* and *Norse Dairy Systems* point out that S&OP visibility has triggered accuracy improvements in inventory records, bills of materials and manufacturing specifications.

Profitability

All of the hard benefits mentioned above, and all of the soft benefits mentioned below, are key ingredients in improving the company's bottom line:

> ➤ Profitability and ROI have increased at *Pyosa* significantly with the careful use of S&OP to optimally allocate scarce capital to the appropriate products and customers

> ➤ *"During the last four years, almost half of the company's increase in earnings has come from supply chain savings: inventory down, manufacturing efficiency up, purchase and transportation costs down. All of these are due to improved planning."* Ken Reiff, Vice President, Product Planning, *Scotts*

Soft Benefits

Though soft benefits may not be expressed in quantifiable numbers, they represent improvements in processes and people that will eventually generate quantifiable hard benefits as described above. They also fall in several categories:

Customer

This is a case where the hard benefits of improved on-time deliveries and shortened lead times lead to soft benefits such as improved customer communications, credibility, relations and satisfaction. As customers begin to perceive greater reliability due to consistent processes and predictable performance, they become much more willing to collaborate with their supplier in areas such as forecasting and new product development. And all of this can lead to an increase in business.

"We use sales and operations planning as a marketing and sales tool, because it enables us to give better customer service. We give prospective customers a write-up of how we do it, along with a copy of Tom Wallace's book." Ross Bushman, President and COO, **Cast-Fab Technologies**

People

Virtually every company describes significant improvements in the performance and interaction of their people once an effective S&OP process is in place. S&OP by its very nature engenders and demands this kind of improvement. If the changes below do not occur, not only has S&OP been ineffective, in all likelihood it will be abandoned.

> ➤ **Clear understanding and acceptance of individual roles and responsibilities**
>
>   o   This includes a much clearer mutual understanding of the problems, issues and responsibilities of each function.
>
>   o   *"S&OP is a great process to help people learn the roles of other functions: what they do and what they're responsible for. This leads to better decisions made more quickly, because people know who to talk to."* Marilee Cameron, former Director of Planning, Ortho/RoundUp Business Unit, **The Scotts Company.**
>
>   o   With S&OP integrating the more detailed demand and supply processes such as customer order management, forecasting and master scheduling, people throughout the organization understand how they personally are involved in the overall process. When appropriate, this can mean the direct involvement of key customers, third-party manufacturers and suppliers.
>
>   o   The organizational structure should clarify and emphasize the defined responsibilities of each function.
>
>   o   *S&OP has allowed us to integrate, simplify and solidify our combined organization structure (value-streams on the supply side and customer industries on the demand side). It's amazing how we look differently at the business today because of this orientation. This is one of the keys to our growth and profitability!* Lach Perks, President, **Eclipse.**
>
> ➤ **People are held accountable for their responsibilities**, which are monitored at the appropriate step of the S&OP process, generally through KPI's and follow-up on action plans

- o   S&OP focuses on several key objectives that by their very nature require cross-functional communication and cooperation. These include improved customer service, lower inventory levels and decreased costs. Multiple functions share the responsibility for achieving these company-wide objectives.

- o   This means a reduction in "finger-pointing", "sandbagging" and other forms of gamesmanship.

- o   *"S&OP is the catalyst for reaching consensus. It significantly reduces people's ability to play games."* Ken Reiff, Vice President, Product Planning, **The Scotts Company**

➢ **Structured, periodic, open, cross-functional communication**, based on commonly accepted data, at clearly identified steps or meetings within the process

- o   *"By managing our S&OP we achieved a common language in our team, with clear plans and goals for the period. All of this translates directly to lower inventories and better customer service."* Jose Fernandez, Vice President of Operations, **Pyosa**

➢ **Improved teamwork, with decisive, consensus based decision-making**

- o   With accurate data, clear responsibilities and a structured process, better decisions are made more quickly and more confidently.

- o   With better communications, clear responsibilities, and joint ownership of critical company objectives, multiple functions join together to make decisions that are best for the company, not just a single department.

- o   This means on a monthly basis the right people are supplied with actionable information, and are called on to update their plans and confront clearly identified issues, problems and opportunities.

➢ **Empowerment**

- o   As the S&OP process matures, and confidence grows, the level of decision-making is pushed down. More decisions can be made earlier, at lower levels of the organization, by people closest to the detailed data, in a manner consistent with the overall philosophies and guidelines of top management. Sometimes this means decisions can be made cross-functionally even before the formal meetings, in other cases the decisions are made in the partnership meetings. (See **AGFA, Interbake Foods** and **Norse Dairy Systems**)

- o *"From the 'people' perspective, our S&OP process is about empowerment. Everyone is very clear with respect to roles, responsibilities, and decision-making authority. Decisions are in fact made at the appropriate level (often at the partnership meetings between business segments and operations). Senior executives have to 'referee' less and less."* Denise Bullock, Vice President and General Manager Front Royal Plant, **Interbake Foods**

- o *"S&OP has enabled us to push decision-making lower in the organization. For example, decisions on overtime, hiring and layoffs are now made by production managers and production control people. That was not the case before S&OP."* - Ross Bushman, President and COO, **Cast-Fab**

➤ **All of this leads to less anxiety, reduced resistance to change and better team spirit**

- o S&OP makes people more effective, leading to a better working environment and greater job satisfaction.

Visibility

"We now have better visibility." Didier Pradeilles, Vice President Global Operations, **Danfoss Commercial Compressors**

S&OP forces the management team to learn from the past, listen to each other, look to the future and understand the implications of making or delaying decisions. To support this, accurate data must be sorted and distilled into meaningful and actionable information over the decision-making horizon, ensuring that **visibility is expanded:**

➤ to at least twelve to twenty-four months, to support manufacturing and supplier capacity planning, headcount and equipment planning, and budgeting and financial planning

- o *Pyosa* started with a twelve month horizon, then cut back to three months, due to concerns about future forecast accuracy. They are now moving back to a twelve month horizon, having realized that planning with lead time, based on the best number you have, is better than no planning at all.

➤ with S&OP acting as an early warning tool, predicting problems before it's too late to avoid them (helping to minimize last-minute "firefighting" and damage control) and giving everyone more lead time to act on the issues and take advantage of the opportunities o   In global companies it is critical to share and reconcile regional demand plans, plant production plans and inventory in all locations globally. This is especially critical in large complex companies like *Eli Lilly*, which has 8000 end items sold in 161 different countries, through 130 sales affiliates, with products produced by twenty-four plants and eighty third party manufacturers.

➤   to highlight business, capacity, inventory and production issues, opportunities, plans and progress against those plans

➤   through clearly defined KPI 's that monitor performance to targets

➤   making the decision-making process more objective

➤   allowing the company to focus on continuous improvement

"The S&OP process provides a great way to routinely review company performance, critical issues and opportunities. It keeps all of us on the same page and provides a great forum to keep critical issues and action plans at task." Nick Kosanovich, VP Sales, *Norse Dairy Systems*

Planning

S&OP integrates, synchronizes and directs all of the detailed and functional planning efforts in a company, to ensure that they do not cause sub-optimization or interference and that they are reconciled and mutually support overall company goals, especially strategic and financial plans.

➤   Individual functions sharing their future forecasts and plans helps ensure that they are realistic and pass the "sanity test" of all who see them.

➤   *AGFA* spends far less time developing their annual budget, using the rolling S&OP plans as a starting point. And it has been a key process to help them rationalize their product lines, and move production responsibility to different plants in a way that maintained high customer service, with no increases in inventory.

➤   *At Amcor*, S&OP helps plan for future demand in a way that minimizes costs and overtime, while still enabling people to take time off over the holidays.

➤   *Eclipse* is able to update their business plan monthly based on the review of information coming from the S&OP process.

> At **Norse Dairy Systems**, S&OP helps integrate the engineering planning and activities in designing engineer-to-order equipment. By adjusting resources to match future forecasts, activities are properly prioritized, the schedules stabilized, utilization of capacity is optimized, while waste is minimized.

Business Improvements

Properly constructed S&OP can be the "control room" for continuous improvement. It can be used to identify and oversee the implementation of other improvement processes including postponement, new product development, lean manufacturing, TQM/6 Sigma and supply chain management. This interaction is described in chapters 6 through 9.

Below is a list of specific business improvements achieved by our model companies:

> more predictable business results

> better connection between operating objectives and business strategies

> improved supply demand alignment

> more flexibility in responding to customer requests and business opportunities

> the ability to deal with problems or opportunities in a way that balances costs vs. inventory vs. resource utilization

> manufacturing performance that is more stable, reliable, lean and efficient, with fewer personnel layoffs

> more effective planning for inventory builds to support new product launches, seasonal or cyclical demand fluctuations or anticipated supply interruptions

> more effective allocation of capital

> quicker and more effective completion of assigned action items

> a wider sense of ownership and support of changes

Summary

S&OP - is it worth it? The evidence is indisputable. And what's even better is the ROI. There isn't another process or business improvement initiative that costs less in out-of-pocket dollars, resources and time, while still producing this level of benefits.

And the bonus is that S&OP will enhance the performance of every other business process and improvement initiative, increasing the benefits that they produce.

Coming up next: a review of the lessons learned by our thirteen model companies.

Chapter 5

Lessons Learned - S&OP Success Factors

What can we learn from these thirteen manufacturing companies from across the globe concerning:

➢ *How can S&OP be best implemented?*

➢ *What accelerates the process and leads to the best results?*

➢ *How can the S&OP process be managed for optimum results?*

"Virtually all business processes center around people, and S&OP is certainly no exception. We've been saying for years that people are the A. item, as in ABC - Pareto's Law. The B item is data, and the computer is the C. Very simply, people are by far the most important element in sales and operations planning, and thus the people part of the project must be done very well."[7]

People - The "A" Item

As discussed in the previous chapter under Soft Benefits, the power of people working collaboratively, in a predictable and structured manner, dwarfs the sum of their individual or functional efforts. Communication, consensus and teamwork, across functions, and through the levels of the organization (from the CEO to the sales person and to the plant floor) needs to be developed.

Top Management

For this to occur, there must be leadership and support from **top management** for the clear definition of roles and responsibilities in the process, and for the sense of ownership and responsibility that each function and individual must accept. Senior managers must understand their own involvement, as leaders and final decision makers in S&OP. They lead by setting an example, and by insisting on full participation and compliance with S&OP as the company's main process for resolving forecasting, planning and all related supply and demand issues.

They need to set high standards and communicate large expectations, while providing resources and insisting upon timely completion of tasks.

---

[7] Chapter 6 of **Sales & Operations Planning - The How-To Handbook** by Thomas F. Wallace

Cross-Functional Participation

Top management must assign responsibility for the S&OP process design and operation to a cross-functional team. Then they must ensure that all functions participate and remain enthusiastically committed to the process, especially during times of organizational, personnel, product, or other major changes.

By following the process, all of the key business functions and appropriate organizational levels will improve their communication, mutual understanding, consensus building and joint decision-making. Sales, marketing, manufacturing, supply chain management or planning, finance, and design and development (engineering) must always be involved. Depending on the business issues and organizational style and structure, purchasing, quality management, information systems and human resources may also play regular roles.

In larger, multi-location companies, each sales location, business unit, and manufacturing location needs a clearly defined part in the process. Both as an implementation guide at the start, and as a quantity control and continuous improvement benchmark for the future, a **well documented process policy and procedure** needs to be developed, maintained, and widely distributed.

S&OP must necessarily lead to (and at the same time require) much improved **teamwork.** This goes hand in hand with:

➢ Developing and operating to a "single company game plan", reached by consensus through the participation of all functions and appropriate levels within the organization

➢ Breaking down functional "silos of excellence" by eliminating the maximization of local or functional targets and objectives, which interfere with achieving optimum company-wide performance

➢ Less effort spent on "finger pointing", or trying to avoid the blame for problems

Since the process forces focus on the future, decisions are made sooner. Small problems are prevented from growing into major crises, while the company is able to take advantage of more potential business opportunities. Top management spends more time guiding, directing and monitoring, and less time making last-minute, "least worst" choices. Cross-functional middle management makes more of the decisions.

"You really don't appreciate the value of true demand/supply alignment until you're in a situation where a strong SOP process doesn't exist. When Interbake acquired Norse, information was incomplete, of

questionable quality, and not shared with all the parties who needed it. After putting the SOP process in place, there was an immediate and noticeable improvement in the way everyone focused and coordinated their efforts on the same critical issues." Gunther Brinkman, Vice President Marketing, **Norse Dairy Systems**

Education

This is required at multiple levels of the organization, both early and ongoing, to ensure a common understanding of the objectives, principles, concepts, mechanics, terminology and required participation for success with S&OP. The end result is a common language in every functional area of the company, used to establish, monitor and achieve business objectives. And top management needs to be willing to gain a complete understanding of the process by participating early and often in education and the S&OP process design reviews.

Training in the procedural aspects of each company's specific S&OP process design is also critical, so everyone has a clear understanding of the tasks and activities that are required.

"The organizational capability of our people is our greatest asset and a foundation for our S&OP processes. We also have excellent documentation, defined roles and responsibilities, education and training programs to support and sustain the processes." Kenneth Thomas, Manager, Supply Chain Capabilities **Eli Lilly**

Accurate Information, Not Precise Data - The "B" Item

"S&OP would have never worked well without "fixing the holes in our systems." But without S&OP, AGFA may never have fixed those holes or improved the accuracy and timeliness of data." Malcolm Jaggard, Director Supply Chain Management, **AGFA US Healthcare**

For S&OP to work, inventory, sales, forecast, production plan, and capacity data have to be made reliable. Perfect 100% accuracy is not required, but consistently predictable and valid information is. Generally this means 95% accuracy on inventory, production and capacity data. Forecast accuracy can vary from company to company and industry to industry, but a predictable range of deviation needs to be identified so that plans can be made to accommodate demand variations over time.

The processes that maintain and execute these plans therefore need an equal level of reliability. These include manufacturing resource planning - MRPII, enterprise resource planning - ERP, customer relationship management - CRM, supply chain management - SCM and total quality management - TQM processes. It is especially required in the areas of customer order management, forecasting, inventory tracking and management, distribution resource planning - DRP (for supply chains, with multiple finished goods warehouses), production planning, master production scheduling - MPS, plant scheduling, and capacity management (usually rough cut capacity planning - RCCP).

As well as quantitative expressions of historical and future supply, demand, and inventory information, there must be an easy and routinized methodology that **documents underlying assumptions and root causes** of the quantitative data.

If you don't manage the daily and weekly steps that maintain accurate information and execute the plans, then you will lose the potential benefits of the S&OP process." Hector Gil, Vice President, Finance, IT and HR, **Pyosa**

Information must be presented in a focused and usable format. This means getting not just the data that's easily available, but the right data in a timely manner, presented in a way that highlights issues and fosters quick and confident decision-making.

> ➤ A detailed, **tabular display of quantitative data** needs to be developed and maintained as the basis for performance reviews and planning. But this level of detail need not be reviewed by every participant in the S&OP process.

> ➤ Wherever possible, **graphical representations** of the underlying quantitative data should be used, especially for senior management.

> ➤ Since the purpose of S&OP is to balance demand, supply, backlog and inventory volumes, not individual item mix, the data should be displayed and analyzed **in appropriate aggregations such as families**, subfamilies or groupings appropriate and specific to demand and supply viewpoints. For example, a family forecast may be broken down by geographical region, for sale review, and a family production plan may be broken down by resource for manufacturing review. But for each family, actual sales, future forecast, actual production, production plan, current inventory and projected future inventory are displayed together on a single screen, so that their interaction can be reviewed. For a make-to-order family, backlog would normally be shown instead of inventory.

> ➤ These companies maintain **four to thirty family** groupings, with each being reviewed monthly, in one or more partnership meetings, to identify problems, issues and opportunities. The families most critical to total sales, profit, or customer service, often get the lion's share of attention in the monthly meetings, especially at the executive level.

> ➤ The forecasts and production plans can be developed at an item level and then aggregated up to the S&OP family groupings. Or they can be developed at the family level, and subsequently disaggregated down to an item planning level.

Forecasts and plans must be consistent between the S&OP process and all detailed planning and execution processes such as customer order management, detailed forecasting, and master scheduling.

➤ Though virtually every company uses simple, Excel-based data presentations, many find it helpful to augment this with more powerful analytical tools

    o *Eli Lilly* and **Scotts** have developed tools to access and integrate data from multiple systems in multiple locations and divisions in their company worldwide.

    o *Eli Lilly* uses a sophisticated APS package quarterly to identify overloads, underloads or unbalanced situations with product made in multiple locations across the globe. The system suggests changes to the plan, which are reviewed and fine tuned by experienced planners.

    o *Eclipse* has developed clear and focused ways of presenting information to facilitate decision-making.

"Information is shared, we have a common language. Transversality throughout the supply chain is making our work easier." -Philippe Duchêne, Sales and Marketing Manager, ***Danfoss Commercial Compressors***

"Timing is Everything"

Frequency: Every one of our model companies has a one month S&OP cycle, since marketplace, customer and supply source dynamics have the potential to vary considerably from month to month. This doesn't mean that every, or even any of the forecasts or plans need to change every month, just that they deserve to be reviewed for potential problems or opportunities.

Daily or weekly issues involving product mix, sequencing, and customer priority considerations are handled outside of S&OP by the customer order management, master scheduling, and detailed supply scheduling processes.

Using S&OP as a basis for updating business plans, financial plans, budgets, capital spending plans, etc. may mean that in certain months additional steps are taken with the S&OP data to review, update or establish new financial or strategic plans. These activities typically occur no more often than quarterly and sometimes only once or twice a year.

A **planning horizon** of at least twelve rolling months, and in many cases eighteen to twenty-four months is needed to help management focus on the future, away from the short term, and on the implications of demand and supply changes over time.

The data should be presented in **monthly periods** for at least the next six months. Thereafter, some companies summarize into quarterly increments if month-to-month variations have no effect on planning that far out.

There should be a focus on discovering root causes for past variation, with the majority of time spent considering the potential implications of changes in the future, especially **two to six months** out.

Computer Hardware and Software - The "C" Item

Process design, not software tools is seen as the key to success by all thirteen companies. None of the companies utilized commercial S&OP software. Virtually every company developed their own S&OP analytical and presentation tools, based on Microsoft Excel spreadsheet logic, supported by some custom databases (often Microsoft Access) and retrieval programs which accessed data stored in ERP and demand management systems or subsystems.

All companies started with the standard five step S&OP process (see chapter 3), shaping and customizing it as they went along, to accommodate their particular business issues and conditions.

Implementing S&OP - You Can't Plan Forever

"... though this process itself is very straight-forward and easy to understand, it is difficult to implement it successfully
- *because it's a new process...it means change in some aspects of how people do their job*
- *so people need a solid understanding of the process and a vision of the future*
- *top management people are typically very busy, so progress must be made quickly and consistently, or the implementation project may stall out and never reach a successful conclusion*
- *during implementation incremental experience and expertise are gained only once each month."*[8]

A **documented, disciplined process**, consistently implemented and operated in all locations and functions of the company, was a common theme in these thirteen companies.

---

[8] Chapter 5 of **Sales & Operations Planning - The How-To Handbook** by Thomas F. Wallace

Step-by-step, phased implementation

A solid **process design with input from all functions and levels** of management should be developed. **Plagiarize**, guiltlessly:

> ➤ Learn from others, avoid their mistakes, follow the 5 step process, the principles of good management and project management, and the specific guidelines for success in S&OP (see *Sales and Operations Planning - The How-To Handbook*, by Thomas F. Wallace)

> ➤ Where available, learn from the experiences of other divisions of the same company (see *AGFA, Coca-Cola MIDI, Interbake Foods, Norse Dairy Systems* and *UMC*)

> ➤ Follow the guidance of an experienced consultant who's done it before (see the consultants mentioned at the end of each company chapter in Part III of this book)

"If we do something uniquely or in a different way, I worry!" Hector Gil, Vice President, Finance, IT and HR, *Pyosa*

Measure It

What needs (or gets) improvement, must be **measured.**

Well defined and balanced performance **measurements, metrics, or KPI's (key performance indicators)** are the nervous system for the healthy operation of the corporate body. If well designed, they tell everyone, at every level, in every function, how well they're doing their part, how well the processes are working, and how well the objectives of the customer and the company are being met.

Every one of our thirteen model companies has clearly identified KPI's that are reviewed at the appropriate steps of the process. *Interbake Foods* and *Norse Dairy Systems* formally follow a "balanced scorecard" approach. The other companies pursue the same underlying principles of cascading, connected and balanced KPI's, that act as checks and balances on each function and location, to ensure that the proper trade-offs are made, and attention given to issues that affect customer service and overall company performance.

Many companies see S&OP as the key driver for ongoing continuous improvement efforts. This could apply to business objectives such as improving customer service or lowering inventory or costs. It could apply to improving the reliability of the processes supporting S&OP, such as forecast accuracy, production plan reliability, and inventory accuracy. This could also include making improvements in detailed planning and execution systems, such as ERP or some of its major components. Or it could include launching major business improvement initiatives, such as lean manufacturing, total quality management or 6 Sigma, supply chain management, etc. The KPI's that are tracked should reflect these efforts.

Personalize It

Unique circumstances or issues specific to a particular company or industry need to be addressed, but often they can be handled using standard approaches or techniques applicable to most companies. For example, in addition to tracking finished goods inventories, *AGFA* also monitors critical semi-finished inventories of large master rolls of film.

For most companies, an **initial process design should be developed in two to four months**. Since various functions and levels of management will request changes to the process once they actually experience it after implementation, it is important not to spend extra time trying to "perfect" the process before it is launched.

Some large, global, multi-division or multi-location companies may need to define, develop and fine tune processes and tools to capture and share data between different systems and company locations.

It is wise to implement a **pilot product line** (or for large, global, multidivisional, multi-location companies, a business segment or division) first, followed rapidly (over several months) by the remaining lines or segments. But all plant locations producing products in a given line or business segment, and all sales and marketing locations in a given region or business segment need to be included in the implementation concurrently. See *AGFA, Coca-Cola MIDI, Eli Lilly* and *UMC*.

Making It Work

"With the process standardized across all product lines and locations, it is easier for everyone to focus on performance to target and opportunities for improvement." Glen Melanson, Vice President of Reagent Manufacturing, *UMC*

Early on, the process must be carefully monitored, validated and fine tuned until it is institutionalized and followed in a standard way across the entire organization. If not properly addressed, the presentation of incomplete or inaccurate information to senior management for decision-making runs the risk of undermining their support of, and participation in the process. The less the members of the top management group are "bought in" to S&OP, the greater this risk becomes.

This is not to say that it's advisable to delay involving senior management until all the information is totally complete and 100% accurate. In many cases (forecast accuracy, for example) that time may never come. But the information presented must be based on data that is valid, meaningful and actionable, not necessarily precise. And where the data is less than perfect or complete, its reliability should be explained to the people using it to make decisions.

"Time is of the essence." The goal should be to get the process up and running for least the pilot product family within two to three months, with the other families following as quickly as possible. Fine-tuning should occur each step of the way, based on gaining more experienced input and recommendations from the participants.

"You have to stick with it, it takes time." Malcolm Jaggard, Director of Supply Chain Management, *AGFA*

A few companies are unhappy with the results at first, and find they need to go back to the basics and get the process working better months or even years after the initial implementation (see *Eclipse*).

Others find the discipline, the level of participation and execution, and the accompanying results, may diminish over time. This is often caused by the distractions of other large changes in the company such as reorganizations, changes in ownership or management, relocations, adding or closing sales or plant locations, major product introductions, or shifts in business strategy. Once this is realized, those companies that devote their energy to getting the S&OP process back in full working order find it worthwhile.

The companies that don't let S&OP slip during these times of change, and in fact use it to manage through the change, find their level of control and results greatly enhanced (see *AGFA, Eli Lilly, EMS, Interbake Foods* and *UMC).*

"El secreto esta en pegarse!" or *"The secret is sticking to it!"* Alberto Fernandez, former President and current Chairman of *Pyosa*

Ongoing Improvements

The S&OP process can be streamlined as the concepts of continuous improvement, lean manufacturing and total quality management or 6 Sigma are applied to the activities, steps and meetings that make up the S&OP process. Aim for *quicker, fewer, shorter, lower,* and *sooner,* to streamline it and make it more efficient and timely.

Some companies, when the process and people are operating reliably and consistently for a period of time, start running the review meetings **"by exception"** only. Here only families with performance outside acceptable parameters, or action items not progressing to a schedule, are actually reviewed in the partnership or executive meetings. But be careful, no company starts out successfully this way! It can take months or years to reach a level of reliability where this can be effective. (See *AGFA* and *UMC*)

It's like red wine! S&OP doesn't get "tired and old" over the years, it becomes richer, smoother and more robust. It becomes inextricably embedded in a company's culture and business management processes. It becomes "the way" to get issues on the table, to get problems solved and to get opportunities captured. We often hear managers say: "How did we ever get along without it?" or "I never want to work in a company without a good S&OP process again!"

Companies like *AGFA, Coca-Cola, Eli Lilly, Interbake, Pyosa* and *UMC* have been using S&OP for over thirteen years, and feel more committed to it now than at the start.

Don't just store it in the wine cellar, actively pursue continuous improvement through:

> Regular, structured self-critique of the effectiveness and efficiency of the meetings and other steps in the process

> Setting quantifiable targets for improvement, and monitoring progress against these targets each month

> Use of any one of several generally accepted S&OP effectiveness checklists, at least annually, to identify process performance slippage and/or opportunities for improvement

Summary

Not surprisingly, success with S&OP requires knowledgeable and involved people from many functions and levels of the organization, supported by top management that is involved and insistent on success. It requires and helps foster a company culture of communication and consensus, based on good listening and understanding other viewpoints. A decisive atmosphere emerges, where people are prone to take action early, based on projected, but reliably monitored information, while there's time to avoid problems and secure success.

S&OP's hallmarks are leadership, teamwork, communication, and consensus decision-making. Properly applied, its results are consistently outstanding.

Coming up next: Part II of the book, which focuses on how our best practice companies use S&OP in a variety of operating environments and with a variety of other tools and processes.

Part II

Environments and Processes

Chapter 6

Getting the Product to the Customers

Where does S&OP work? With which kinds of products? With which kinds of customers? Does it help with the new product development and design process?

Our best practice companies sell to a wide array of customers, specifically:

Mass merchandisers
Retailers
Distributors
Wholesalers
Government agencies
Equipment manufacturers
Consumer goods manufacturers
Food and beverage producers
Textile producers
Hospitals
Laboratories

Their products range from cookies to 20-ton castings. Processes span cookie dough mixing and baking, liquids blending and filling, and chemical reactions, to metal casting, machining, fabrication and assembly.

Order fulfillment strategies - what is done when a customer order arrives - vary for our best practice companies. Some manufacture their product in anticipation of getting orders, and then ship from finished goods inventory. Others produce it partially, hold the finished components or semi-finished materials until they receive the customer order, and then finish the product and ship it. Others don't even start producing until after they have the customer order firmly in hand. And a few companies custom design certain aspects of some products for each customer

In the first part of this chapter we'll cover how S&OP works in different customer, product and order fulfillment environments, and how it works specifically at our best practice companies. Later in the chapter we'll discuss how S&OP supports a key process that is common to all companies and probably key to the success of your company as well: new product design and development. .

Meeting the Customer.

A company's order fulfillment strategy need not be industry or even product specific. It can be a *conscious choice* to achieve competitive advantage, or it may be guided by the intersection of customer lead times and supply chain lead times and flexibility. Virtually all of our model companies employ more than one strategy. Sometimes the strategy varies by product line, sometimes by product within a product line. And strategies can be changed over time - as lead times, customer expectations, market conditions, or a competitor's actions change.

Figure 6-1 - **Order Fulfillment Strategies** - lays out the primary options: make-to-stock, finish-to-order, make-to-order, and design-to-order. "Value Added" indicates how much labor and material is invested in the product prior to the receipt of the customer order. "Time to Complete the Customer Order" indicates how much time is required after the receipt of the customer order to complete manufacturing and get the product ready to ship.

Figure 6-1

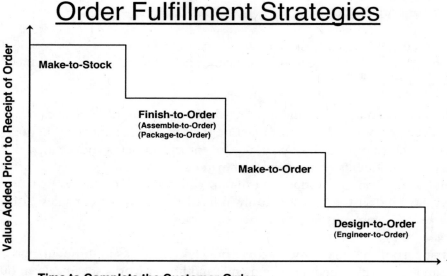

What's S&OP Got to Do With It?

Before discussing each of the different order fulfillment environments, it is important to point out one very important fact - **the basics of S&OP don't change when the order fulfillment strategy does.**

The basic approach, objectives, structure, meetings and participants in the S&OP process remain the same regardless of the order fulfillment strategy. The same communication, problem-solving, identification of opportunities and decision-making remain at the heart of the process.

What does vary is the information that is tracked and displayed. For example, for make-to-stock families, "sales" data represents anticipated or actual shipments and the S&OP display shows it and the actual and projected finished goods inventories. For families using the other strategies, where there is no finished goods inventory, "sales" data represents the rate of incoming orders - "bookings" - and for them, the S&OP display shows the projected incoming orders and the current and projected backlog[9] of customer orders.

In some finish-to-order situations, the available and projected inventory of key components or semi- finished product is displayed for planning purposes. The S&OP display for a family with different fulfillment strategies may show inventory and backlog, as well as bookings, shipments and production.

Whatever data is displayed, an effective S&OP process always does one thing very well: it provides long range visibility on projected business performance, highlighting potential issues that may be hidden in the details of individual product forecasts, master schedules, and inventory by item. It pulls management's vision back from all the detail to get a sense for what's really happening in the business - seeing the scope of the forest, instead of just staring at individual leaves.

It highlights:

> Incoming customer order rates versus revenue and profit targets and plans

> The impact of seasonal, cyclical or temporary changes in demand patterns, on revenue and supply plans

> Current customer order backlogs versus desired backlog levels, and customer lead times versus required competitive lead times

> The scheduled shipping dates of the current customer order backlog versus their order booking dates (which could affect revenue and capacity plans)

> Incoming customer order rates versus supply (production) plans and capacity limitations

---

[9] Backlog is the total quantity of a product that has been ordered by customers, but has not yet been shipped at a specific point in time

➤ How fast production needs to ramp up or down. How the required volume shifts affect critical lead times, or management guidelines (time fences) used to manage the impact of change on internal and external resources.

➤ The potential impact of supply disruptions on overall sales, inventory and revenue plans.

     o   For example, how a planned shutdown will impact inventory levels

     o   Or is there capacity to produce more in advance of the scheduled shutdown?

     o   And the financial impact of holding more inventory?

➤ Current and projected inventory levels versus desired targets (of finished, or in some cases, semi-finished product)

➤ The impact of new product launch dates on revenue, sales, supply and inventory plans

Let's now look at the different order fulfillment strategies one at a time and see how some of our best practice companies use them.

Make-to-Stock

What do you do when a customer order arrives? If you say, "we pick it, pack it, and ship it," you're following a make-to-stock (MTS) strategy. Products are manufactured to a forecast of some kind, put into finished goods inventory, and await customer orders. All of our best practice companies except *Cast-Fab* employ a make-to-stock strategy on some or all of their products.

Make-to-Stock and S&OP:

An example of a simple MTS sales and operations planning display is shown in Figure 6-2. It shows the basic data needed for S&OP in a make-to-stock environment: sales (shipments), supply plans, and finished goods inventory. This example only shows a six month future horizon, so that the numbers will be large enough to be legible on this page. Typically, companies would display planning information at least twelve months into the future, and often as much as eighteen to twenty-four months.

Figure 6-2

Make-to-Stock S&OP Display

Family	AXY		
Description	Large Widgets	Crit Time Fence	4 weeks
Unit of Measure	EA	Customer LT	2 days
Turns Target	12		

	History			Current		Current Year	Next Year			
	AUG	SEP	OCT	NOV	DEC	Expected Results	JAN	FEB	MAR	APR
Sales										
Sales Plan	280	324	190	286	232	3200	335	353	453	318
Actual Sales	240	190	190							
Difference	-40	-134	0							
Cum Difference	-40	-174	-174							
Supply										
Production Plan	280	324	190	270	240	3100	290	400	460	300
Actual Production	300	210	140							
Difference	20	-114	-50							
Cum Difference	20	-94	-144							
Inventory										
Plan	320	320	320	334	342	342	297	344	351	333
Actual	380	400	350							
Difference	60	80	30							
Turns	10.0	9.8	11.5	12.1	12.2	12.2	12.3	12.3	12.4	11.2

Note: Turns for any given month = Sum of next 12 months sales (actual sales in the past, sales plan in the future) divided by month end inventory.

The projected **finished goods inventory** level represents a critique of the current balance between anticipated sales and planned production. The inventory acts like a shock absorber between demand and supply, absorbing minor variations from the demand plan, so that continual adjustments to the supply plan aren't necessary.

If the projected inventory is too high, perhaps the supply plan is now higher than need be. If the projected inventory is too low, then the supply plan may be too low, or the forecast may now be higher than the supply side of the business can support during that time period. The S&OP process will highlight these situations.

The size of the finished good inventory is also a key competitive variable, and as such should be managed through the S&OP process. It affects the level of customer service, but ties up capital. If the inventory is too low, customer service can suffer and the company is less competitive. If the inventory is too high, too much money may be tied up in working capital (inventory), excess inventory may prevent rapid response to new product opportunities, and cash flow and the company's financial results may suffer.

The inventory targets that are authorized by S&OP should represent a reasonable trade-off between carrying inventory versus the costs of constantly adjusting the supply plan to actual customer orders. These costs may include not only increased changeovers, overtime and premium freight, but also the cost of maintaining (and under-utilizing) resource capacity levels to accommodate the highest demand peak that could occur during the year.

Inventory target levels may be expressed as a single number, or as a range: lowest acceptable inventory to highest acceptable inventory. This kind of "high/low planning" reflects the fact that changes occur in both demand and supply, and that the job is not to hit a single arbitrary inventory number, but to adjust future plans in such a way as to stay within reasonable pre-determined inventory ranges.

The S&OP process is the best way to periodically monitor the impact of the latest demand and supply plans on the inventory targets, and to simulate how different demand and supply scenarios will affect this.

Seasonality

This often plays a key role in make-to-stock environments. In some cases, a relatively short selling season prevents the entire volume of product from being produced during that time. Some production, perhaps quite a bit, must occur early: weeks or months ahead of the selling season, and S&OP can help manage how much is produced and inventoried in advance.

Often, some hard decisions must be made about which specific products should be stocked in anticipation of the selling season, and which should be produced only at the last moment. While S&OP deals with the aggregate volumes, and not the detailed schedules for individual products, the S&OP process provides a forum for developing guidelines for which products to produce when.

For example, some companies choose to produce and stock more of their most predictable items, to avoid excess inventory at the end of the season. Other companies may have shelf life issues that dictate how much in advance of the season any given item can be produced. In the end, a more accurate inventory budget can be developed based on the S&OP projected inventory calculations.

The impact of seasonality on both supply plans and financial projections for revenue and profitability is a direct byproduct of the S&OP process. Simulation of various supply strategies may be helpful in developing the best overall game plan for handling seasonality.

A Best Practice Example:
Make-to-Stock with Seasonality at *The Scotts Company*

The Scotts Company is a make-to-stock manufacturer, selling its lawn care and related products into a highly seasonal marketplace. For its line of lawn products, over 90 percent of the sales occur within three months. See Figure 6-3:

Figure 6-3

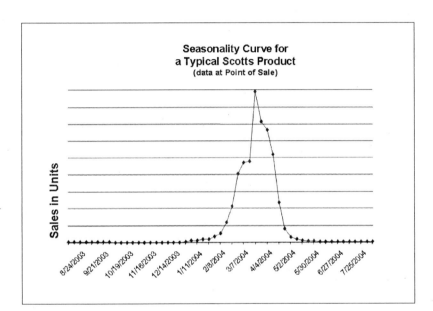

Scotts credits S&OP with helping it to better cope with this extreme seasonality. Most manufacturers in seasonal businesses do not have enough capacity to produce all of the required sales volume during the selling season, and *Scotts* is no exception. Therefore, a critical decision is when during the off-season to start production (the *pre-build*) for the high selling season. There's a trade-off here that must be recognized:

➤ The earlier the *pre-build* starts, the more inventory that will be carried for a longer period of time - and that costs money, ties up cash in inventory, and may increase the risk of obsolescence if the wrong products are produced

➤ The later the *pre-build* starts, the greater the production rate must change - and that costs money due to increased resource requirements

Highly seasonal product lines, such as those at *Scotts*, represent arguably the most difficult kind of make-to-stock environment. For virtually all of its product families, *Scotts* uses S&OP to find the "sweet spot" regarding timing on the *pre-build*, minimizing the combined costs of carrying inventory and varying the production rates.

S&OP projects what the finished goods inventory will be during the *pre-build*, both in units and dollars, important for projecting cash flow during the low-selling season. Then, S&OP tracks performance against those plans to insure that the inventories are where they're supposed to be.

The benefits from S&OP at *Scotts* includes order fill performance at above 98% and inventory that is one-third less than just a few years ago. A sizeable number of mass merchandisers have designated *Scotts* as a vendor of the year.

Additional Company Experiences with Make-to-Stock

Amcor Flexibles manufactures specialty flexible polyethylene packaging. In this extremely price sensitive industry, Amcor's customers hold only small inventories and demand short lead times, with major changes in requirements on very short notice. For this reason, 55% of their products are make-to-stock, with the inventories carefully managed through the S&OP and detailed resource planning processes. The results have been outstanding:

➢ Inventory has fallen by 40%

➢ DIFOT (Delivered In Full On Time) - customer service rose by 10%

➢ Distribution cost fell by 30 %

➢ Improved customer retention

➢ Reduced obsolescence

Interbake Foods is one of two manufacturers that produce six million cases of eight different varieties of Girl Scout cookies in the USA. Shipping schedules from 130 local storage and delivery agents drive shipments out of Interbake's finished goods inventory by 5 PM the next day.

S&OP coordinates weekly production schedules within minimum and maximum inventory levels that are adjusted each month throughout the highly seasonal Girl Scout Cookie season.   Capacity is planned to provide flexibility to increase the schedule quickly if the Girl Scout demand suddenly increases.

Make-to-Order

What do you do when a customer order arrives? If you say, "We don't start the production process until we receive the customer order, and sometimes we buy special material needed for the order," that's a make-to-order (MTO) strategy. Or if you have significant product variations that aren't known until the customer order is received, and you can't afford to maintain all the product variations in finished goods inventory, then you are making-to-order (or possibly finishing-to-order - covered in the next section of this chapter). Our model companies with significant make-to-order volumes include *Amcor, Cast-Fab, Danfoss, Eclipse, EMS, Interbake, and Norse Dairy Systems.*

Make-to-Order and S&OP:

An example of a simple MTO sales and operations planning display is shown in Figure 6-4. It shows the basic data needed for this environment: sales (bookings), supply plans, and backlog. This example only shows a six month future horizon, so that the numbers will be large enough to be legible on this page. Typically, companies would display planning information at least twelve months into the future, and often as much as eighteen to twenty-four months.

Figure 6-4

Make-to-Order S&OP Display

Family	BHK									
Description	Large Pumps			Critical Time Fence		10 weeks				
Unit of Measure	EA									
Backlog Target	12 weeks									

| | History | | | Current | | Current Year | Next Year | | | |
	AUG	SEP	OCT	NOV	DEC	Projected Results	JAN	FEB	MAR	APR
Sales (Bookings)										
Bookings Plan	210	270	260	260	200	3200	200	200	220	220
Actual Bookings	200	235	250							
Difference	-10	-35	-10							
Cum Difference	-10	-45	-55							
Supply										
Production Plan	210	270	260	260	210	3000	220	220	220	220
Actual Production	208	272	260							
Difference	-2	2	0							
Cum Difference	-2	0	0							
Backlog										
Plan	785	785	785	730	720	720	700	680	680	680
Actual	777	740	730							
Difference	-8	-45	-55							
Backlog in Weeks	12.8	13.2	13.8	14.6	14.2	14.6	13.8	13.4	13.0	13.4

Note: Backlog in weeks is calculated here from month end backlog divided by the next three months production (actual production in past months, production plan in the future) times 13.

The size of the **customer order backlog**, current and projected, expresses the balance between demand (anticipated incoming orders) and supply (planned production or shipments) in a make-to-order environment. The current customer order backlog is the total of all customer orders in house, not yet shipped. The projected customer order backlog is the expected total of all the unshipped orders at the end of each period. Like inventory for make-to-stock products, the order backlog acts like a shock absorber between demand and supply for make-to-order products, absorbing minor variations from the demand (or supply) plans, so that continual adjustments to the supply plan aren't necessary.

If the projected backlog is too high, perhaps the supply plan is lower than it needs to be. If the projected backlog is too low, then the supply plan may be too high, or the forecast of incoming orders may be lower than the supply or production rate set for that time period. S&OP will highlight these potential imbalances.

The size of the backlog is a key competitive variable for MTO products, and like finished goods inventory for MTS products, should be managed through the S&OP process. If the backlog grows, customer order lead times get longer, often making the company less competitive. If the backlog shrinks too much, it may be difficult or impossible to maintain a smooth flow of work into and through the plant. Trying to maintain a smooth flow may encourage early release of work which may be counterproductive if the backlog remains too small due to a low rate of incoming customer orders.

The backlog can be expressed in a variety of ways:

1. Some companies show backlog as a quantity: the current quantity of unshipped product and the quantities projected to be unshipped at the end of each future period considering the projected bookings and shipments in those periods.

2. Other companies like to see backlog expressed as the average customer lead time - how quickly will future orders ship based on the current or projected backlog

3. Some display both the backlog quantity and the projected lead time

4. Still other companies prefer to also see the backlog spread over the future periods based on the scheduled shipping dates for each order. This helps companies clearly see revenue shortfalls in periods where bookings are running as anticipated, but where either the customers are requesting shipment at dates later than normal, or where shipping is being delayed due to material or resource availability.

A Best Practice Example:
Make-to-Order with Highly Cyclical Sales Volumes at *Cast-Fab*

At *Cast-Fab Technologies*, all of their products are custom designed for each customer, with about 15% of their sales each year generated by new products. Most new products result in repeat business from the customer over a two to 5 year horizon.

But largely they are a make-to-order manufacturer that's subject to extremely variable demand. This is because they're at the outer end of the overall supply chain: the company's products are used by machinery manufacturers whose products are sold to producers of other products, which may go directly to an end consumer or, in many cases, are sold to other manufacturers.

For example, a *Cast-Fab* casting might go to a machine tool manufacturer whose product is sold to a "tier 2" automotive supplier, who in turn sells to a "tier 1" supplier, who supplies an auto assembly plant, which produces and ships cars to dealers, who stock them and then deliver them to people like you and me. As the fortunes of the automotive business ebb and flow, signals for more or less demand are sent back through the supply chain and the notorious "bull whip effect" takes place. This refers to the phenomenon of demand changes amplifying through each successive stage in the supply chain, due to manufacturing, and/or transportation lot sizing, and/or inventory adjustments at multiple steps within the supply chain.

Thus the demand streams coming to *Cast-Fab* tend to be highly variable and erratic. Figure 6-5 shows the tonnage of castings shipped by year since 1992, and it certainly is a highly variable picture.

Figure 6-5

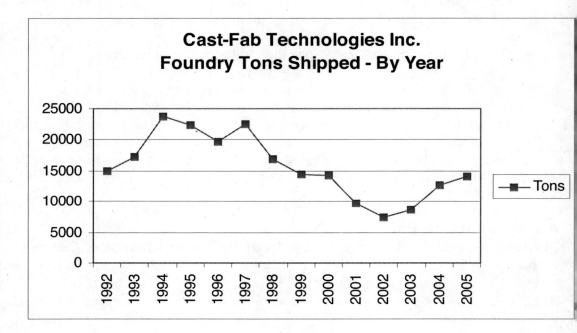

Looking at the individual year-to-year changes in Figure 6-6 paints an even more dramatic picture:

Figure 6-6

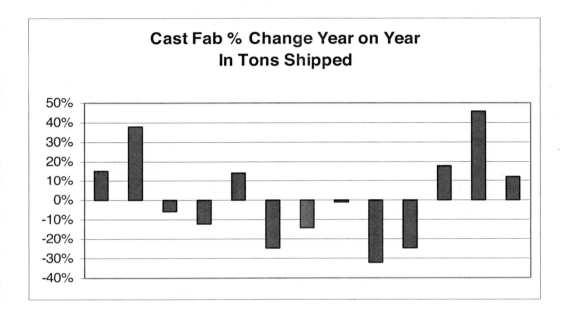

Cast-Fab has used S&OP to manage its backlog since 1995. By looking forward and identifying shifts in demand, and carefully monitoring the actual backlog, they were able to adjust future production rates without letting the backlog get out of control. In fact, they've increased market share by actively managing backlog to lower levels than the competition. The relatively short lead time of four weeks (for their industry) is a great selling tool. When customers ask Cast-Fab how they do it, the answer they give is a detailed explanation of their S&OP process!

And when business increased sharply during 2004, up 46%, *Cast-Fab* realized a productivity increase of 2% on the year, despite all of the hiring, training, retraining, and new people on the job. The company is very proud of this achievement and points to it as another benefit from S&OP: a productivity increase during a period when, in the past, it would have declined.

This is yet another example of how S&OP provides a "window into the future," allowing companies to get a head start on volume shifts, and respond to them in a cost-effective manner.

Additional Company Experiences with Make-to-Order

Eclipse manufactures a variety of products ranging from individual piece parts all the way to complex systems - including burners, control systems and support services for industrial process heating equipment

➢ Some of the products are high volume while others are low, made from standard parts and assemblies

➢ Over a recent three year period over 18,100 different line items were sold

➢ Thirteen percent (13%) of their products are make-to-order, with lead times of two to four weeks

➢ Assemble-to-order products represent 60% of the total, with lead times of one to two weeks (see the next section of this chapter on finish-to-order products)

➢ Design-to-order products account for 22% of the total, with lead times of eight to twelve weeks (see the section of this chapter below on design-to-order products)

➢ With earlier visibility of increases in business coming from the S&OP process, *Eclipse* is able to add sufficient production and/or engineering staff gradually to meet the increased demand without extending lead times

➢ Customer order delinquencies have been greatly reduced, while on-time shipping performance has remained steadily high, even as sales were growing. These service levels are considered the best in their industry.

➢ S&OP has changed how the company negotiates delivery dates with their customers so that loads on key resources are leveled, and all customer commitments are met. And with the visibility S&OP provides, they know when to turn down business when they cannot support the customer's requirements economically.

Finish-to-Order (Postponement)

The approach called finish-to-order (FTO) sits between make-to-stock and make-to-order. It's like make-to-stock in that a substantial amount of production is done before receipt of the customer order, typically to a semi-finished product level. It's like make-to-order in that it requires the customer order before the product can be completed. At the last possible moment, the product is configured to the customer's specification. If the finishing process can be done really quickly, the finish-to-order fulfillment strategy is often called "postponement[10]".

Significant product variety, a product design that allows configuration to the customer's requirements in the finishing step(s), and short customer lead times are typically the key factors in causing a company to select a finish-to-order fulfillment strategy.

A variety of terms are used to describe products that are finished to a customer's specification. In some companies, particularly traditional fabrication and assembly type operations, the term "assemble-to-order" is used; in chemical plants it's sometimes called "blend-to-order". At Dell Computer, the term "build-to-order" is used to describe this kind of manufacturing. These all mean essentially the same thing.

A finish-to-order fulfillment strategy is used at *AGFA, Danfoss, Eclipse, EMS, Norse* and *UMC.*   Interestingly, all of these companies also have significant lean manufacturing initiatives in place. Both finish-to-order and Lean were pursued to efficiently support short lead times to their customers. See chapter 8 for more on lean manufacturing.

Finish-to-Order and S&OP:

> Typically the S&OP data display is similar to a make-to-order situation: bookings, production and backlog.

> The critique of the balance between supply and demand is most often expressed by the size of the current and future customer order backlog. However, since this backlog is often small - when expressed as a customer lead time it may only be slightly longer than the finishing time, some companies display the projected semi-finished inventory to serve as a feasibility check on the supply plan.

> S&OP in a finish-to-order environment, like the others, must answer these questions: What is the actual rate of incoming orders versus the planned rate? Is demand changing and how fast must adjustments be made to production levels? Are the customer lead times competitive? And sometimes, are the (semi-finished) inventory levels appropriate?

---

[10] Postponement is explored in depth in *Building to Customer Demand* by Tom Wallace and Bob Stahl, 2005, T. F. Wallace & Co.

A Best Practice Example: Finish-to-Order/Postponement at *UMC*

UMC makes medical devices and consumable materials. They are an accomplished user of S&OP and lean manufacturing, and have put those tools to good use in developing their postponement processes.

For their line of medical devices, they've become able to defer the final assembly of the product. They don't finish the product in their plant; rather they finish it at the customer's site, which is often a laboratory within a hospital. There the *UMC* technician "final assembles" the semi-finished product by adding the last few components shipped directly by their suppliers to the customer's site.

S&OP at *UMC* keys on the inventory level of the semi-finished devices. These semi-finished models are forecasted and scheduled in a make-to-stock manner. But due to their lean manufacturing efforts, the assembly lead time is very short and the process is very flexible, so that the schedule can easily be adjusted to actual customer demand as it is received during the month..

The units are more than 90% complete when they leave *UMC's* assembly area, but they lack certain optional features. If these options were added to the product during assembly at the *UMC* plant, there would be a much larger variety of different items in finished goods inventory, with the attendant risks of high inventory, stockouts, obsolescence, and so forth.

This approach allows *UMC* to provide their customers with wide product variety and high customer service (over 98%) but with inventories drastically lower than before they began postponement. S&OP serves as the overall coordination tool for this superb supply chain process.

Additional Company Experiences with Multiple Order Fulfillment Strategies

Danfoss uses S&OP to manage multiple market channels with different order fulfilment strategies:

➢ They sell direct to major customers in three regions (Europe, North America and South America) using a modified make-to-stock strategy:

  o for their OEM customers, they build five to ten days of inventory in advance and store it at customer sites.

> o three to four weeks of inventory of their highest selling compressor products is stocked at five major distribution centers and some sales affiliates

> ➤ The strategy for one of their major product lines is assemble-to-order (postponement) since demand is highly variable and the customers require short delivery lead times. To support this, lean manufacturing initiatives are being pursued at all manufacturing locations.

> ➤ No finished inventory at all is held for slow movers, since the compressors are assembled-to-order in twelve hours. Some subassembly and component inventory is held ahead of finishing, but lean manufacturing has helped shrink this inventory from two weeks or more to about two days worth.

EMS' product lines have slowly evolved from low mix, high volume, to high mix, low volume. They include special "bimetal" and "clad material" components and electrical contacts for industrial customers. Today they use basically the same equipment that was purchased for the high volume environment, but it has been redeployed and managed using lean manufacturing techniques.

S&OP has helped focus sales and marketing attention so that forecast errors on the subfamilies that are planned have been reduced by 90%. And the S&OP supply planning process maintains capacity-smoothed, realistic plans by integrating the three categories of items:

> ➤ Make-to-stock: 60 "A" items (high volume, consistent demand items) with finished goods inventory allowing flexibility to smooth fluctuations in customer demand, anticipate seasonal surges and level production volume in the factory

> ➤ Finish-to-order: 1100 items with semi-finished goods inventory held to accommodate minimum run sizes

> ➤ Make-to-order: 60 items

Design-to-Order[11]

Design-to-order (DTO) means designing or engineering at least some of the product after receipt of the order from the customer[12]. A design-to-order product is often for a unique application in a specific customer environment. A design-to-order environment

---

[11] Also called engineer-to-order (ETO)

[12] Although some product design has probably been done in order to quote price and delivery, the *detailed design* of the product typically begins once the order is received.

is make-to-order taken to its extreme - almost no work is done in advance of the actual customer order. Our model companies that offer some design-to-order products are: *AGFA, Cast-Fab, Danfoss, Eclipse, EMS,* and *Norse Dairy Systems.*

Companies operating in a design-to-order environment place great emphasis on managing pre-production processes: product development, design, laboratory testing, product engineering, drafting, model shop, and the like. These resources are on the critical path to getting the product made and shipped.

If the total demand for pre-production services is greater than their available capacity, then:

> ➢ backlogs of unfinished work build,

> ➢ lead times stretch out,

> ➢ some, possibly many, of the orders are late going into production,

> ➢ and production will probably not be completed on time to meet the customer promise date.

Here's where S&OP can help.

Design-to-Order and S&OP:

➢ The rough cut planning and monitoring of pre-production services is an essential part of S&OP in this environment. Just as MTS, MTO and FTO products require visibility into the manufacturing processes, DTO requires essential visibility into the demand/supply balance for important non-manufacturing resources. While rough cut capacity planning is a key technique for evaluating any key resource in any fulfillment environment, it is indispensable to S&OP here.

➢ The overall balance between incoming orders (bookings) and shipments (after design and production is completed) is expressed by the size of the customer order backlog. As in the case of the other two "to-order" environments, managing the projected backlog is vital in maintaining a competitive customer lead time.

➢ Typically the S&OP format used for DTO is the same as that used for MTO: sales (bookings), production, and backlog.

A Best Practice Example:
Design-to-Order at Norse Dairy Systems

One of *Norse's* businesses is equipment: the design and manufacture of equipment for filling and packaging ice cream products. Seventy-five or more machines are produced each year, with thousands of options and attachments, many of them unique to the customer. Much of this equipment is managed via a finish-to-order strategy, but a substantial portion is design-to-order. Engineering design lead times range from four to one hundred weeks, based on the complexity of the design to satisfy the customer requirements and specifications.

Norse uses S&OP to manage, schedule, and allocate the time and resources of the engineering department (product design). Key points include:

> ➤ The engineering department is planned and scheduled in a manner similar to a production work center

> ➤ Engineering on-time performance on drawings, material specifications, and bills of material is monitored, with defined root causes for any issues or problems used to plan the appropriate corrective actions

> ➤ A capacity plan for each engineer is tracked for actual hours versus a plan based on the design complexity and actual hours spent on previous orders

In their partnership meeting, engineering capacity and related issues are reviewed and problems are examined for root causes and corrective actions. Engineering personnel are key players in this process. At the executive meeting, engineering capacity, manpower needs and overtime are approved and prioritized.

S&OP has helped the *Norse* engineering people reduce design time by 27% and simultaneously gain a 30% improvement in efficiency and a reduction in order configuration time from forty-five days to four days. Equally impressive is that *Norse* engineering routinely achieves 98% on time performance for completion of drawings, specifications and bills of materials.

Norse's use of S&OP to manage its critical engineering resource is an excellent example of how companies use S&OP to get a handle on the truly important parts of their business, and to manage them effectively over time.

Additional Company Experiences with Design-to-Order

AGFA's digital imaging equipment is assembled to customer order using the modules, components, and software specified by the customer. The lead time here is one to six weeks, depending on the product and options specified. The proprietary software is custom designed at their software design subsidiary in Ontario, Canada. This process encompasses:

> three thousand possible SKU's

> twenty major typical units forecasted and planned

> various options planned by historical percentages

> a large customer backlog providing most of the demand planning required

> S&OP used largely to monitor business performance, projected revenues, backlogs and lead times, and long term resource issues

New Products

Sooner or later, for each product line, every company must face the lagging sales that come with the end of the product lifecycle. These must be replaced by new product additions, or in some cases, entirely new product lines or approaches. Here S&OP is critical in providing future visibility for changing demand patterns: shrinking sales for some and fast growing for others.

Supporting increasing sales on existing or new products represents the happier, but often tougher set of challenges for many companies. S&OP helps focus on the future implications of this growth, and identifies when major resource adjustments are required.

What's the difference between S&OP for design-to-order products and a formal new product development (NPD) process? Conceptually, not much. But generally the new product development process has a broader scope and longer lead times, since its goal is to design products that can be sold to multiple customers in the future. Because of that scope there are typically many more resources to manage. And with a broader objective, and longer lead times, the accuracy of hitting target dates and utilizing a planned amount of each resource is often quite variable.

As we saw with **Norse Dairy Systems**, some companies use their S&OP process and the related detailed planning tools to manage product development and design resources, material availability, and suppliers, just like any other product.

That is not the case with new product development (NPD). Here all the resources and sample materials used in the design process may be managed separately from the ongoing manufacturing activities. (There are well established methodologies to help companies manage these activities, and they are beyond the scope of this book.) However, NPD must be properly integrated with the S&OP process to help manage the transition from design and development to active products managed by sales, marketing and operations.

S&OP and NPD

Conceptually, it's pretty simple. If any new product being developed in the NPD process will have an impact on sales or production within the S&OP planning horizon, then demand and supply plans need to be developed to represent the impact on business volume.

In actual practice it's much more difficult: difficult to predict future sales volumes on products that have never been sold before; and difficult to project the impact on production and supply resources, especially since the final product and process designs are rarely complete within the S&OP planning horizon.

Given this level of difficulty, why not just let the folks in design and development worry about it? After all, most of the time it only affects the far end of the S&OP horizon anyway, right? While that might be true most of the time, when a major new product is about to hit manufacturing, and shortly thereafter, the marketplace, it's probably already too late to manage this well, if the proper planning didn't happened months before.

Despite the uncertainty, S&OP provides management a monthly opportunity to revisit product launch dates and the latest new product sales forecasts, review their potential impact on manufacturing, suppliers and sales resources, and determine when the next steps need to be taken. This includes ordering materials, lining up resources (people and equipment), and preparing to sell the new products in a way that is cost effective, while minimizing any disruption in getting the new product to customers.

By ensuring that new product launch information is updated and fed into the S&OP process monthly, painful surprises can be avoided, such as:

➤ not being able to meet revenue goals or financial commitments that were predicated on the new products

➤ impacting other existing product lines, which may share critical resources or materials with the new product

➤ unplanned overtime and premium freight charges to rush the new product out at the last minute

> ➤ shortages and delays in getting the new product to customers, after it's been introduced to the marketplace

Often S&OP helps management monitor the achievement of major milestone dates and targets for product development and launch.

A Best Practice Example:
New Product Development at *Eli Lilly*

Eli Lilly launched ten new products from 2001 through 2005, a rate over *five times higher* than the pharmaceutical industry average. Further, **Lilly** can bring products to market *faster*, averaging less than eleven years from product concept to market, versus an industry average of over fourteen years.

At **Lilly**, new product launch is complex and lengthy due to FDA regulations. So there is a significant devotion of both time and resources to new product launches.   Managing the unique molecule for each drug through its life cycle: clinical trial testing, submission, launch, growth and patent expiration, is critical. It also includes outsourcing of late-life-cycle products to make room for new ones.

Many of the product development projects have highly variable conditions and timing. This has resulted in a great dependence upon supply chain principles, organization and processes to effectively manage this challenging opportunity, with S&OP providing a forum to document the current assumptions and manage change effectively.

S&OP provides the planning mechanism for **Lilly** to time-phase the rollout of their new products across the 146 countries in which they do business. This timing is key in helping each of the regional sales organizations reconcile their current sales forecasts to their financial revenue targets.

Lilly rigorously follows a formal new product development and launch process with capacity addition and sourcing decisions made when the probability of success of a product launch is still only 20 to 40%. These are also key inputs to the S&OP planning process, since worldwide utilization and allocation of capacity at their twenty-four plants is critical to **Lilly's** success.

Additional Company Experiences with New Product Development

For **Amcor's** customers, the average life of a product is only six months. Because of this, **Amcor** is subject to the unpredictability of many product launches and pipeline fills, as well as constant promotional and counter promotional activity.

The majority of **Amcor's** business is won by bidding on large customer contracts, which are typically decided on cost. But incumbent suppliers have an advantage if they have been providing excellent service, which may enable the retention of business at a premium equal to the value placed on the superior service by the customer.

Amcor's S&OP process coordinates the demand and supply planning on these many new product launches to insure a high level of customer service is maintained at a reasonable cost. New item lead times and performance on short lead time requests are constantly monitored to insure customer satisfaction.

AGFA, like any company in the imaging industry, is carefully managing the transition from the film-based approach (cameras and x-ray machines using film) to digital imaging (digital cameras and digital radiography machines that produce electronic images that can be stored and printed on paper as needed). All their company's revenues were once based on the former, which now produce lower revenues and profits, as they are being replaced by the newer, growing, more profitable digital products.

They have used S&OP to carefully manage the rationalization and reduction of the old product lines, while simultaneously introducing new ones. And this has been done while the company's gone through two changes of ownership, and multiple plant closings and consolidations (see more on this in chapter 10).

"S&OP allows us, from a marketing perspective, to seamlessly manage product life cycle issues (phase-in/phase-out). The impact is that our customer service is uninterrupted, allowing us to concentrate on selling the features and benefits of the new product without us having to concern ourselves with supply issues." Ray Russell, Director of Marketing, **AGFA US Healthcare**

Coca Cola Midi has developed specific expertise for developing and releasing new products prior to widespread commercialization and volume production. The activities here span all activities associated with new product development on a rapid launch basis. Once commercialized, many of these products will be produced elsewhere in the company

This activity requires a close partnership and coordination between and among Division HQ, Research and Development, **Coca-Cola Midi**, and the bottlers.

New product development reviews are a key part of the S&OP process. New products people provide information for new ingredients, new finished SKU's and launch feasibility updates to the S&OP process. In addition, information about near term middle term (six to nine months into the future) launch plans are all reviewed in the executive S&OP meeting.

Danfoss Commercial Compressors division has ambitious growth objectives of 24% over six years in a highly competitive market. A large part of this growth will come from regular introduction of new products in their two major product lines. The percent of annual sales from new products will stay at 20% to 30%. S&OP is the main top management tool for managing this high growth.

Interbake Foods and *Norse Dairy Systems* follow a formal NPD process they call Design Control Initiation Process (DCIP). It is used to formally introduce new products, change the existing products or processes, transfer existing products from plant to plant, then pass the information to the S&OP process.

At *Coca-Cola MIDI, Interbake, Norse Dairy Systems* and *UMC*, the formal NPD reviews are synchronized with S&OP meetings so that the latest new product information can be reviewed monthly

Summary

The basic structure and focus of the S&OP process remains unchanged, regardless of the order fulfillment Strategies, or the varying impact of new products over time.

The order fulfillment strategy affects what S&OP information you display - sales or bookings, finished goods or semi-finished inventory, backlog and customer lead times.

This information needs to be augmented with planning information from the new product development process, with S&OP being a vital tool in overseeing the successful and timely launch of the new products.

S&OP is management's control room, monitoring progress on all the critical factors listed above, as well as providing the visibility of many traditional KPI's such as customer service, customer lead times, inventory turnover and various operating costs.

S&OP helps management identify when things are working well, and when they're not. It then becomes a forum for discussing and deciding when changes are needed, whether they are in order fulfillment strategies, new product development resourcing or any other tactical or operational approaches.

Chapter 7

Tools for Linking Volume with Mix: S&OP and Resource Planning

How are the demand and supply plans for the detailed product mix managed in a way that is consistent with the volume plans from S&OP?

The essence of S&OP is setting an overall game plan consistent with the business strategies. As we saw in chapter 2, it focuses principally on the product volumes of family groupings and relies on other processes to reconcile these plans with detailed forecasts and schedules. But what are those processes and what ensures that they work properly to communicate the detailed plans to the people who must execute them?

In this chapter we will cover the methodologies and tools that support detailed planning and execution. These fall under the term "resource planning" - which you may know as MRP, MRPII or ERP.

Terminology, again

As described in Chapter 2, resource planning evolved in a series of important steps:

- Detailed material planning (material requirements planning - MRP)
- Closed loop demand and supply planning (manufacturing resource planning - MRPII)
- Integrated planning processes supported by highly integrated software (enterprise resource planning - ERP)

Sales and operations planning, a key element of resource planning, evolved similarly from production planning, the manufacturing focused aggregate planning process, to an integrated process encompassing functions beyond manufacturing and supply planning. This expanded S&OP played a critical role in providing the visibility and tools needed to manage the business in an integrated way with all these functions.

In parallel, assessment and certification programs evolved to help measure how effectively companies were using the tools of resource planning. Ollie Wight created the first checklist in 1975. The ABCD Checklist, originally twenty questions, has grown over the years to a significantly more detailed checklist and associated process for benchmarking performance. Today, as in 1975, the companies using resource planning tools up to their full potential are rated **"Class A"**. Companies not using it as well are classified **Class B, Class C,** and **Class D,** in descending order of effectiveness.

Today this ABCD Checklist can be used for benchmarking a variety of methodologies, including:

- Resource planning (MRPII or ERP)
- Lean manufacturing
- Quality management (TQM/6 Sigma)
- Strategic planning
- New product development

Hundreds if not thousands of companies are rightfully proud of their Class A certification in resource planning. Hundreds of others are still pursuing it. Some large global companies, such as Coca-Cola, still see Class A certification in each of their divisions and locations as an effective approach to ensure critical core competency.

Of our thirteen model companies, the following seven have been certified Class A in resource planning: ***Amcor, Coca-Cola Midi, Eli Lilly, Interbake Foods, Norse Dairy Systems, Pyosa*** and **UMC.** All the others also effectively employ the detailed tools and techniques of resource planning. Each company emphasizes the critical need for guiding the detailed demand and supply planning with their S&OP process.

You can't achieve Class A results without S&OP and detailed resource planning working hand in hand. Concurrent implementation isn't necessary, but for either to work effectively, both must be in place and highly integrated.

S&OP without the detailed parts of resource planning is like going on a diet by just buying a scale and setting overall goals for weight loss, calorie intake and exercise, without breaking that down into a daily schedule and routine.

Resource planning without S&OP would be like buying exercise equipment, running shoes and low-fat and low-carb foods, without having overall goals and a plan to utilize them.

The Basics of Resource Planning
- The Demand Side

It all starts with the customer.

Even before it was fashionable and captured in a catchphrase ("demand driven"), the best companies knew that effective planning and resource management starts with managing customer demand. Demand management is the term often used to describe customer order management[13] and sales forecasting processes, although it may also include distribution resource planning (DRP) and sales force management. While sales force management is beyond the scope of this book, the other three processes will be discussed in detail below.

Customer Order Management

This handles the processing of customer demands and associated data from quotation to acknowledgement to shipping. S&OP utilizes this data to monitor backlog, actual sales and the accuracy of the forecast. This is typically accomplished during data gathering and review - Step 1 of the S&OP process when monthly totals are summarized and passed into the S&OP process.

By analyzing sales and the current backlog, S&OP highlights performance against lead time targets set by product family or category. It also provides a forum to identify problems caused when backlogs and lead times grow or shrink from planned levels, and spot opportunities for competitive advantage in those same situations. These may lead to changes in aggregate or detailed demand or supply plans, or in the targets themselves (triggered either by changes in the marketplace or in the company's ability to deliver in the short term).

Sales Forecasting

This is a process at the heart of S&OP. For many companies even today, their initial interest in S&OP is driven by a desire to improve forecast accuracy. In demand planning - Step 2 of the S&OP process, the primary focus is on developing the sales forecasts and reducing their variability. Here companies update both their family and item level forecasts on a monthly basis.

The way that forecasts are developed, as well as the level of forecast detail, may vary from product to product. Sometimes companies (typically for make-to-stock products, or make-to-order products with a relatively few number of customers and product variations) start at the item level, then aggregate those forecasts up to family totals, both as a validity check and to feed the S&OP planning process.

In other cases, companies (typically for make-to-order, finish-to-order, and design-to-

---

[13] The term customer relationship management - CRM has become popular in recent years. It typically is used to encompass the functions of customer order management, customer communications, the development of customer contracts and agreements, customer collaboration, and other related interfaces with customers.

order products with many product variations) develop the forecasts at a family, sub-family or product group level, and where necessary aggregate these numbers for the S&OP family. Since individual, shippable product configurations are not produced until a customer order is received, individual forecasts for each of these are not necessary.

One particular strength of S&OP is its ability to monitor actual sales against the forecast, and to project the future implications of current activities and trends. S&OP provides the structure for the responsible sales and marketing people to periodically review and update the forecasts, while documenting the underlying activities and assumptions that affect the demand patterns. These numbers are then reviewed by multiple functions in the company during the partnership and executive meetings - Steps 4 and 5 of the S&OP process.

These reviews within the S&OP process show that the most effective forecasts are more than computer generated statistical projections. When done properly, final forecast numbers will typically include human input from a variety of sources. The numbers can and should be adjusted by responsible managers based on their knowledge of the marketplace, including changing trends and factors in the future compared to the past. The process can also accommodate input and collaboration from customers, demand chain partners and field sales personnel (see chapter 9 on "The Extended Demand and Supply Chains").

Besides including essential human input, the most successful forecasting processes are those that are kept simple, understandable, reliable and usable in a way that is easily integrated into the supply planning step. The focus is not on an unrealistic expectation of perfection, but on constantly minimizing the forecast error and adjusting the numbers to match reality as things change. S&OP keeps the spotlight on this by its monthly review of key KPI's, such as customer service, inventory turns, backlog levels, average customer lead times, and forecast accuracy.

See the best practice examples for "Collaborative Forecasting with Customers at *Scotts"*, and "An Additional Company Examples of Customer Linking" at *Interbake Food* in chapter 9, under the Collaborative Forecasting section. See also *AGFA, Amcor, Danfoss, Eli Lilly, EMS, Norse Dairy Systems* and *UMC*.

Demand Management in a Distribution Environment: Managing Finished Goods Inventories through the Supply Chain Pipeline

Many companies manage their make-to-stock products through a network of warehouses, distributors, wholesalers, retailers and/or dealers, each of whom may maintain finished goods inventories of designated items. Depending on the volume, geography and market characteristics, these companies may use any number of steps and partners between their plants and the ultimate customer.

For truly enlightened companies, the goal is to optimize service and inventory performance throughout the supply chain, regardless of who owns the inventory at each point. Having just the right amount of inventory at the right links within the chain will satisfy the customer and minimize the capital that is tied up. This is better for every one of the supply chain partners, each of whom can share the benefits of decreased working capital, reduced cost, and improved supply chain responsiveness.

To accomplish this, the interaction with the distributors and customers needs to focus on inventory levels and replenishment plans, as well as forecasts and future customer orders. This demand planning and management of the inventory, as well as the flow of product throughout the chain, is best done collaboratively, integrating the knowledge and attention of each partner in the supply chain.

The major tool to achieve this is a proven one: **"distribution resource planning" - DRP.** Our colleague Andre Martin was a pioneer in developing, defining and spreading this approach beginning over thirty years ago at Abbott Labs of Canada.

DRP is quite simple. It's just applying time phased planning logic (first developed for manufacturing as material requirements planning - MRP) to the finished goods inventory network.

> ➢ it starts with the sales forecast for each region served by each distribution center

> ➢ the forecast may be updated monthly, or more frequently

> ➢ these forecasts are compared to current regional inventory levels

> ➢ following prescribed inventory and restocking rules, predicted replenishment plans are generated for each item over the planning horizon

> ➢ the predicted replenishment plans are updated on a weekly or daily basis based on the latest demand, supply and inventory information

This logic can be applied to multiple links in the supply chain (for instance, retail stores, retail distribution centers, supplier distribution centers and finally back to supplier plant locations). It is the most effective way of directly linking actual customer demand, using the inventory throughout the network, back to the manufacturer.

DRP is done at the finished goods SKU level. It provides the detail that can then be aggregated to family totals, and reviewed in the demand planning step of the S&OP process. Here management can accurately monitor sales, inventory and customer service performance, and where necessary, decide upon tactical adjustments to improve performance.

In this way, DRP broadens demand planning by monitoring and managing finished goods inventory in every location of the company, its demand chain partners, and sometimes its customers, regardless of the legal ownership of the inventory. The information is often shared with the demand chain partners and customers, and in some cases they actually participate in the company's S&OP process.

A Best Practice Example:
DRP at *Eli Lilly*

Lilly has four networks of over twenty plants in total, producing 65 different products (over 8000 SKU's), sold through 130 worldwide sales affiliates. The global inventory ($1.7 billion) and customer orders are managed through four regional distribution centers who distribute to over sixty local distribution centers (both internal and third party).

All of these links in the supply chain use sound demand and supply chain principles, documented business processes, and effective DRP and MRPII / ERP tools, with capable, trained people to operate them.

Additional Company Experiences with DRP

Pyosa uses DRP to manage regional forecasts, demands and inventories through the network of six Pyosa distribution centers in North and South America, each of which stocks up to 340 items. In addition, 25% of their sales is through distributors (2 in Mexico and fifteen in South America), each stocking about ten products.

All of these activities feed into and are guided by their S&OP process.

The Basics of Resource Planning
- Balancing the Supply to the Demand

"The key is providing the correct planning tools, empowering the individuals using these tools and strong support from the senior management team." Jeff Crawford, Director of Manufacturing, Engineering and Packaging, ***Norse Dairy Systems***

Once the latest demand plans are established by combining customer order backlogs, updated forecasts and DRP replenishment plans, supply plans need to be developed to ensure that all the materials and resources required will be available when it comes time to begin manufacturing.

Master Scheduling

As mentioned above under forecasting, for make-to-stock and simpler make-to-order product lines, the demand plans are usually developed at an item level. This supports a supply planning process by item, typically specifying sequenced weekly scheduled amounts. Often, beyond the critical (material and/or capacity) lead time, these plans are expressed as monthly totals. This process is called **master production scheduling** or **MPS**.

For make-to-order, finish-to-order and design-to-order products, the MPS is not by item, but rather by family, sub-family or model, again at the same level of detail as the forecast. Often a planner will establish an MPS schedule for the entire family, and an individual schedules for major components or product options whose frequency must also be forecast. This is called **two-level master scheduling,** and it ensures that specific semi-finished, component and raw material inventories, and differing resource requirements are planned appropriately for each of the product option schedules.

In some cases, detailed master schedules are summarized to set the aggregate supply plan for S&OP. In other cases (often for make-to-order products), the aggregate supply plans are set at the family level and then reconciled to the total of the detailed master schedules.

The **master scheduling** process includes production rules for sequencing, production lot sizes, and the frequency of manufacturing. If lean manufacturing is being pursued, these are set to improve the flow of product through manufacturing.

To insure that the supply plans are feasible, capacity planning tools are utilized to ensure that enough people, equipment and supplier resources will be available when needed. At the MPS level, typically only the critical resources are checked through a process called **rough cut capacity planning** or **RCCP.** RCCP is often applied to the S&OP family level as well, to ensure that the monthly rates of production across all families can be accommodated by critical resources.

The aggregate supply plans, master production schedules, and capacity planning checks typically are reviewed and updated during supply planning - Step 3 of the S&OP process. However, this is not the only time during the month that master scheduling and capacity planning happen. They are nearly continuous processes. Throughout the month, some adjustment and fine-tuning of the master schedules and capacity plans can be triggered by the receipt of actual customer orders and the monitoring of actual production. But once a month, when the new forecasts are developed, a major replanning occurs as a critical step in S&OP.

Detailed Resource Planning

The master schedule triggers plans for the appropriate mix of raw materials, components and capacity resources, by driving the following:

> Based on the bills of material, future requirements for every manufactured and purchased item are calculated using a planning tool called **material requirements planning** or **MRP**. This takes into account inventories of every item at every level, as well as all open manufacturing and purchasing orders.

> In some environments, particularly those that have been streamlined by lean manufacturing, the product mix and inventory levels are stable enough that the requirements for some materials (typically those used most frequently and steadily) can be calculated directly from the family S&OP plans. This is accomplished using a technique called **rough cut material planning**, or some equivalent method that does not involve a traditional bill of material explosion using lead times, inventories, lot sizes, etc..

> The key point here is that material requirements planning (MRP) as described above isn't always used, but there does need to be a way to project future requirements for the suppliers.

> The feasibility of these plans can be checked, using manufacturing routing information, by detailed **capacity requirements planning** or **CRP**. The logic here is the same as for RCCP, but it checks each work center, process or resource, not just the critical ones.

> This results in a full horizon of projected plans for all manufactured and purchased items. The latter are often called **supplier schedules**. These can then be shared with the manufacturing, purchasing and supplier personnel, who can insure that they're prepared to meet them once they are released.

> In some manufacturing environments, the planning system can trigger the release of manufacturing orders (sometimes called **plant schedules**) and purchase delivery orders based on manufacturing and supplier lead times.

> Alternately, in a lean manufacturing environment, the actual release of work to production, or to suppliers, may be triggered by a "demand pull" or "kanban" mechanism. Here, regardless of the forecast or plan, actual work doesn't begin until inventory or previous production is either shipped to the customer or consumed downstream in the manufacturing process. This better synchronizes production to the downstream consumption by customers, irrespective of the "accuracy" of the forecast.

Putting It All Together

Decades of experience with resource planning proves that detailed planning and execution systems do not work to their full capability without an integrated monthly S&OP process. S&OP ensures that demand and supply plans are balanced at a family, volume level, so that the detailed item and mix level can be properly managed day-to-day and week-to-week. It does this by directly connecting to the MPS and RCCP processes, and using these to guide the other detailed processes.

Without this connection to detailed resource planning tools, the objectives and plans established in the S&OP process will never be consistently met.

A Best Practice Example: Resource Planning at *Interbake Foods*

Interbake has been certified Class A in manufacturing resource planning (MRPII) in three manufacturing plants, four business segments, and enterprise-wide.

➢ Sales forecasts are developed for each product line, in each business segment, based on input and collaboration between marketing, field sales people, and where appropriate, major customers.

➢ The forecasts are by family, and by item for major products, and include any planned promotional or other marketing activity.

➢ They use the customer backlog, individual item forecasts where available, and for all other items, a family planning bill of material to derive the item mix from the family forecast.

➢ *Interbake* maintains a weekly production schedule by item for up to eight weeks out, depending on the plant, with a weekly master production schedule covering twenty-six weeks.

➢ In some cases, they convert the family level forecast to an eighteen month family production plan, which drives long range material requirements, crewing, and line capacity for months three through eighteen.

➢ In other cases, they generate a monthly production plan for each end item to drive their material and capacity requirements.

➢ At *Interbake*, senior management approves the plans at the executive meeting, but leaves all the tactical decision-making to their partnership level managers, who ensure that the S&OP plans are driven down through their MRPII system to each supplier and production resource.

*"The end result is a **vertical partnership** between operating management and senior management regarding a single company game plan, and a **horizontal partnership** between the functional areas of the business that are responsible for achieving the business plans and financial results."* John Civerolo, Consultant

Additional Company Examples

At *AGFA, Pyosa* and *Eli Lilly,* S&OP and detailed resource planning are tightly interwoven. Volume and detailed mix planning are not separated conceptually, only practically by who does the review and decision-making, and at what stage of the process: customer order management, detailed forecasting, distribution planning, master production scheduling, or S&OP family planning. None of these companies really differentiate between S&OP and detailed resource planning (MRPII). They see them as interconnected methodologies in one company-wide process.

Pyosa was the first "Class A" manufacturing resource planning (MRPII) user in Mexico, linking management strategies through S&OP plans to detailed manufacturing and supplier schedules, all to support the business plan and performance objectives.

Amcor manages with a well integrated, closed-loop resource planning and control process having achieved Class A MRPII accreditation during December 2003.

At *Coca-Cola Midi (CCM)* their MRPII process is driven by S&OP, and has been key in dealing with the competitive challenges in the rapidly changing nature of *CCM's* business. They achieved Class A MRPII certification ten months after the site was opened in 1990 and have maintained that level of excellence for over fifteen years. Rough cut capacity planning is vigorously utilized to validate the monthly production plans and weekly master schedules. It is the major tool used for managing manpower levels.

At *UMC* the S&OP monthly production plan directly drives requirements for key component suppliers, via rough cut material planning. Then the weekly Master Schedule, derived from the monthly production plan, is used to drive requirements planning on all other required materials.

At *Danfoss*, rough cut purchase requirements are derived from S&OP, by multiplying the production plan by quantities from a resource planning bill of material.

Resource Planning in the New Millennium
Advanced Planning Systems - APS

In this section we had hoped to share with you the extensive successful experiences of many companies using the newer, more "sophisticated" demand and supply planning tools called APS. In fact, two years ago, we undertook a study with one of our associates, Jack Gips, to catalog the experiences of companies successfully using APS. We asked over thirty of our consulting associates (who have worked with thousands of clients during their long consulting careers) to provide us with reference companies. We also contacted eleven software suppliers and seven consulting firms. From all these sources we could only find one company that actually successfully used these new APS tools in a significant way. Their story is described at the end of this section.

The Promise of the Black Box

The promise of APS is enticing. It is to apply sheer computer power and use clever programming to more effectively automate demand, distribution and supply planning. Some software vendors even hint at mostly taking humans out of the equation, and letting the computer automatically reset the plans. And given the computer's tireless nature, some suggest that all the plans can be readjusted daily, hourly, or perhaps every time a new customer order is received.

If this could be done effectively, it would be impressive indeed. The problem is that while these approaches sound good, they haven't been proven to work in practice. No company that we know of has used APS extensively in this proposed way. And the more you think about it, if plans could be changed that quickly, how could the humans working in sales, marketing, manufacturing and planning possibly ever keep up with it? And that's not to mention the various pieces of equipment that would have to be constantly redeployed to react to the constant changes in plans. One writer suggests that the most effective users of APS are actually the ones that are updating it the least frequently.

The Problems with APS

We see several significant problems with using APS systems as envisioned above:

> They require the user to load and maintain data, criteria, rules and factors into the program, so that the computer can iteratively crunch the numbers until it comes up with an optimal plan given current demand and supply data. In some cases, it is difficult to express these factors in a quantitative way that the program can utilize.

➤ With the marketplace constantly changing, and supplier and manufacturing resources being adjusted, can these planning factors be updated frequently enough?

➤ APS systems assume that most of the factors needed for planning future demand and replenishment activities are known or can be reasonably foreseen in advance. This is the same weakness that exists with any statistical sales forecasting package: the factors and elements in the past can be clearly defined, but will they continue in the future, and how and when will they change?

➤ Users are unwilling to be held accountable for executing a plan where they can't reconstruct how it was calculated, or why the system changed it from the last plan that they agreed to. If the APS system is run as frequently as some recommend, this could be as frequently as every few minutes!

For these reasons, and because (we believe) of the inherent complexity of the tools, many of these software packages have been purchased, but only a very few have actually been implemented and used on an ongoing basis.

The Real Value of APS

Where APS has been effective (and we believe will be effective in the future) is as a simulation or what-if planning tool. Load some factors, and test out the implications of a given set of numbers. Adjust the factors and try it again. Let knowledgeable, experienced humans prescreen the significant factors and the potentially effective solutions, rather than have the computer test every possible combination of factors and data.

We believe APS is the latest evolution of computerized automatic scheduling and modeling tools. We do not believe that APS will ever effectively replace human managed communication and decision-making processes like S&OP and ERP/MRPII. Rather APS should be seen as a set of decision support tools that can be used in circumstances where major change is occurring or seems imminent.

Think of APS as a power tool, but one that still depends on good architectural plans, and the skills of a craftsman to be effectively put to use.

A Best Practice Example:
APS at *Eli Lilly*

Only one of our thirteen model companies uses or has even attempted to use APS. As we mentioned earlier, in our study of two years ago we were unable to find any other companies that had gotten much further.

Eli Lilly uses APS as an integrated tool within their MRPII / ERP system, to plan and schedule their over-twenty manufacturing sites across the supply chain in a way that avoids overloads, and minimizes inventories and lead times. Their APS tool provides the capability to view data globally in many different units of measure, by region or by plant, with a drill down capability for analysis and simulation. They use APS quarterly to rebalance global production plans and capacities, allocate capacity and production responsibility, adjust the source of supply, and where necessary, give feedback to sales affiliates to adjust the timing and source of their warehouse replenishment demands.

After extensive training on, and testing of the APS system capabilities, they have chosen to use the software in the simplest manner to optimize only two major constraints. They feel that using the system to optimize any more constraints or criteria would result in information that was so complex that it would be impossible for the responsible planners and managers to utilize it effectively.

Summary

S&OP is the driver, the windshield, the dashboard and the steering wheel. The detailed resource planning and execution systems of ERP and MRPII are the rest of the car, insuring the rubber meets the road in the right direction, in the right gear, and at the right speed.

Without S&OP, detailed resource planning systems lack the ability to effectively balance supply and demand and ensure that all of the efforts of the individual sub-processes and people are reconciled, synchronized, and integrated for the greatest potential performance.

Without effective, integrated resource planning tools, the plans and targets set by an S&OP process cannot be effectively and profitably met.

S&OP can provide a forum for management to: review current status; identify where improvements are needed, or need to be continued or accelerated; and authorize new improvement targets or processes, both in the accuracy of data and in the effectiveness of the detailed planning and execution systems.

Chapter 8

S&OP and Continuous Improvement through Lean Manufacturing and TQM/6 Sigma

Is S&OP really needed in a company using continuous improvement methods like lean manufacturing or TQM/6 Sigma? Is S&OP part of continuous improvement or an alternative to it? What are the experiences of companies that have used all these methodologies - S&OP, Lean, and TQM/6 Sigma? How do they work together?

For almost three decades now, leading companies have been implementing effective S&OP processes in order to plan and execute strategy, to prioritize market and plant improvement opportunities, and to monitor results.

At the same time, much of Western manufacturing has "gone Lean", using the tools of lean manufacturing and 6 Sigma[14] to drive continuous improvement - reduce defects, cut setup times and order quantities, slash lead times, increase productivity, reduce obsolescence, and cut costs.

We believe the widespread adoption of continuous improvement through lean manufacturing and 6 Sigma, and of sales and operations planning, have been the outstanding events in manufacturing in the last twenty years.

But do they actually help each other? Can a company using S&OP leverage it to get even better results with continuous improvement? And can a company effectively using the lean manufacturing and 6 Sigma tools of continuous improvement, get even better results from their S&OP process?

Our thirteen best practice companies certainly think so. According to Malcolm Jaggard, Director, Supply Chain Management, ***AGFA US Healthcare***: *"Continuous improvement is embedded in the S&OP process, and continuous improvement cannot be maximized without S&OP."*

With regard to continuous improvement, many (including us) believe that lean manufacturing and 6 Sigma go hand-in-hand. You probably can't do an effective job of lean manufacturing without using the problem solving and statistical tools that are part of 6 Sigma. Conversely, if you have a manufacturing environment where any key Lean

---

[14] The terms TQM (total quality management) and 6 Sigma are both in widespread use today. There are some differences between the two, but there are many, many similarities. Since many companies today use the term 6 Sigma to describe their quality improvement activities, we are going to use the term 6 Sigma alone to refer to all quality improvement initiatives. If your company is doing TQM and not 6 Sigma, don't worry, our comments about S&OP and quality apply just as much to your situation.

concepts - like standardizing work activities and instructions, leveling of production, reduced setup or mistake-proofing - are not applied, you'll probably have problems making headway with 6 Sigma.

Yet even though many people correctly see the two toolsets going hand in hand, the vast majority of companies implement them as two separate initiatives. As matter of fact, according to a 2004 Census of Manufacturers by Industry Week magazine, in the US:

> ➢ 42% use lean manufacturing
> ➢ 14% use 6 Sigma
> ➢ 11% use lean manufacturing and 6 Sigma

For that reason, we will talk about lean manufacturing and 6 Sigma separately in this chapter.

S&OP and Lean Manufacturing

Sales and operations planning and lean manufacturing go hand in hand. They do different - and very necessary - things, and you need them both.

A principal objective of lean manufacturing is to create the physical environment that will allow material to flow - from raw material to finished product to the customer. Doing this means eliminating waste and wasteful practices, reducing costs and cutting lead times - while synchronizing all production and purchasing activities. S&OP, integrated with the other detailed tools of resource planning, is a set of forward planning tools to help balance future demand and supply, to predict capacity and material problems with enough time to do something about them, and to understand the financial consequences of production and purchasing decisions.

If you create a manufacturing environment where material flows with minimum waste (Lean), but you can't predict capacity and material availability problems in enough time to avoid them (S&OP), you will inevitably revert to firefighting, finger-pointing and poor results. Similarly, if you do an excellent job of future planning but have poor flows, you can almost count on higher inventory levels, longer lead times, and lower profitability.

Traditionally lean manufacturing has been stronger on workplace management; S&OP on decision-making for the future. The tools and methods of lean manufacturing have tended to look most closely at the plant, and its immediate customers and suppliers, mostly over a short horizon. This leads to improvements like: "shorter, quicker, fewer, lower cost, more flexible, and better aligned".

S&OP provides distance vision - providing the ability to predict capacity and material availability problems before they become crises, to identify market issues while they are still opportunities, and to prioritize improvements in a way that will create the most favorable results.

What company wouldn't want both? Hundreds of companies have proven that you can have both, and that each approach amplifies the benefits of the other.   In other words - they work best when they work together.

Bill Kerber, the consultant for **EMS,** who specializes in lean manufacturing and S&OP says "*The S&OP process fits nicely around Lean concepts such as leveling volume and mix for a value-stream and using inventory as a strategic buffer for customer service. As management's steering wheel for the business, it serves as the logical starting point for any Lean transformation.*"

Let's take a look at the areas where lean manufacturing and S&OP complement each other:

Objectives and Key Tools of Lean Manufacturing

A key objective of lean manufacturing is to get inventory to flow to the customer, ideally without interruption - and ideally one piece at a time. To achieve uninterrupted flow, several Lean concepts have important connections to S&OP. These include:

➢ **Takt time** is the key Lean concept for synchronizing production rates with customer demand, and as such is arguably the most important idea in Lean. Takt times drive cell designs and operator balancing processes, are used for leveling production, for scheduling finishing processes, and for monitoring production performance in time increments small enough for rapid response to problems.

Takt time expresses the sales rate - how fast must the plant must produce a product in order to be perfectly synchronized with the customer. One unit every twenty-three seconds in a company making visors for automobiles, one unit per hour in an organization producing large pumps, or one unit every two weeks for a manufacturer of fighter jets would be practical examples takt times in real companies.

"Operational takt time" expresses the anticipated build rate, taking into consideration finished goods inventory adjustments or work time adjustments like overtime. For the examples cited above, the operational takt time might be one unit every twenty-three seconds (no inventory adjustment or overtime), one unit per 1 hour 15 minutes (finished goods inventory is being lowered to reduce working capital), or one unit every 1.5 weeks (overtime has been added and the build rate increased because of a subsequent planned shutdown).

Since S&OP also tries to synchronize the plant (supply) with customer demand, it shouldn't be surprising to hear that Lean and S&OP are complementary. In many Lean companies, the demand plan from S&OP establishes the takt time and the supply plan from S&OP sets the build rate and the operational takt time. And over time, as supply and demand are brought into balance through S&OP, takt time and operational takt time converge as well.

➤ **Value-stream mapping and improvement** is an essential methodology for a very specific kind of process mapping. Basically the idea is to document every value-adding and non-value-adding activity for each product - start to finish, raw material to finished product - and then use this as the basis for improvement. The current value-stream map shows what the overall flow is today. Future value-stream maps show what the desired future state should be.

Comparing value-stream maps of the current states to the future states then drive improvement projects to streamline and simplify the manufacturing environment by reducing setups, improving yield rates, cutting unplanned downtime, etc.

Generally speaking there are two important connections between S&OP and value-stream mapping:

First, value-stream mapping is oriented towards identifying distinct product families and then, as much as possible, disentangling any shared manufacturing processes so as to make the simplest, most streamlined production environment. Distinct value-streams here typically correspond to distinct product families in S&OP.

Second, this mapping tries to improve each value-stream by reducing waste and improving flow, increasing flexibility and reducing lead time. These improvements enhance S&OP's ability to respond to changes as well.

➤ Equally important from a lean manufacturing perspective is a **balanced and managed capacity plan.** Rough cut capacity planning (performed during the supply planning step of S&OP) provides distance vision to Lean. Imbalances between supply and demand, and between planned capacity and required capacity can be predicted long in advance, and fixed long before they become a problem for the Lean execution systems.

And S&OP provides future visibility for internal manufacturing, new product development resources, and for key supply chain partners.

➤ **Streamlined production means simplified planning processes** and that certainly holds true for S&OP. Shorter lead times mean improved flexibility to respond to changes, the possibility of reduced planning horizons, less inventory with the same or better customer service - all big benefits to the business. And in a simplified environment, S&OP can be used to directly calculate and communicate future detailed requirements to suppliers and partners. This might come directly out of a rough cut planning calculation, rather than the traditional method of deriving it from a detailed material planning technique like MRP.

Kanban (or *demand pull*) is a primary execution technique of Lean that can simplify or eliminate traditional execution or ordering systems, and reduce even further the need for MRP type techniques. Kanban can be used anytime material cannot be made to flow continuously between two processes. For example if the supplying process and the consuming process cannot produce at the same rate (the cycle time is different, they have significantly different setups, operate to a different work day, or a host of other reasons), kanban can be used to signal when more material is required from the supplying process. In a kanban system, the only work that happens is that authorized by a kanban pull signal - without the use of traditional work orders or purchase orders. The use of kanban has no direct effect on the mechanics of S&OP.

Notable Practices of Our Model Companies:

Lean Without Good S&OP:

> *EMS* started to implement lean manufacturing, only to realize that their existing S&OP process was not working as well as it should. Before launching full stride into Lean, they had to upgrade both their forecasting and S&OP processes.

Takt Time:

> At *EMS*, the supply plan rates for each S&OP family are used to calculate takt times, and the inventory plans authorized by S&OP link to the production rates used in both S&OP and Lean. While it isn't always the case, at *EMS* the families as defined by Lean matched fairly well with the pre-existing S&OP groupings. This made it very easy to use S&OP to set takt times and provide valid demand numbers for each value-stream.

> At *Danfoss*, operational takt time derived from S&OP is now being implemented to govern the Lean production processes in the factories.

Value-stream Mapping and Improvement:

> At *EMS*, value-stream mapping was used to prioritize Lean initiatives and to implement one S&OP product family at a time. For each family, a current

state value-stream map and multiple future state maps guide improvement activities.

➤ Thanks to several years of lean manufacturing initiatives at **UMC**, S&OP is seen as "*easier*" and less linked to short term decision-making. Overall, lean manufacturing led to better responsiveness to mix changes and improved inventory turnover.

Specific Lean improvements that helped with improved flexibility at **UMC** included:

o   plant flow improvement (moving from functional plant arrangements to cellular manufacturing, arranged by product line)

o   moving to a demand pull finishing schedule concept where production is triggered by customer pulls from small finished goods inventories (*supermarkets* in "lean speak")

o   redesigned products, allowing some product options to be installed at the customer site

o   improved material availability due to the high reliability developed in manufacturing and at the key suppliers

o   lead time reductions on manufactured and purchased materials ranging from 25% to 75%%.

➤ Since reorganizing its factories into cellular configurations several years ago, **Danfoss** has pursued a variety of lean manufacturing initiatives: value-stream mapping, synchronizing to takt time, cycle time reduction, streamlined changeover, utilizing kanban, implementing total preventive maintenance, and pursuing a range of small group improvement activities.

Generally speaking, results in manufacturing have been very good. For example, in one process, lot sizes of two weeks' usage have been eliminated. Today, every part is produced every day, increasing the line's responsiveness to the final assembly process and customer needs.

For a second product line in another factory, customer order lead time from order placement to delivery was reduced from eight weeks to ten days, a 75% reduction. And the ten days includes order processing time of two days and transportation time of five days, which means that assembly takes only three days.

At **Danfoss,** the impact of Lean with its shorter lead times, along with better planning guided by S&OP, has been significant in other areas as well:

- o   Customer service increased from 60% to 99%

- o   Total inventory has been cut in half while control of inventory is better

- o   Seasonality is managed better

- o   It's easier to anticipate customer demand

- o   The S&OP meetings are shorter

But the most important aspect of implementing Lean within the context of their existing S&OP process was the integration of sales and marketing people into the improvement process. Instead of having manufacturing people decide which improvements to make, sales and marketing people had a chance to help prioritize these efforts based on actual customer data.

Capacity Management:

- ➤   Key managers at **UMC** feel that lean manufacturing is somewhat "*shortsighted*" when it comes to future demand shifts and capacity concerns, and that S&OP and its related detailed planning tools provide the required vision to deal with these issues in the future

- ➤   At **EMS**, rough cut capacity planning is used to validate S&OP plans both against the current state value-stream (over the shorter horizon) and the future state value-stream (over the longer horizon)

Streamlined Production Means Simplified Planning Processes:

- ➤   *At UMC*, planning in general, and S&OP specifically, has been simplified due to the decreased variability, shorter lead times and improved confidence in data.

Additional Company Experiences with Lean

Eclipse started their initial Lean activities in 1999 due to cost and lead time competitive pressures. S&OP has very nicely complimented their previously existing lean manufacturing efforts

At **Norse Dairy Systems,** the S&OP process drives a continuous improvement focus on reduction of customer complaints, cost, waste, and labor, using Kepner-Tregoe problem solving and decision-making tools, to find the root causes of problems and develop corrective actions. All US plants have had outstanding results from these lean manufacturing efforts, including: increased capacity utilization, less inventory in queue and the stockroom, shorter manufacturing lead times and improved manufacturing flow.

Cast-Fab has pursued lean manufacturing to build on their S&OP successes. "*We cut some batch sizes, did some 5S* (a methodology for organizing the manufacturing workplace for cleanliness, safety, ergonomics and efficiency) *and did some work on balancing load.*" Ross Bushman, President and COO.

Eli Lilly has extended their quality programs to include lean manufacturing. Most of the company is in the early stages of education and certification of internal "black/green belt" experts, with specific project identification and rollout of implementation activities just beginning.

The Scotts Company has implemented Lean at a plant in California and has organized just-in-time deliveries from suppliers of packaging materials (for example bottles from a key supplier located near the Iowa plant).

S&OP and Lean Work Best Together

Overall S&OP is a very effective way to monitor company performance improvements coming from lean manufacturing: customer service levels, demand variability, the flexibility of supply, on-time performance, reductions in lead times, and capacity availability in key resources. These documented improvements can be communicated to the marketplace to emphasize a company's competitive advantage.

As Glen Melanson, Vice President of Manufacturing at **UMC** says: "*Use lean manufacturing to drive continuous performance improvements. And use S&OP to focus on the new opportunities that are possible because of the flexibility created by lean manufacturing.*"

S&OP and 6 Sigma

As mentioned earlier in this chapter, many companies view quality methods, particularly 6 Sigma, as an indispensable part of their lean manufacturing efforts. Both Lean and 6 Sigma seek to identify and eliminate variation, and as a consequence, waste in manufacturing processes. However they can be implemented independently, so it's worth saying a few words about how quality initiatives can support and complement S&OP, and looking at some of the experiences of the model companies.

The Development of Quality Methods

As was the case with terminology related to resource planning, the terms we use for quality improvement have gone through several changes in the last fifty years. For example, the roots of 6 Sigma are in TQM (total quality management) whose roots are in Deming's TQC (total quality control) which can be traced to Shewhart's statistical process control (SPC) methods. It has been implemented in a variety of ways, ranging from Japan's quality circles to today's project-focused, "black belt" driven projects. Yet regardless of the terminology changes and various implementation methods through the years, some observations are as appropriate today as they were fifty years ago. Whether your program is TQC or TQM or 6 Sigma:

> **Quality is conformance to requirements**, not "gold plating". A high quality product meets the requirements as determined by its customers. In this way, an inexpensive car - say a Hyundai - is a high quality car when it meets the requirements for its target customers, just as an expensive car with more chrome, fancier paint, a larger engine, a more aerodynamic design, etc. would be a low quality car if it doesn't start reliably.

> **Variation is the enemy.** It causes defects and must be monitored and minimized or eliminated.

> **You can't inspect quality in**. You can sort out defects, but the damage is already done. The only way to ensure quality at minimum cost is to meet the requirements the first time.

> **Defects are most often caused by the "system"**. Generally speaking, people don't go to work intending to produce defects. But less than optimal equipment and tools, unrealistic quotas, the inability to monitor a process, etc. - the production system - may not allow them to produce defect-free products.

> **A process is never optimized**, it can always be improved.

> **Improved quality doesn't cost more**, it actually leads to lower cost.

What is 6 Sigma?

As we explained earlier, we've been using the term "6 Sigma" as the generic description of a modern quality initiative. 6 Sigma is a results-oriented, project-focused approach to quality improvement. The basic idea is to focus problem solving tools in general, and SPC in particular, to the 4% of the issues that create 50% of the problems or defects. Using these tools, assisted by skilled experts ("green belts" or "black belts"), processes can be improved so that defects are fewer than 3.4 per million - or six standard deviations from the average or mean. This is the source of the term "6 Sigma". As we heard someone express it once: "6 Sigma is TQM on steroids!"

And What Does 6 Sigma Mean to S&OP?

So imagine operating in an environment where fewer than four defects occur in every million products produced. Planning (S&OP) works better - because there are fewer defects, less scrap and rework, things are more predictable, plans are more often met! And the same statistical tools and problem solving skills can be used to reduce demand variability as well. Again S&OP works better - less need for high inventory to hedge against highly variable forecasts.

And S&OP helps 6 Sigma by providing a more stable operating environment to measure and improve. And as mentioned before, S&OP can help select and prioritize improvement opportunity areas and then monitor progress against goals.

It should be noted that most companies can draw a very direct link between lean manufacturing and S&OP (using S&OP to determine takt times for example). But 6 Sigma's connection is somewhat more subtle - tools for improving forecasting, customer order management and product development processes, more predictable supply output and the comfort factor that goes along with this.

Here are some of the most interesting 6 Sigma stories from among the best practices companies.

Notable Practices of Our Model Companies:

Reduced Variation, Competitive Advantage: The advocates of 6 Sigma - include us in that group - are convinced that focused problem solving to reduce variation inevitably leads to competitive advantage. Quality up, cost down, less scrap and rework, and more flexible capacity: it's not long before the S&OP process starts to see lots of additional opportunities for improving market share and overall profitability.

> ➢ *Interbake Foods* has become a "worry-free" supplier to their customers. They offer both high quality and low cost - through their business systems (superior planning tools including S&OP) and manufacturing processes (high automation coupled with statistical process controls to ensure a good quality product). They are registered ISO 9001:2000 (one of only a handful of baking companies in North America).

Interbake has a very strong internal quality management system called Integrated Process Management (IPM). IPM uses statistical process control (SPC) and team problem solving, and focuses on the key input and output variables (KIV's and KOV's) for each process under its control.

To drive continuous improvement, *Interbake's* manufacturing plants use process capability analysis, "R&R" (measurement) studies and designed experiments to continually improve their processes. IPM is functioning in seven plants and is sometimes used in the sales and marketing areas. Engineering, Maintenance and Quality Assurance support IPM. Customer Service has begun to implement IPM. There is an internal and external IPM audit process similar to the resource planning MRPII Class A audit process.

Using the tools and techniques of IPM, *Interbake* has:

o   Significantly reduced process variability

o   Improved product quality

o   Reduced scrap and overweight (packages of product that weigh too much based on set limits)

o   Reduced manufacturing costs

➢   When acquired by *Interbake, Norse Dairy Systems* implemented the IPM process. As it did at *Interbake*, IPM has led to significant improvements in quality and reduced customer complaints.

Improved Business Processes Outside of Manufacturing: The tools of 6 Sigma apply to any kind of process, even business processes outside of production itself. As mentioned above, creative use of the 6 Sigma tools may lead to improvements in administrative or planning processes.

➢   At *Interbake* and *Norse Dairy Systems,* IPM has lead to an even stronger emphasis on product quality and on resolving customer complaints. Quality and quality metrics are reviewed at each step in their sales and operations planning processes.

➢   At *Pyosa,* a Mexican chemical company using a Japanese quality model, people have become so adept at applying the techniques and identifying real the root causes of problems, that every business process has become a potential target for improvement. For example, as a result of focusing on the processes for data accuracy and demand variability, this methodology helped them improve bill material accuracy significantly, and increase forecast accuracy from 25%, up to 45%.

Additional Company Experiences with 6 Sigma

Coca-Cola Midi has been involved with major quality initiatives since the plant opened. ISO registered, they are audited annually as part of the corporate quality program TCCQS (The Coca-Cola Quality System).

EMS implemented 6 Sigma across all areas of the plant when Texas Instruments owned the business. It is still an important part of the overall management process.

UMC expanded their lean manufacturing efforts to a focused quality improvement program that has reduced quality rejections by 50% per year for each of the last two years. Though not a formal 6 Sigma program, the process is well structured and effective, and has reduced variability levels from three sigma to five sigma.

At *The Scotts Company,* 6 Sigma efforts have been in process for about a year.

Summary

Often, lean manufacturing, and/or TQM/6 Sigma drive continuous improvement, with S&OP facilitating this by providing information and a management communication and decision-making structure guiding everyone's participation.

As we said in the chapter 7 summary on resource planning, S&OP is the driver, the windshield, the dashboard and the steering wheel, guiding the future direction of the company and helping to identify obstacles along the way. Lean manufacturing and 6 Sigma, optimally guided by S&OP, are initiatives and methodologies that enable detailed process improvement and the achievement of better business results. They are the pit crew and the mechanics, constantly fine-tuning and improving the operational processes and tools, so that the business finishes ahead of the competition.

Lean manufacturing and 6 Sigma make planning easier and more predictable. Applied to the S&OP process itself, they can make startling improvements in efficiency and effectiveness.

S&OP can provide a forum for management to: identify where improvements are needed, or need to be continued or accelerated; review current status and progress; and authorize new improvement targets or processes.

S&OP can monitor multiple initiatives on many fronts, tracking progress through a review of time-phased action plans.

Chapter 9

S&OP and the Extended Demand and Supply Chains

How does S&OP work outside the company, with customers, and with suppliers?

The nature of competition has changed, and so has S&OP. Although the core processes of S&OP have remained largely the same, its application and the business processes it integrates with have changed significantly. As we saw in chapters 6, 7 and 8, leading companies use S&OP in combination with approaches such as finish-to-order, new product development, two-level master scheduling, advanced planning systems - APS[15], lean manufacturing and 6 Sigma. This has helped them deal with increasingly demanding and competitive marketplaces that expect suppliers to:

➢ deliver with short lead times

➢ provide more flexible product design and delivery options

➢ control costs and then reduce them

➢ launch new products more quickly

➢ organize all the resources of the supply chain to respond to market shifts faster

➢ collaborate with upstream and downstream partners for everyone's benefit

Now S&OP has also evolved to encompass approaches like third party manufacturing, "partnerships", collaborative business processes, outsourcing and "off-shoring". Our model companies have shown how S&OP can deal with a wide array of demand-side and supply-side configurations, as well as a varying range of customer and supplier relationships.

---

[15] APS systems attempt to provide more sophisticated computer modeling techniques to develop sales forecasts, supply plans, optimized distribution networks, and improved resource and capacity allocations

Supply Chain Management: The Definition

Before talking about all the various customer, supplier and partner configurations that are emerging during the first decade of the 21st Century, we need to understand the terms "supply chain" and "supply chain management". These terms are widely and variously used, most often in reference to a company's supply side (their suppliers, inbound transportation providers, their suppliers' suppliers, etc.).

Most accurately, these terms refer to all of the linkages from the ultimate customer, through all the distribution partners[16], through the manufacturing company and all of its functions and divisions, and then back through all the suppliers, and their suppliers, including transportation providers. This encompasses both demand and supply, and all the planning that goes with it.

The tools for managing this extended supply chain are mostly encompassed in the processes of resource planning, new product development, TQM/6 Sigma and lean manufacturing. They include forecasting, planning, tracking, measuring and continuously improving:

>   -sales and customer order management
>   -production
>   -purchasing and supplier management
>   -product and process design
>   -inventory management
>   -logistics and transportation
>   -and all operational and administrative support processes

In this chapter we will use the term "supply chain management" (SCM) to encompass all these approaches, tools and activities that work well *inside* the company, as they are applied *outside* the organizational boundaries of a single company[17].

---

[16] The term "demand chain" is sometimes used to describe the part of the supply chain from the manufacturer out through wholesalers, distributors, dealers and retailers to the ultimate customer
[17] Recently a term that has gained some popularity is "demand driven supply networks - DDSN". We like this term because it implies that demand coming from the customer, not capacity from manufacturing or supply capabilities, is the driver of the supply chain. Too often, even today, we see traditional capacity measurements and considerations driving supply chain decisions. But in the end, the approach and mechanics behind DDSN are much the same as those in supply chain management.

Managing the Chains

Several things pass up and down through the demand and supply chains: product inventory, financial payments, and perhaps most useful of all - information. We'll leave it to our friends in finance to help you manage the accounting activities. But S&OP is a major tool in managing the other two.

For finished inventory, in chapter 6 we discussed how S&OP helps manage make-to-stock products. In chapter 7 we covered distribution resource planning - DRP, which guided by S&OP, is the key planning function for managing and coordinating all of the inventory in the downstream supply chain.

S&OP enables sharing information regarding demand, inventory and capacity that spans multiple links in the chain. Using this information for more thoughtful and measured decision-making with different supply-chain partners is at the heart of "supply chain management". And it is what we will cover in detail for the balance of this chapter.

Now let's talk about the specific demand side issues that are particularly relevant to S&OP.

The "Demand Chain"

What's the difference between a "supply chain" and a "demand chain"?
Only one thing - the direction in which you are looking. If you are the customer, looking up the chain to your suppliers and their suppliers, it's a supply chain. If you are a supplier, looking down the chain at your distribution partners, dealers and customers, it can be referred to as a demand chain. In either case, the issues are the same: lead times, inventories, capacities, forecasts, customer orders and supply plans.

The information and interaction that every company wants from its customers, is just the same information and interaction that its suppliers also desire from them.

And in this increasingly competitive world, these can be best managed collaboratively with the demand/supply chain partners working together to improve the efficiency and effectiveness of the chain in total. In the ideal situation, each partner shares fairly in all improvements made in the flow of material and information up and down the chain.

Let's first look at the view of the supplier towards their customers.

Linking to the Customer – Collaborating for Competitive Advantage

Leading companies have learned the advantages of better communication and collaboration with their customers. In the best examples, customers actively participate in forecasting, planning, and inventory management.

Talk about being right up S&OP's alley! At first, S&OP was the process that helped companies get their internal departments and functions talking, and making consensus based decisions. Why not broaden its scope, and apply the same approaches to engaging the participation of customers and distribution partners?

"The S&OP process provides a great framework for sharing information coming from the customers. Having all the parties around the table allows us to listen to and then share different points of view. Regardless of whether we get good news or bad news in the S&OP process, we are able to create sustainable actions plans to make timely deliveries. The Customer Services Department looks forward to this open discussion every month." Antonio Egido, **Coca-Cola Midi** Commercial Director.

Improved communication and collaboration can take different forms depending on the situation. In these cases, S&OP (particularly the demand planning step) can provide a disciplined structure and framework[18] for trading partners across the chain:

> **Multiple sales inputs:** Where a company sells through multiple regional or market channel sales locations and affiliates (see especially **Danfoss, Eli Lilly, Interbake Foods, Norse Dairy Systems** and **Scotts**), the individual locations are in some ways treated like a customer. Often, each location or office will manage their own customers and generate a sales forecast that is then aggregated into a company total.

> **The customers plan their own manufacturing requirements:** Where a company (like **Amcor, Cast-Fab, Coca-Cola Midi, Danfoss, Eclipse, EMS** and **Pyosa)** sells to other manufacturers, instead of simply trying to predict what the customers will buy (a "forecast"), the customers share their requirements as calculated by *their* manufacturing planning systems.

> For example, at both **Amcor** and **Cast-Fab**, some major customers provide them with weekly requirements updated monthly, and **Coca-Cola Midi** gets

---

[18] It should be noted that for most of our model companies forecasts for make-to-stock products (as well as for higher volume products made-to-order for a few large customers) are developed at the individual item level, and then aggregated into family totals for the S&OP process. For other make-to-order, finish-to-order, and design-to-order products, where typically the customer is offered many different product options, the forecasts are developed at the family, sub-family or product model level

requirements directly from the Coca-Cola bottling plants.

➤ **The customers can share retail sales information:**   Where a company (like *Coca-Cola, Interbake Foods, Norse Dairy Systems* and *Scotts)* sells to mass merchandisers, instead of trying to predict what the mass merchandisers will buy (a "forecast"), they get the mass merchandisers to share either the actual retail sales data (often called "point of sale - POS" data) and/or the future requirements as they are calculated by the mass merchandisers' distribution and inventory planning systems.

When this is done with the participation of both supplier and customer, it's often called "collaborative planning". This is sometimes referred to as "CPFR - collaborative planning and forecast review", a term used by consumer goods industries and demand chains that include mass merchandisers like Wal-Mart.

➤ **Pre-sales activity:**   Where information from major customers is a good overall predictor of the future, forecasts may be developed from this primary input.

For example, both *AGFA* and *Unicorn Medical Company* sell assembled devices, and consumable products used with the devices (x-ray film and consumable materials, respectively). Actual sales of the devices is a "leading indicator" of the follow-on sales of the consumable products. And even before the actual sale is made, the number of potential customers in the pipeline, the number of outstanding quotes or bids, and other presales information is used as an input for forecasting not only the assembled devices, but the consumable products as well.

➤ **"Demand shifting or demand shaping" opportunities:** Where customer demands don't match predictions, it is sometimes possible to shift them from one product to another, so as to take better advantage of the supplier's inventory, material and capacity resources, while still satisfying the ultimate requirements of the customers. In other words, "sell 'em what you got or what you can easily make!"

➤ **Varying availability and reliability** of information can exist in all the scenarios listed above (multiples sales divisions, multiple manufacturing customers, multiple mass merchandising customers, pre-sales activity and "demand shaping"). The following points can apply in any of these cases:

o   if the company has numerous customers or sales divisions, the process may be only done with the major ones, with the balance of the demand for the minor ones forecasted as a single number by product or family

o   for those customers unwilling to share their numbers or who simply do not plan in a suitable fashion, their share of the demand must be "forecasted" like the minor customers or sales divisions. In the words of our fondly remembered mentor, Oliver Wight: "Best is the enemy of better". In other words, some good information is better than none, take advantage of whatever you can.

o   the accuracy of the numbers need to be monitored; if the customers or sales divisions are not good at planning, adjustments may need to be made

o   rarely are these customers or sales divisions regular participants in S&OP meetings, but often there is periodic communication with them as part of the demand planning step

A Best Practice Example:
Collaborative Forecasting with Customers at Scotts

Scotts has a highly concentrated sales volume, selling mainly to a relatively few immediate customers: home centers (Lowe's, Home Depot), mass merchandisers (Wal-Mart, K-Mart), club stores (Sam's Club, BJ's, Costco), and hardware co-ops (Ace, Pro). These larger customers can be challenging.

Their S&OP demand planning step includes "consensus" meetings by their Business Development Teams, which are *Scotts'* sales, marketing and supply chain people based on the ground at Wal-Mart, Home Depot, Lowe's, etc.

With input from the customer, they generate the POS (point-of-sale) forecast for retail demand at the stores, then the resultant projected replenishment demand from *Scotts* to the customer, based on pipeline inventory at stores and the customer's distribution centers. Replenishment demands are calculated using a DRP approach.

This represents about 80% of *Scotts'* total volume. The other 20% is forecasted, back at the home office, based on history, using a standard forecasting software package, but adjusted based on marketing judgment.

These planned demands are aggregated and reviewed at their Brand Consensus Meetings for each of their business units (Lawn Products, Miracle-Gro, Ortho, and Round Up). Because they operate largely at an SKU level, the meetings take four to six hours.

Scotts has reduced the number of their finished goods warehouses by two-thirds. Most of this reduction was because they were no longer needed due to better transportation management, and improved tools for managing the supply chain - especially S&OP and the collaborative forecasting with their customers.

Scotts manufactures 80% of their products in house. But virtually all of the Miracle-Gro products are fully outsourced. The S&OP process looks at this product line and its source suppliers separately.

"During the last four years, almost half of the company's increase in earnings has come from supply chain savings: inventory down, manufacturing efficiency up, purchase and transportation costs down. All of these are due to improved planning." Ken Reiff, Vice President, Product Planning

An Additional Company Example of Customer Linking

Interbake Foods has a combination of several of the above situations, including:

➢ retail products sold to mass merchandisers, with a "vendor managed inventory" - VMI[19] program in place at Wal-Mart

➢ Girl Scout cookies sold to 330 Girl Scout council locations through 130 local agents for storage and delivery, plus several distribution centers and floating stock warehouses

➢ "contract" products sold through their customers' (large baking companies) own channels

➢ dairy products shipped direct to customers or customer warehouses

➢ separate sales and marketing organizations dealing with each of these market channels and responsible for the forecasting of their products

➢ all of this coordinated by their S&OP process

S&OP Managing the Demand Chain

S&OP provides the forum and visibility for sales departments, distributors, partners and customers to share collaborative planning, forecasting, inventory, and inventory replenishment information at an aggregate level. It can coordinate the involvement of field sales, demand chain partners and customers, making the collaboration easier, which in turn makes partners even more likely to participate. S&OP guides and controls the detailed processes that manage customer orders, inventories, SKU forecasts, etc., which also can be shared between the partners.

---

[19] "vendor managed inventory" - VMI programs can vary, but in general they hold the supplier primarily responsible for managing the inventory levels held at the customer's sites

The visibility that comes from S&OP helps identify potential problems (like revenue shortfalls or overloaded resources), which then can be addressed by changes in the timing of marketing activities, new product launches or inventory build plans; or in more difficult cases, the "demand shifting or shaping" activities described above.

S&OP can also provide the forum to discuss potential demand opportunities to either beat or reach original targets, or to take advantage of emerging customer or market place desires or opportunities.

The "Supply Chain"

Working with Supply Chain Partners

Supply chains are many splendored, complex and varied things! They can range from a single plant location supported by a network of suppliers, to a multi-layered grouping of suppliers, their suppliers, multiple plants in parallel and feeding each other, with "supply chain partners" making some finished products, and some semi-finished manufacturing activity subcontracted or outsourced.

These supply chain partners go by a variety of names including *manufacturing partners*, *third party manufacturers*, *sub contractors*, *co-producers*, *toll manufacturers or tollers*, *contract manufacturers*, *joint venture partners* and others.

And with globalization, the locations of the suppliers, plants, and supply chain partners are spread more widely across the globe, with a fast-growing percentage in Central America, Eastern Europe, and increasingly Asia, due to lower labor costs. There are many combinations and permutations of these supply chain sourcing networks utilized in virtually every industry, and in more and more companies, large and small.

S&OP in Extended Supply Chains

Does the objective of S&OP change in these more complex environments? No! Better customer service, lower costs and inventories, and meeting all the business plans and targets is still the goal. And this is accomplished by managing inventory, information, plans and orders.   But the complexity of the chain, and the number and geographic dispersion of the partners makes this more of a challenge.

As we discussed above under "demand chains", S&OP can provide more structured communication and decision-making regarding demand planning and inventory management with customers and distribution partners. And it can do the same thing for "supply chains", whether the process is initiated by the supplier or the customer.

When the customer is a manufacturer, there is always a strong emphasis on managing inventory at every link in the chain. This should be true regardless of who owns the inventory, since holding inventory adds cost, which will inevitably be passed on to the customer in one form or another. And to properly manage the inventory means that the customers' demand plans (and the suppliers' supply plans) that produce inventory require careful attention. The points made in the "Linking to the Customers" section above apply equally well here.

Even further benefits can come from using the S&OP process to monitor capacity planning, lead times, costs and product quality issues, through standardized planning displays and KPI's. For optimal collaborative decision-making, this information is shared on a monthly basis between all involved supply chain partners. It can then be used for making timely decisions on:

➢ demand and supply plan timing and quantity changes

➢ the use of overtime and premium freight

➢ the need to add capacity (people and/or equipment)

➢ the need to temporarily "subcontract" to other supply chain partners

➢ the need to more permanently "outsource" some requirements to new supply chain partners

➢ the need (often cost driven) to "offshore" some requirements to new partners in Asia, Eastern Europe, Central America, etc.

Often S&OP can identify issues early enough so that the least costly and difficult alternatives can be chosen to solve a problem.

Supply Chains in the Thirteen Model Companies

Even the smallest and simplest at least have multiple manufacturing locations within the same vicinity (*Amcor, Cast-Fab,* and *Pyosa*).

Coca-Cola Midi has only one manufacturing location, but 72% of their product volume is manufactured and distributed by third party manufacturers. For their concentrate and beverage base business they are one of roughly a dozen Coca-Cola manufacturing operations around the world, typically serving a distinct geographic market.

Interbake Foods and *Norse Dairy Systems* have multiple locations in North America.

Norse's ice cream wafer products are made at *Interbake* plants in Richmond, VA and Elizabeth, NJ. Thus *Norse's* S&OP process generates the demand plan as an input to the supply planning process at *Interbake*.

Danfoss, Eclipse and *EMS* are actively adding regional manufacturing locations in other continents. *AGFA, Eli Lilly, Scotts* and *Unicorn Medical Company* already operate with multiple plant locations across the globe.

Most of these companies have a variety of supply chain partners across the world, producing finished goods, semi-finished product and key raw materials. At the moment, only *Amcor, Cast-Fab, Interbake* and *Norse* do not venture beyond their home continent for major sources of supply.

Managing the Supply Chain with Partners in Our Model Companies

So what can we learn from the varied experiences of our thirteen companies?

First and foremost, each company relies heavily on the S&OP process to coordinate the demand, inventory and supply planning (and balancing) across these multiple links in their supply chain.

Secondly, the inputs and participation of the "supply chain partners" vary depending on the situation:

> ➢ they may be simply treated as a capacity constraint in the rough cut capacity planning validation of the supply plans

> ➢ the partners may supply information and input through individual communications with those responsible for the supply planning and/or partnership review meetings

> ➢ for major partners, there may be a separate production plan for their product line, subfamily or family

> ➢ sometimes there are separate supply reviews or partnership meetings that exclusively review products supplied by major third party manufacturers. *Norse Dairy Systems* actually holds a separate partnership meeting with the demand manager and direct ship purchasing personnel to discuss demand and supply issues specific to the third party manufacturers.

> ➢ some partners may collaborate in decision-making on supply plans, inventory, tactics, lead times, etc.

➤ sometimes major partners actually attend supply planning meetings to provide real-time input and participate in the decision-making

➤ often, the partners are the recipient of numbers and notes from the S&OP process

➤ five of our companies currently have significant sourcing from partners in Asia. Eight use European sources. Doubtless those numbers will rise in the future. They have the following characteristics:

   o generally the S&OP process is conducted no differently, regardless of the location of the source

   o teleconferences or video conferences, rather than just face-to-face meetings, are used to cope with geographic dispersion

   o for remote supply chain partners the biggest issue is lead time - this is dealt with by carefully making changes at the right spot in the future planning horizon

A Best Practice Example:
Supply Chain Management with a Supplier at *Coca-Cola Midi*

Coca-Cola Midi (CCM) is the Center for Juice Expertise for The Coca-Cola Company, overseeing the juice processing used in canning and bottling operations across Europe, both at Coca-Cola and customer locations. Minute Maid is one of the most recognizable brand names.

There are multiple third party suppliers of ingredients and juices. In addition to Coca-Cola plants, there are also multiple third party customers who produce products from these juices and ingredients. Their end products are finished consumer beverages delivered to customer distribution centers and direct point-of-sale locations.

CCM coordinates all the planning, scheduling, inventory management, and transportation resources that result in the direct delivery of the juices to the bottling operations, third-party packers and customer locations. This is a process they call Direct Products Supply (DPS). And they provide specialized analytical testing capabilities for juices supplied direct to canning and bottling operations or Coca-Cola concentrate plants in Europe, including *CCM*.

DPS activities have required more intense coordination and communication with customers, including regularly scheduled meetings with customers as part of the S&OP

process. As a part of DPS, new product volume information is sent to the suppliers who have approximately three to four days to respond if there are issues. *CCM* has linked S&OP to strategic business reviews with both customers and suppliers.

Over the last fourteen years, S&OP has been continuously expanded, improved and used to manage beyond just manufacturing. S&OP today covers internal manufacturing as well as the extended supply chain (DPS for juice), where it has integrated suppliers, customers, manufacturing resources (mixing and blending) and manufacturing support activities (analytical lab capacity, warehouse and cold storage space).

Another Best Practice Example:
Supply Chain Management with Sister Plants and Third Party Manufacturers at *Eli Lilly*

Eli Lilly has four networks of over twenty plants, producing sixty-five different products (over 8000 SKU's), sold through 130 worldwide sales affiliates.

> ➤ There are eighty third party manufacturers in thirty-three countries used for selected manufacturing operations or as flexible capacity alternatives. Most provide local, country specific finished packaging. A few provide filling, compression or bulk formulation operations.

> ➤ Many of these eighty "supply-chain partners" are managed as part of two "Hubs" in North America and Europe, which have their own S&OP supply planning processes and meetings. The others are incorporated into the supply planning processes of the local plant site that coordinates their activities.

Other supply chain processes such as product rationalization, make-buy decisions, supply chain design, and risk management are connected to *Lilly's* global S&OP process, when decisions, approvals and communications are needed. This includes, for example, where and how much strategic inventory should be held.

At *Lilly*, this has resulted in a great dependence upon supply chain principles and processes to effectively manage it all, with S&OP providing the forum to manage change effectively.

All of these links in the supply chain are guided by a global supply chain organization established in the mid 90's, with one person responsible for the overall S&OP business process, and another one who actively coordinates and facilitates its execution at all sales, manufacturing and corporate sites.

Another Best Practice Example:
Supply Chain Management with Asian Suppliers at *Pyosa*

Pyosa's marketplace demands high quality, but is driven by low prices. It is increasingly affected by competition from Asia, is tightly regulated in the use of certain of its products, and is hindered by worldwide shortages of certain raw materials.

➤ This *Mexican* company procures 12% of their finished products (forty-two items) from China, India or the U.S.

➤ Semi-finished products going into 25% of the product line are also purchased from China and India.

➤ Some suppliers with very inflexible capacity have forty-five to sixty day lead times.

➤ One critical raw material is on allocation from the supplier, who is given a rolling three-month forecast, but maintains a six day delivery lead time.

➤ The S&OP process, along with its detailed resource planning tools, carefully monitors and fine tunes the demand and supply plans on products affected by these long lead time suppliers.

➤ S&OP provides rolling projections over the longer horizon needed to manage these long lead time suppliers. This provides ***Pyosa*** an early warning system to anticipate volume changes much sooner, and plan around the suppliers capacity constraints.

Summary

Supply chain management is all about applying tools and methodologies outside the boundaries of a single company. It requires timely and usable information in a consistent format. Its effectiveness is based on the mutual participation in key decision-making processes by the supply chain partners - in other words, enlightened collaboration.

S&OP provides visibility up and down the demand and supply chains, to a level of detail that is appropriate and significant to management, supporting timely decision-making on demand, inventory (at the right spot in the chain), and supply plans and resources.

S&OP monitors partner performance, and provides early warnings to the partners where improvement is needed and when it's time to adjust volumes.

And most importantly, S&OP provides a clear framework that identifies when and how decisions need to be made, along with the roles and responsibilities of each supply chain partner.

Linking and collaboration are the keys to successful supply chain management, and S&OP provides the structure to ensure timely and accurate interaction between supply chain partners.

Chapter 10

Organizational and Size Issues

In what size company does S&OP work best? How does it work in privately-held companies, global companies and companies using a matrix organization structure? Does S&OP survive ownership or organization changes? Can it help with these changes?

Cross-functional planning, communication and decision-making are at the heart of the S&OP process. These activities can be affected by company size, and organizational style and changes. In this chapter, we'll see how.

Smaller Companies

Communication and cross-functional planning processes are generally simpler in smaller companies. This is because they often have:

➢ Fewer products, customers, locations, suppliers, people

➢ Fewer customer orders, forecasts, manufacturing schedules and purchase orders

➢ Simpler, flatter organization structures, often only one or two levels of management

At the same time, smaller companies have additional challenges. With limited finances come fewer resources and less sophisticated tools. Leaner staffing and broader individual responsibilities may make it difficult to free up time to work on improvement projects like S&OP. And sometimes, small companies take cross-functional communication and decision-making for granted, feeling that formal business management processes such as ERP and S&OP are needless, complex, bureaucratic overkill, which will merely stifle the agile and creative environment that they've worked hard to nurture.

Despite this perception, our experience in working with hundreds of companies, large and small, over the past thirty years, is that generally small companies suffer from the same inconsistencies in communication and decision-making as large companies.

So the bottom line for small companies is this: fewer things to manage and a simpler environment, counterbalanced by fewer people and less resources to manage them.

S&OP in Smaller Companies:

In figure 1-2 in chapter 1, we classified our thirteen model companies by size: those that had annual revenues of less than $100 million as small companies, those having revenues of greater than $1 billion as large companies, with medium size companies in between.

The small companies were: *Amcor, Cast-Fab, Eclipse, EMS,* and *Pyosa.* In these companies:

> ➤ S&OP provides a structure to ensure that cross-functional communication and decision-making is consistent and complete.

> ➤ With less complex communication, planning and decision-making, and fewer people involved, S&OP and detailed resource planning processes are simpler, quicker and less time-consuming.

> ➤ A flatter organization often means overlapping attendance at S&OP partnership and executive meetings. So sometimes, like at *Amcor* and *Cast-Fab,* there is no separate partnership meeting. Typically this means that the discussions in the executive meeting go into a lot more detail, and will include a review of every family and every issue.

> ➤ In some cases, a company will alter their process and the number of meetings until they arrive at something satisfactory for them. For example, initially *Eclipse* held just an executive meeting, allowing the executive managers to play a very hands-on role in leading and designing an effective S&OP process. But once this became institutionalized, they added a partnership meeting (with several attendees who are also part of the executive meeting), so that their most senior executives only had to deal with the major issues.

> ➤ The lack of sophisticated tools to support detailed resource planning and tracking is often overcome with the relatively inexpensive ERP software that is currently available.

> ➤ The S&OP planning data is managed using customized spreadsheets, based on Microsoft Excel or an equivalent[20].

> ➤ Most key people who need to be involved in designing and participating in S&OP are already overloaded, and have no extra time to work on S&OP. They, like most people, never get to the bottom of their "to-do" list. So the trick is to make sure S&OP is high enough on that list to receive the attention it needs, when it needs it. This means that top management must clearly prioritize S&OP

---

[20] This is also true of our other best practice companies, and of virtually every other company we know

as a critical organizational imperative, one that must be addressed in a timely manner, by all appropriate participants.[21]

S&OP in small companies is successful because management insists that it be so. This is no different from any other size company.

Privately-Held Companies

Privately-held companies are different from public companies in several obvious ways. The question is whether these differences really affect S&OP.

First, size may be an issue, since there are many more small privately-held companies than large ones. What this means of course is that the factors that affect S&OP in small companies also affect most privately-held companies.

Second, the line between ownership - often a family - and executive management can be blurry or non-existent. In a typical privately-held company, at least a few members of executive management are also owners of the company. If not, the owners typically play a very strong role in operational decision-making in other ways. Decisions having a financial impact on the company can directly affect the personal financial situation of the owners.

But is this really so different? Most senior executives of publicly held companies are specifically measured and rewarded based on the overall financial performance of the company. Often this is in the form of stock ownership, frequently through stock options. Therefore the financial impact of any S&OP decision probably has a similar personal impact on the senior executives of a public company, as it does on the owner/executives of a private company.

The owners of a privately-held company do tend to be more directly involved in S&OP than the owners in a public company. But this is mostly due to their typical roles as senior operating managers. This was the case for our five model companies listed below.

S&OP in Privately-Held Companies

The five privately-held best practice companies are *Pyosa, Cast-Fab, EMS, Danfoss* and *Eclipse.*

Pyosa is one of the Mexico's largest domestically owned companies, and the leading manufacturer of inorganic pigments in Mexico. They also produce dyestuffs. Three

---

[21] This is also true of our other best practice companies, and of virtually every other company we know of

other specialty chemical divisions of Pyosa are jointly owned with Asian and European companies.

Cast-Fab and **EMS** are privately-held, spun off from larger public companies. **Danfoss** is a Danish company, owned by the second generation of the founder's family. **Eclipse** is an American company, owned by the third generation of the founder's family.

These five companies successfully use S&OP in ways that match their particular business situations. But in no case could we identify any differences in the S&OP process itself that we could attribute to the ownership issue.

So what is done differently using S&OP in a privately-held company? Arguably not much. But the owners need to emulate the role of executives in a publicly held company, including:

> participating and becoming actively involved in the S&OP process itself, not just approving and resourcing the process

> seeing S&OP as a key tool for managing the business, based on good cross-functional communication and decision-making

> using S&OP as a primary driver for achieving customer service and inventory targets

> ensuring that the S&OP process directly addresses their (the owners') specific business goals and objectives, including new product introductions, geographic expansion, overall growth, and improvement in profit margins

The bottom line: S&OP operates just as it does in publicly-held companies, but with the owners playing a prominent role.

Global Businesses

What is a global business? In its simplest form, it could simply mean a company has customers and/or suppliers located in other countries or continents. Where these do not represent a significant portion of a company's business, very little changes when it comes to S&OP.

But sometimes management of a company's demand and supply chains is greatly affected by people and organizations located outside their home country. In these cases the company's demand and supply chains require intense coordination in order to achieve competitive advantage, and issues that we might label as "global" become important to S&OP and other internal business processes in the company.

These "global" companies fall into one or more of the following categories:

➢ Sometimes there are customers or suppliers in other countries that are actually part of the same company. This can include plant locations, distribution warehouses, or even subsidiary operating divisions. ***AGFA, Danfoss, Eclipse, Eli Lilly, EMS*** and ***UMC*** have these situations.

➢ Sometimes there are customers or suppliers in other countries that are actually other divisions of the same corporate parent. ***AGFA*** and ***Coca-Cola Midi*** have this situation.

➢ Sometimes the sales organization is broken into separate offices, divisions or companies for different countries or regions. Possibly some products are produced in regional manufacturing locations, and others produced in locations in different countries or continents, to take advantage of centralized economies of scale and technology. ***Danfoss, Eli Lilly, EMS, Pyosa, Scotts*** and ***UMC*** operate in this manner.

➢ And of course, there is the situation where the key suppliers and customers in other countries are parts of entirely different corporate entities, but still need to be coordinated as part of the overall S&OP effort.

In each situation there are people who need to participate in the S&OP process who are located remotely from headquarters, often multiple time zones away. They may report through a different chain of command within the same company or corporate entity, or actually work for an entirely separate company. This can result in:

➢ **Different levels of S&OP understanding, engagement and commitment** from local management and staff members, whose participation is needed. In the case of participants who work for different divisions of the corporate parent, or for different companies entirely, they and their associated management teams may not ascribe to the same S&OP process design being followed by the reference company. In the worst case, they may have no experience or interest in S&OP at all.

➢ **Difficulty in gaining the required data** and information in a consistent format, and on a timely basis. This is sometimes due to different and un-integrated systems. In other cases it can be due to different data structures and hierarchies, such as product family designations, financial account numbers and codes, etc..

➢ **Different KPI calculations**

➢ **Different data display and formatting**

> ➤ Different, and sometimes **conflicting operating objectives** (for instance, one location is intent on reducing inventory, while another is focusing more on lead time reduction and customer service improvement)

> ➤ **Difficulty in easily facilitating face-to-face communication** between the appropriate people, throughout all the steps of the S&OP process. Many companies use teleconferencing, video conferencing or web-based conferencing to minimize the travel expense and lost travel time that could result from everyone attending every monthly meeting in which they should participate. But even this is not a perfect solution, as can be attested by anyone who has sat in their office at midnight participating in a teleconference based halfway across the world.

> ➤ **Additional steps required in the S&OP process** to accumulate, review and readjust plans by regions and products. Some global companies have multiple partnership, and/or executive meetings looking at the regional or business line numbers, that are then rolled up into global totals for corporate management. When these steps are added, we refer to this as a **"global S&OP"** process[22]. Without these extra steps, we will refer to a **"standard S&OP"** process, used by a company doing business globally. We will expand on both of these below.

In all these cases, the challenge is really getting everyone who should be involved to participate in a consistent and timely manner, by ensuring that they follow a common S&OP process design that can identify problems and opportunities, reconcile conflicting objectives, and meet the overall business objectives of the participants in the process.

"Standard S&OP" in a Global Business

For companies who operate in environments where the impact of global participants can be channeled through the traditional five step S&OP process we described in chapter 3, the S&OP process will not look much different.

But there may be global, regional, family and sub-family aggregations of data that are developed, reviewed, monitored and discussed at the appropriate points of the process, to help the "global" participants clearly focus on their parts of the strategies, tactics, plans and objectives. There will doubtless be extensive use of teleconferencing, videoconferencing and web-based conferencing to facilitate the communication.

For S&OP to work as well as possible in this environment requires a sensible process that develops the numbers through a well-defined five steps. And this requires upfront education and training of all the "global" participants, so that they will share a common understanding of the objectives, design and activities within the S&OP process. A very

---

[22] see the end of Chapter 3 for a more detailed description of "global S&OP"

careful and thorough documentation of the S&OP process can be used as a procedural reference document and the basis for the training.

Best Practice Examples of "Standard S&OP" in a Global Business

At *AGFA US Healthcare* strong relationships have been developed with both parts and OEM suppliers of major components for equipment, and suppliers of critical raw materials for film. In all of the following examples, planned requirements are calculated by the receiving location and shared with the sending locations. In many of the situations, inventory is carried at both points in the supply chain based on negotiated guidelines. These include:

> ➤ master rolls of film produced in the central global *AGFA* plant in Belgium to the US finishing plant in South Carolina

> ➤ equipment produced in an *AGFA* plant in Germany going to the US distribution center in New Jersey

> ➤ key digital equipment components from IBM, Dell, Sun, HP and EMC, purchased to customer order to the central US assembly location

> ➤ custom programming for digital equipment from their subsidiary in Canada going to the central US assembly location

The S&OP process at *AGFA* orchestrates the demand and supply planning, and the communication and collaborative decision-making that goes on between the various divisions of *AGFA* and their key suppliers.

Eclipse, EMS and *Pyosa* also follow the basic five step process, with global participants included where appropriate.

"Global S&OP"

In more complex environments like the ones described below, additional steps typically need to be added to the S&OP process design.

For example, in an environment where both sales and production is largely divided on a regional basis, each region may go through its own five step S&OP process, the results of which are then rolled up into a final, "global" step that includes either just a global executive meeting, or possibly a global partnership meeting as well.

Where sales and inventory management is regionalized, but manufacturing is not, there may be multiple steps for planning demand (by region) and supply (by product type or source where third party manufacturing is used extensively), feeding into single global partnership and executive meetings.

There is no single model that fits all situations, and most companies in these environments gradually add, subtract and consolidate steps in the process until they've found the most efficient way of getting the right people participating in appropriate stages of the process.

Unquestionably S&OP is more difficult to implement and operate in these environments. It's more work, it takes longer, and there are many more people to get on board. And once running, it's more fragile, since just a few individuals can start to degrade the entire process.

All of this shouts for one, critical, absolutely irreplaceable ingredient: **strong and continued top management support and insistence** on everyone's complete compliance with the process design and guidelines.

The best practice companies who operate "global S&OP" processes demonstrate that the following must be in place to support an effective global process:

> - **common process design and terminology**

> - **precise completion dates**, communicated and strictly enforced for each step of the process

> - **data organized in common product families,** resource categories and other groupings, or least in a way that can be clearly and easily accumulated

> - **clearly identified and enforced roles and responsibilities** for each participant at every location (including those who just provide input or data to the people directly participating in the S&OP steps)

> - clear **recognition and understanding of** the global, regional, local, business line, product and functional **targets, interests and KPI's** for which each of the participants are accountable.   Where these may be in conflict, to avoid sub-optimization, either they need to be adjusted, or overtly reviewed each month with the appropriate trade-offs made through a cross-functional, consensus based decision-making process.

> - **"data capture" tools** that make it as easy as possible for each participant to review, update, adjust and pass on the data and information for which they are responsible. With multiple participants, and extra steps in the process, often

people only have a day or two to execute their responsibilities and insure that their data is passed on to the next step in the process by the exact time it is needed, so there can be complete aggregations across multiple regions, products, families, etc..

Though S&OP is more difficult in these environments, it is also much more needed to gain economies of scale and global optimization, and to avoid falling into the traps of regional and functional sub-optimization. This sub-optimization can be fostered by individual budgets and objectives which are set at the beginning of the year, and then doggedly pursued by the responsible management.

In some cases, when the global mix of demand and supply is altered during the course of the year due to internal or external circumstances, S&OP can highlight the need for adjusting local or functional targets in support of achieving better overall global company performance.

In fact, we believe S&OP is the single best process to communicate, integrate and manage demand, supply and inventory in a global situation.

A Best Practice Example of "Global S&OP" at *Eli Lilly*

Lilly sells in 146 countries thru 130 sales affiliates (local, regional or country-specific Lilly sales organizations) to wholesalers (like McKesson), large retail pharmacy chains (Walgreen's, CVS, and Wal-Mart), other pharmaceutical partners, hospitals and government agencies.

The diagram below shows the steps in their global S&OP process.

Figure 10-1

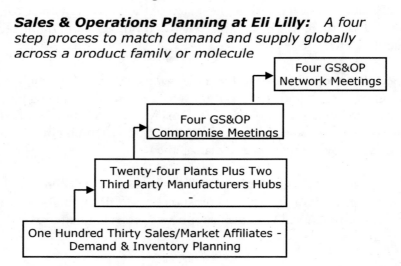

Sales & Operations Planning at Eli Lilly: *A four step process to match demand and supply globally across a product family or molecule*

> A Global Demand Management Center (fifteen people in four locations: part of the supply chain management organization) consolidates, validates and measures the accuracy of the 130 affiliate forecasts (which are updated each monthly, twenty-four months out), insuring that robust forecasting processes are in place, while providing a communications link between twenty-four plants, in sixteen countries, organized in four global Network groups, divided by manufacturing technology and the type of product for global capacity utilization and allocation.

> Eighty third party manufacturers in thirty-three countries produce both semi-finished and final packaged products:

> o many are managed as part of two "Hubs" in North America and Europe, which have their own manufacturing S&OP processes

> o the others are incorporated into the S&OP processes of the local plant site that coordinates their activities

> Every month, the plants update production plans considering capacities, inventories, cost and customer service over a twenty-four month horizon.

> For years three to seven, over twenty Global Marketing Product Teams maintain a forecast for each key product (including planned new products).

> There are four quarterly global S&OP (GS&OP) "Compromise" meetings, where the affiliate and plant plans for the next two years are extended to seven years. This process, by molecule or supply chain family, looks to support product launches, product outsourcing, and strategic facility expansions. It insures that

the worldwide production plans will satisfy the worldwide demand plans in a way that minimizes customer service problems, inventories and supply chain costs, well best taking advantage of the capabilities and capacities of ***Lilly's*** internal plants as well as their third party manufacturing partners.

➤ Four quarterly top management level "Network" GS&OP review meetings are then held to review the critical issues and decisions from the four global "Compromise" meetings.

➤ All of the S&OP steps follow a formal documented process and use common templates to assure consistency in data gathering, review and decision-making.

➤ Each of the steps provides visibility into issues and opportunities that drive contingency planning and action plans to meet the market demands, and mitigate as much of the risk as affordable.

➤ The annual business plan can be modified on a quarterly basis based on changes identified in the S&OP process.

*"**Eli Lilly's** global S&OP process was developed and implemented based on the success of identical processes already operating at our manufacturing sites and sales/marketing affiliates. It wasn't so much that we needed to develop something entirely new for our culture, as it was just expanding and escalating the process upward to gain higher levels of visualization, impact and resolution, with a longer (seven year) horizon."* Ron Bohl, Supply Chain Adviser

Additional Best Practice Examples of "Global S&OP"

Eclipse sells through various sales channels, and then ships product out of supply centers in Rockford, Illinois; Gouda, The Netherlands; Suzhou, China; and Pune, India.

There are four divisions within ***Eclipse***, two that are organized regionally, two that are product based: Americas and Asia, Europe, "Algas-SDI", and "Exothermics". While one executive team at the corporate level leads them all, each division has its own general manager with a full supporting staff. Things like R&D and administrative support are centralized.

S&OP has allowed us to integrate, simplify and solidify our combined organization structure (value-streams on the supply side and customer industries on the demand side). It's amazing how we look differently at the business today because of this orientation. This is one of the keys to our growth and profitability!" Lach Perks, President, ***Eclipse Inc.***

At **Danfoss** the regional S&OP processes which were recently created will help to deploy decisions worldwide. Previously, decisions made at headquarters were not easily deployable at the factory level or in the **Danfoss** sales companies. **Danfoss** has evolved toward local, regional assembly of product, then local machining and fabrication of the major components, from central manufacturing of all products.

Matrix Organizations

Here we refer to company organization structures where there may be "general managers" who are responsible for the success of a particular product line, measured by a balance sheet and a P&L statement, but who do not have each of the functions supporting their product line reporting directly to them.

For example, there might be a president who has reporting to her several product line general managers, one or more directors of manufacturing (whose plants each may make products for more than one of the product line divisions), several regional sales directors (each of whom may be responsible for the sales of all product lines in their region), a director of research and product development (whose people work on projects for various of the product line divisions), a CFO who is responsible for financial practices and reporting across all divisions, a director of HR and perhaps a director of IT.

Sometimes some portions of the centralized or "corporate" functions of finance, HR and IT are decentralized within the product line divisions, and/or the manufacturing organizations. Different combinations and many versions of this approach are possible and are used.

Some managers are responsible for activities and business results over which they do not have total control or authority. And consequently, at lower levels of the organization, people's priorities may be set by more than one manager in the organization, even though in some instances these are not direct reporting relationships.

Often these matrix type organizations exist within larger, global companies, who find it is not economical and effective to build regional subsidiaries, each of which have all the business functions reporting to a local executive. Economies of scale, and the need for global focus, may dictate that functions such as product design and development, marketing, and sometimes even manufacturing, be done centrally at a "center of excellence." In this way those functions can focus on becoming their very best under a single leader, with a single vision and a single set of plans and processes.

In other cases, a matrix organization is established in an effort to decentralize the responsibility for product or business lines, so that a single leader and team can focus on optimizing all aspects of performance of their assigned product or business lines.

The difficulty in any matrix situation is that corporate objectives for customer service, customer lead times and flexibility, revenue levels, inventory levels, product costs, and profit margins are greatly affected by multiple parts of the organization, who may have their objectives for each of these prioritized in different ways.

For instance, manufacturing may be focusing on lowering product costs and inventories, while the product line divisions are emphasizing the support of sales growth through higher customer service and shorter lead times. These don't necessarily have to be conflicting objectives, but to achieve them all, and in total, all the different organizations within the company must have their specific goals and approaches integrated and reconciled with each other.

Characteristics of matrix organizations include:

> ➤ shared responsibility among multiple organizations and senior executives for customer and financial objectives

> ➤ incomplete authority on the part of any single executive or organization to achieve all of their objectives

> ➤ critical shared resources, with multiple "internal customers" vying for higher priority and a bigger share of constrained resources

> ➤ no single executive directly in charge of all the functions, responsibilities, activities, resources and objectives of an entire product line

> ➤ lots of meetings, and long ones if the company hasn't got its arms around this style of management

> ➤ a corporate philosophy or culture which minimizes top-down decision-making, and requires cross-functional, consensus based communication and decision-making to best optimize all functional and company objectives (Wow, where have we heard of a process that works like this?)

S&OP in Matrix Organizations

Of our best practice companies, the following have some form of matrix organization: *AGFA, Coca-Cola Midi, Danfoss, Eli Lilly, EMS, Interbake Foods, Norse Dairy Systems* and *UMC.* Based on their experiences, we believe that S&OP is the single best process to highlight the issues and monitor the progress towards concurrent achievement of all organizational goals.

An effective S&OP process for a matrix organization:

> ➢ encompasses the key responsible functions and individuals

> ➢ provides a forum for all interested parties to describe problems and suggest solutions

> ➢ forces issues and problems out into the open, every month

> ➢ insures that capacity constraints and conflicting objectives are openly reviewed and resolved each month

> ➢ identifies **when** decisions need to be made

> ➢ clearly outlines the potential impact of **not** making a decision

> ➢ helps to foster open communication, build trust and teamwork, and facilitate decisive, consensus based decision-making

A Best Practice Example of S&OP in a Matrix Organization at *UMC*: Five Teams - No Bosses!

The management of the business is done by five product teams, one for each of the business lines, encompassing twenty-seven individual product lines. Each business line includes both assembled devices and consumable products.

But there is no business line or product team general manager. Each team is comprised of a cross-functional group of vice presidents who operate in a matrix or consensus style. There is a designated facilitator for each team (sometimes a manufacturing person, sometimes a marketing person, etc.) who guides the process, the discussions, the meetings and everyone's participation.

Generally the teams reach consensus on all decisions that need to be made. If not, in those rare cases the issues are forwarded for final resolution to corporate management at the company headquarters.

Every month, there are two full days of meetings for each product team, with extensive use of video and teleconferencing for these meetings. One full-day is devoted to new product development. The other day is devoted to quality, marketing and sales, finance, HR and S&OP. The S&OP portion of the meeting typically takes three hours.

Though difficult, this management approach works because everyone is fully committed to team principles, values and standards of behavior. Also critical are the well defined processes guiding the teams' communications and decision-making, particularly the S&OP process.

Changes in Ownership

Just as there are lots of variations on how global enterprises are organized, there are many ways in which a company's ownership can change significantly:

> **Being acquired**, as *AGFA US Healthcare* was first sold by Du Pont to Sterling Diagnostic Imaging (SDI), and then to AGFA; and as *Norse Dairy Systems* was acquired by *Interbake Foods*, which in turn had been acquired by Weston Foods

> **Acquiring others**, as *Scotts* acquired Miracle Gro and Danfoss acquired Maneurop Compressor Company (which became the basis for *Danfoss Commercial Compressors,* our best practice company)

> **Mergers**, as the five component companies joined to form *UMC*, originally under the ownership of two holding companies

> **IPO (Initial Public Offering)**, as *UMC* was divested by its two holding companies and went public on the NASDAQ exchange

> **LBO (Leveraged Buy Out)**, as *Cast-Fab* was spun off by Cincinnati Milacron, and *EMS* was spun off by Texas Instruments

Though each of these types of ownership changes are unique and have their own set of challenges, when it comes to S&OP, there are some strong similarities.

S&OP and Ownership Changes

*"The seamless integration from Du Pont to SDI into AGFA, with minimal impact on customer service, cost containment and inventory management, would have been impossible without the business processes with S&OP at their core." Malcolm Jaggard, Director SCM, **AGFA US Healthcare***

Ownership changes have an impact on S&OP. But maintaining an effective S&OP process through a period of ownership change can greatly facilitate the organization's assimilation of this change, and ensure that business performance is not adversely affected.

Often, a change in ownership triggers concurrent changes in key management positions. The continued operation of S&OP is sometimes put at risk, for one or more reasons. First, because the acquiring company may have no value for S&OP in general, or how it is done in the company they acquire. Secondly, new managers may not embrace the approach of the people they are replacing. And finally, the stress and workload that inevitably occurs in assimilating organization change can provide a temptation to discontinue (temporarily?) processes that require time from key individuals.

So to survive the change, S&OP must be seen as an organizational requirement, similar to GAAP- Generally Accepted Accounting Practices. It must be seen, by both old and new management, as the major process for cross functional decision-making on demand, supply, inventories, and customer backlogs and lead times. The management of the acquiring company must declare that S&OP is a process that subsidiaries or acquisitions are required to follow. It must be clear that all related systems and databases must be integrated into S&OP.

For example, when **Interbake Foods** acquired **Norse Dairy Systems,** it insisted that **Norse** immediately implement an S&OP process very similar to that used at **Interbake.**

UMC was better able to blend its five component companies (each of which was already successful) into a single, cohesive, integrated company by refining a common approach to managing their operations using lean manufacturing, sales and operations planning, and related resource planning tools. This not only improved their business performance, but it also supported the transition to a publicly traded company.

At first, the part of the organization required to adopt S&OP may be resistant. They must then be "sold" on the benefits of S&OP. The experiences of our model companies highlight many of the areas where S&OP can actually facilitate the ownership change.

S&OP can provide an easier transition for new people in key management jobs, since it provides a roadmap or defined process to follow when it comes to balancing supply and demand, and achieving management's business objectives.

But in some cases, the model S&OP process may actually exist in the organization that is being acquired. For example, the **AGFA US Healthcare** S&OP process has attracted the participation of other members of the **AGFA** management team in Europe. And some of its key features are being incorporated in the management processes of other **AGFA** divisions.

"S&OP has been embedded in both our quality system and business processes over the past eleven years, which have been a turbulent time for our marketplace and AGFA HealthCare in particular. When we started, we weren't sure... however when it became evident how powerful it was, we insisted on maintaining the process through two major organizational changes." Bob Pryor, President, **AGFA Healthcare, Americas**

S&OP can also be a powerful tool to identify potential areas of weakness where improvement is required. And it can monitor the implementation of changes in demand and supply chain tactics (which are often reviewed and changed as a result of ownership changes), such as:

> **Incorporating new product lines and customers:** *Cast-Fab* was Cincinnati Milacron's (now known as Milacron Inc.) captive foundry and fabrication shop, supplying the machine tool and injection molding machine businesses. When Jim Bushman acquired what became *Cast-Fab*, Milacron was 100% of the customer base. Over the years, pursuing a deliberate strategy, *Cast-Fab* has been able to diversify its customer base greatly. S&OP has helped plan and monitor the acquisition and retention of significant new customers.
>
> See also *AGFA, Danfoss, Eli Lilly, Interbake, Scotts* and *UMC*.

> **Driving and overseeing product rationalization:** *AGFA* had already been rationalizing film SKU's in a shrinking market, by working with customers to use fewer, common size sheets of x-ray film. This greatly accelerated after the acquisition, since *AGFA* Europe had many, similar, competing products.
>
> *UMC* undertook similar product rationalizations, since a number of the products of its five component companies had overlapping functionality.
>
> *Eli Lilly*, as discussed in chapter 6, maintains an aggressive program of outsourcing older products, to free up internal capacity for producing their many new products.

> **Managing plant consolidation:** When acquired by *AGFA*, *US Healthcare* closed down their film plant in North Carolina and transferred film production to the *AGFA* central film plant in Belgium, and film finishing and packaging to the *AGFA* plant in South Carolina. They also closed down their equipment plant in Delaware and moved production to the *AGFA* plant in Germany. And they consolidated their warehouse operations into the *AGFA* North American distribution centers in South Carolina and New Jersey.
>
> These plant and warehouse consolidation efforts, along with the product rationalization initiatives, allowed *AGFA* to reduce inventories by 67% with virtually no impact on customer service throughout this difficult time of transition.
>
> *"S&OP provided the framework to manage plant shutdowns, and develop cross functional teamwork, with the supply chain management function and the S&OP process guiding the efforts of all other functions."* Malcolm Jaggard, Director of Supply Chain

Management *AGFA US Healthcare*

And, **Interbake Foods** is closing two older, cost-inefficient plants, and moving the production to a brand new plant, plus to the most modern and efficient of their existing plants. The S&OP process is being used as the key planning and monitoring tool by management to ensure that the transition has no negative impact on inventory or customer service.

➤ **Reorganizing demand streams and responsibilities**:   For example, moving the sales or production responsibility for certain products from the acquired company to the acquiring company, or vice versa.

When **Interbake Foods** bought **Norse Dairy Systems**, they had **Norse** take over the marketing and sales of all ice cream products, including the wafers produced at two **Interbake** plants. To help control this, **Norse** has a separate S&OP partnership meeting on this product line, and **Norse** attends **Interbake's** partnership and executive S&OP meetings.

➤ **Overseeing tactical distribution changes:** *Scotts* lowered total inventories (raw, WIP and finished goods) by 33% - a decrease of $100 million. Some of this was as a result of reducing the number of warehouses by two thirds, many of which were overlapping legacies from their previous acquisitions. Most were no longer needed due to better tools for managing the supply chain (guided by S&OP) and better transportation capabilities.

➤ **Managing cash flow (inventory!)**:   This is often critical during ownership changes, as it was at *AGFA, EMS* and *UMC.*

EMS, formerly the Clad Metals division of Texas Instruments (TI), was spun-off via a venture capital backed LBO in 2001. Until then, the emphasis was on helping to reduce TI product development lead times. Thus, large inventories were never an issue.

After the LBO, emphasis on cash flow and profitability increased, as did the challenges resulting from being a stand-alone business. *EMS* used S&OP in conjunction with lean manufacturing to lower inventory levels and improve cash flow to meet the tighter targets set to support the LBO.

Summary

For small companies S&OP is simpler, sometimes there is no partnership meeting, but top management leadership is vital.

For privately-held companies, there is little difference in the structure of S&OP - but the interests, attitudes and requirements of the owners needs to be addressed by their active participation in the process.

For global companies it's harder to get timely inputs and participation in a consistent format from multiple world wide participants, but an S&OP process is vital to balance inventory, optimize resource utilization and allocation across the globe, and identify and reconcile any conflicting regional or functional objectives.

With matrix organizations, S&OP is the best way to insure that there is timely and clear communications, and the proper consensus based decision-making.

When there are ownership changes, the S&OP process can be at risk, but if maintained, S&OP can help manage the change, and identify problems and opportunities that need addressing.

Chapter 11

S&OP and Financial Planning

How can a company be sure that its financial plans match its operational plans?

Boy, that's a slow ball straight down the middle of the plate! S&OP is **the** tool to link financial planning and the achievement of financial objectives, with the detailed unit planning done in the company.

The ultimate objective of S&OP is to help execute business, financial, product and functional strategies. It does this by focusing on the demand and supply plans of families of products in units. But what ensures that these plans, which can change every month, are always equal to the financial plans and budgets?

The Nature of Financial Planning

Sorry, but S&OP does **not** ensure that the financial and operational plans are always equal, nor should it. Financial plans are objectives or targets set by the management team, often to motivate the organization to work harder and smarter to achieve "maximum or optimum" results. When these goals are set very high for this purpose, they are sometimes called "stretch" goals.

Implied in this term is that the goals may border on being unrealistic and may not be met every year. But the idea is that performance will be better if the organization is reaching for a very high goal, as opposed to "settling" for a less aggressive, easier to achieve one.

This scenario probably sounds very familiar to most readers, since many companies use this approach. And though it can cause stress at times, this approach often produces better long term results. For companies operating this way, budgets and operational plans for a new fiscal year will be set based on these stretch financial goals, leading money to be spent and resources utilized at every location and for every product based on these high numbers. And shouldn't money be spent and the resources be utilized this way?

The answer is yes, but only if each and every location and product achieves sales and production at its target level. These targets were derived from plans set months before the beginning of the year, based on market place and supply chain conditions and assumptions which may have already changed, and are quite likely to change even more during the course of the subsequent year.

Because of this, though many companies regularly meet their annual, company-wide, **total** financial targets, the **mix** between product lines often varies during the course of the year, from what was originally planned at the beginning of year.

S&OP, integrated into the financial planning activities of a company, constantly compares the current projected demand and supply plans in financial terms, to the financial plans and targets. During the course of the year, these will exactly match each other only if every plan is right on target, or if the financial plans have been altered to match the changes in the operating plans. These alterations generally occur only if significant variations are identified which make it impossible to achieve the original financial plan for a family.   For most companies, this occurs, if at all, once or twice a year, at most quarterly.

"Making the Numbers"

The fact is that many companies are able to achieve their "stretch" financial objectives. But the reality is that rarely do they do it exactly as they expected when the plan was laid out prior to the beginning of the year. Often due to changes outside the control of people within the company, some sales locations, divisions or regions will not do as well as expected during the course of the year. And the same will be true for some product lines, or products within a product line.

Once they begin to recognize the short falls, companies can try to change their tactics, re-deploy their resources or simply redouble their efforts. Sometimes this will get the lagging locations or products back on target. Sometimes it won't. What then?

Well, if you can't sell carrots in Guatemala, why not try selling more apples in Greenland? In other words, companies make up for financial shortfalls by putting their efforts into beating the original targets in some areas, to make up for the shortfall in others. So if it all works out anyway, what's the problem or risk?

Nothing at all, as long as the supporting plans are adjusted accordingly. But, if the detailed demand, supply and inventory plans are not adjusted to match the new realities, the company may continue to grow carrots and ship them to Central America, instead of growing more apples and sending them to Greenland.

If the plans aren't adjusted to realign how resources are used, the company may be straining to meet the old goals for one family and the new goals for the other. In the worst case, the newly developed sales may not be able to be supported by current resources. Alternately, the company may spend extra resources (overtime, extra labor, premium freight, higher short term material costs, etc.) to adjust the supply plans at the last minute to support the newly developed demand.

This is a scenario all too familiar to many manufacturing and distribution companies. It's one that can be greatly mitigated, if not totally avoided, by an effective, timely S&OP process.

S&OP's Role in Financial Planning

S&OP interacts with financial planning at four different points: monthly reviews of the financial plans, the development of annual plans and budgets, as a basis for some capital investment decisions, and in managing cash flow. Each of these will be discussed in detail below.

Monthly Reviews of the Financial Plans

Can we possibly be suggesting that any modern manufacturing company would want to change its financial plans every month? It's not too far-fetched to think that many companies face competitive situations and rapidly changing markets where this might actually be desirable. But even if companies want to change their financial plans monthly, are they able to? And perhaps even more importantly, could they live with the consequences of constantly changing financial plans and targets?

With an effective S&OP process, and a highly integrated set of operating and financial systems, it is probably possible for a company to change some significant portion of its financial plans and targets on a monthly basis. Actually, it's not a totally new idea - the concept of "variable budgeting" has been around for thirty or forty years. The idea is that spending or expense budgets can vary, depending on some key activity such as sales volume, number of production workers, etc.

For instance, if projected sales volumes for several different families are changed by the S&OP process, the associated supply plans may change as well. This could mean potential changes in purchasing and manufacturing budgets, particularly in the case were certain product lines represent a large portion of a given plant location or supplier's total activity. Changing sales volumes may also affect how management wants to allocate funds to advertising or other sales and marketing activities.

But even a relatively minor change to a single product line could cause changes throughout the entire set of financial plans, including revenue, profit margins, product costs, overhead allocations, selling and administrative costs, and departmental operating budgets. Obviously, it would be no small task to change all of these numbers every month, and redistribute them to everyone in the organization who is tracking their own specific responsibilities against the original targets.

Today's modern, integrated ERP systems could facilitate this process. But what really would take a long time would be the creation of all the human input, understanding and acceptance that would be necessary to make the adjusted budgets viable operational tools. After all, in most companies the initial budget is created in a multi-month process. It's probably unrealistic to think that it can be changed in a dramatically shorter period of time.

And since the factors that change these numbers may change often during the course of the year, this process would have to be repeated each month, if indeed it could even be completed within a calendar month.

Because of this, most of the time companies stick with the original financial plans and budgets, and just track the variances against them.

For example, in Figure 11-1, the sales and operations planning numbers have been converted to revenue, cost dollars and projected profits for comparison against the business plan. Four categories of management information are displayed:

1. **Original Business Plan**: budgeted sales at both the selling price and the product cost, as well as the budgeted and cumulative budgeted profit per period

2. **Current Sales Plan**: actual sales to the current date and projected sales through the end of the year, at selling price and cost, along with current actual and projected profit both by period and cumulatively

3. **Sales Plan to Business Plan Profit Comparison**: the variances between the gross profits based on the current sales plan versus budget, by period and cumulatively

4. **Gross Margins**: the percentage budgeted versus the actual or projected (based on the current sales plan) for each period.

Figure 11-1

Family	BZK
Description	Small Widgets

Average Selling Price	$	1.000
Standard Product Cost	$	0.505

ALL FIGURES IN US DOLLARS

PROFITABILITY	JAN - JUL TOTAL	History AUG	SEP	OCT	Current NOV	DEC	Current Year Expected Results	Next Year JAN	FEB	MAR
Business Plan										
Budgeted Sales (Sales Dollars)	$ 2,823,268	319,326	393,838	408,150	421,066	386,336	$ 4,750,985	440,611	376,083	586,110
Business Sales (Cost Dollars)	$ 1,425,750	161,260	198,888	206,116	212,638	194,596	$ 2,399,247	226,549	189,922	295,986
Budgeted Gross Profit	$ 1,397,518	158,066	194,950	202,034	208,427	190,742	$ 2,351,738	222,062	186,161	290,124
Cum Budgeted Gross Profit	$ 1,397,518	1,555,584	1,750,534	1,952,568	2,160,995	2,351,738	$ 2,351,738	222,062	408,224	698,348
Sales Plan										
Current Sales Plan (Sales Dollars)	$ 3,212,807	399,972	380,555	450,963	440,363	350,125	$ 5,234,785	416,547	440,141	561,599
Current Sales Plan (Cost Dollars)	$ 1,678,184	185,236	175,639	230,145	210,786	175,636	$ 2,665,625	224,935	237,676	303,263
Current Gross Profit	$ 1,534,623	214,736	204,916	220,818	229,578	174,489	$ 2,579,160	191,612	202,465	258,336
Current Cum Gross Profit	$ 1,534,623	1,749,359	1,954,275	2,175,093	2,404,671	2,579,160	$ 2,579,160	191,612	394,076	652,412
Sales Plan to Business Plan Profit Comparison										
Current Sales Plan vs Bus Plan (Gross Profit)	$ 137,105	56,670	9,966	18,784	21,151	(16,253)	$ 227,422	(30,451)	16,304	(31,789)
Cum Sales Plan vs Bus Plan (Gross Profit)	$ 137,105	193,775	203,741	222,525	243,676	227,422	$ 227,422	(30,451)	(14,147)	(45,936)
Budgeted % Gross Margin	49.5%	49.5%	49.5%	49.5%	49.5%	49.5%	49.5%	49.5%	49.5%	49.5%
Projected % Gross Margin	47.8%	53.7%	53.8%	49.0%	52.1%	49.8%	49.3%	46.0%	46.0%	46.0%

So when companies do make changes to their financial plans and budgets during the course of the year, the number of times is small - limited to cases where there are extreme shifts in sales volumes or supply situations. And even in these cases, only those portions of the financial targets, plans and budgets that are significantly impacted, are changed. Only rarely do companies change financial plans each month. See **Interbake Foods** and **Norse Dairy Systems** below.

S&OP's Monthly Role in Financial Planning

"One of the key benefits of working under the MRPII philosophy has been the integration of financials and finance concepts within the operation in the areas of production, inventory management and warehousing. Finance and Operations work hand in hand and feed information to each other to ensure accurate financial figures are provided to Headquarters on an ongoing basis, and to identify and implement opportunities for improvement, cost reduction and optimization with a solid financial justification." Claudio Cerminati, Plant Manager, **Coca-Cola Midi**

If properly interfaced with the financial planning systems, S&OP becomes an early warning system to identify sales or supply variances that affect the short term financial numbers. And if the trends continue, this could have a bigger impact later in the year. S&OP helps identify and address these situations by:

> ➤ Displaying the **cumulative financial impact** of all actuals and projected future changes to demand, supply, backlog and inventory plans. So for instance, at the end of every month, the current monthly sales plans can be converted to dollars and compared to revenue plans, by month or quarter, and for the fiscal year.
>
> For example, Figure 11-2 shows a typical dollarized sales and operations plan with cumulative totals. In the example, four different categories of time phased information are shown:
>
> 1. **Business plan** performance (current sales plan versus budget in sales dollars)
>
> 2. **Sales plan** performance (most current actuals and future sales plan against the last sales plan in sales dollars)
>
> 3. **Supply (production) plan** performance (actuals and current plan against budget in cost dollars)
>
> 4. **Finished goods inventory** performance (actuals and current plan against budget in cost dollars).
>
> The column "Current Year Expected Results" shows projected performance through the end of the current fiscal year. Columns to the right show the latest

projections for the next fiscal year.

Figure 11-2

Family:	All Families		Average Selling Price:	$ 1.960
Description:	All Widgets		Standard Product Cost	$ 1.140

ALL FIGURES IN US DOLLARS x 1000

	JAN - JUL TOTAL	History AUG	SEP	OCT	Current NOV	DEC	Current Year Expected Results	Next Year JAN	FEB
Business Plan (Budgeted Sales Dollars)									
Budgeted Sales Plan	$ 373,576	53,900	46,256	36,652	55,076	44,688	610,148	41,160	43,904
Current Sales Plan	$ 386,904	55,272	46,648	36,848	56,056	45,472	627,200	47,040	48,608
Difference	$ 13,328	1,372	392	196	980	784	17,052	5,880	4,704
Cum Difference	$ 13,328	14,700	15,092	15,288	16,268	17,052	17,052	5,880	10,584
Sales (Sales Dollars)									
Last Sales Plan	$ 383,740	54,880	47,040	37,240	54,300	43,200	620,400	45,500	47,000
Current Sales Plan	$ 386,904	55,272	46,648	36,848	56,056	45,472	627,200	47,040	48,608
Difference	$ 3,164	392	(392)	(392)	1,756	2,272	6,800	1,540	1,608
Cum Difference	$ 3,164	3,556	3,164	2,772	4,528	6,800	6,800	1,540	3,148
Supply (Cost Dollars)									
Budgeted Production	$ 205,884	31,350	26,904	21,318	32,034	25,992	343,482	23,940	25,536
Current Production Plan	$ 211,356	31,920	29,868	21,432	31,920	26,904	353,400	25,080	28,272
Difference	$ 5,472	570	2,964	114	(114)	912	9,918	1,140	2,736
Cum Difference	$ 5,472	6,042	9,006	9,120	9,006	9,918	9,918	1,140	3,876
Finished Goods Inventory (Cost Dollars)									
Budget	$ 30,096	30,096	30,096	30,096	30,096	30,096	30,096	29,640	27,360
Plan	$ 27,360	27,132	29,868	29,868	29,184	29,640	29,640	27,360	27,360
Difference	$ (2,736)	(2,964)	(228)	(228)	(912)	(456)	(456)	(2,280)	-

➢ Monitoring **key KPI's,** such as actual sales versus targets in financial terms, forecast accuracy, customer backlogs, inventory levels, average profit margins, and others, which can highlight the variations from plan, which if continued, could cause bigger problems later in the year.

➢ Provide a basis for **simulation or what-if planning.** With both the unit and financial data in an accessible database, multiple iterations of future demand, supply and inventory plans can be compared based on varying assumptions.

Some companies even maintain a standard practice of "high-low" planning, where they examine the implications of a "highest possible" forecast versus a "lowest possible" forecast versus a "most likely" forecast, for their most variable families or product lines.

Based on these different forecast numbers, they would project the range of future potential inventory balances, revenue totals, backlogs and average customer lead times, and even potential shortages or customer service problems. This could lead to selective contingency planning or at least to more vigilant monitoring of the more critical scenarios.

➢ And, where appropriate, **demand and supply plans are adjusted** at the family level, and then used as a guideline to adjust all the detailed plans and schedules, inventory targets, lead times, guidelines and other tactical data, to properly plan for profitably supporting the new expected sales volumes.

So, for instance, rather than continuing to manufacture and build inventory quantities of a product whose sales are falling below the original expected forecast, by adjusting the demand and supply plans, excess inventories can be avoided, and scarce resources can be devoted to producing the products that are actually selling.

➢ Finally, in those cases where management decides to **alter the financial plans, targets or budgets,** the latest S&OP unit volumes can be used as a starting point for recalculating the new financial data.

➢ S&OP provides a more reliable and rigorous process to replace or provide input into the traditional **business performance reviews** that most top management teams conduct on a monthly basis.

Every one of our thirteen best practice companies uses S&OP in this way, especially *AGFA, Cast-Fab, Coca-Cola Midi, Eli Lilly, Interbake Foods, Norse Dairy, Pyosa* and *UMC.*

➤ In addition, where a company is a division of a larger corporation, a critical output of the S&OP process is unit, financial and KPI **information forwarded to corporate management**.

Of our best practice companies, this occurs at *AGFA, Amcor, Coca-Cola Midi, Danfoss, Interbake Foods* (to its parent Weston Foods), *Norse Dairy Systems* (to its parent, *Interbake Foods), Pyosa* and *Scotts*.

Best Practice Company Experiences with Monthly Financial Planning:

➤ At *AGFA* top management insists that S&OP be the linkage between all business processes. It is the basis for reviewing performance to targets and making adjustments to the business plan two to three times a year. Analysis of the financial impact of critical changes is done by financial personnel, and then input to the executive S&OP Meeting.

➤ At *Eli Lilly* the annual business plan can be modified on a quarterly basis based on changes identified in their global S&OP process.

➤ At both *Interbake Foods* and *Norse Dairy Systems* the S&OP numbers are converted into an updated financial plan each month. Because of this, the focus is on ensuring that the numbers are valid and not inflated or unrealistic. If the financial plan changes by more than +/- 5% over eighteen months, the reasons must be explained and reconciled, before the financial plan is sent to their parent, Weston Foods Corporation.

➤ *"The SOP process and the databases associated with the process have enabled the Financial Department to do timely and accurate financial estimates on a monthly basis. Since it is all coming from the same database that is driving the production plans and inventory levels, the accuracy of the financial reporting is a much more accurate projection than before."* Don Niemeyer, Chief Financial Officer, *Interbake Foods*

➤ At *UMC*, each month the latest sales and production plans are dollarized and compared to budgets and business plans. Based on this process, the business plan is updated quarterly. S&OP provides a reasonable ability to predict business performance, because the underlying data is accurate, and people understand and embrace the process.

S&OP's Role in Annual Financial Planning and Budgeting

Budgeting is one of the most arduous, and at the same time important tasks for managers in any manufacturing company. It feels like a thankless task that's never done, often with many iterations where numbers need to be adjusted (revenues and profits up, spending and expenses down), until the totals come out where senior management wants them.

S&OP, or any other process, won't replace the need for multiple iterations, since they represent the process of bringing together "what we'd like" with "what we think we can live with". And though painful for the participants, this has proven to be a relatively effective way of aligning members of an organization towards a common goal.

But S&OP can help quite a bit with the base or the first set of numbers. Without S&OP, most companies start with the actual numbers year-to-date, plus some data from previous years, plus whatever information they have about future products, markets, customers and trends. Then the obligatory "10 to 15%" growth is added to these numbers. Then the wrestling match begins.

With S&OP, a company can start with the rolling projected demand, supply and inventory plans that exist at the time that the financial planning/budgeting process begins (usually months in advance of the new fiscal year). To support this process, the S&OP planning horizon must be at least sixteen to eighteen months to cover the balance of the current fiscal year plus the next. This is one of the primary reasons why companies maintain an eighteen to twenty-four month horizon for S&OP, even though month-to-month, very little attention is paid to the part of the horizon that falls outside the current fiscal year.

By starting with these S&OP numbers in financial terms, the company is already dialing in much of their product and market intelligence, which is constantly being updated in the monthly S&OP process. Because of that, this first set of numbers is often more believable and defensible to management, especially since they're familiar with the rigorous cross-functional analysis, discussion, and decision-making that occurs within the S&OP process.

Not only is this S&OP set of numbers a better starting point, it's one that is much easier to obtain. Many companies find that the number of hours people need to put into the annual financial planning process can be reduced by as much as 50% when S&OP is used as the starting point. And where a company is a division of a larger company, in a complex corporate structure, this is especially helpful since the timing requirements are usually very strict to get all the numbers put together across the multiple segments of the company.

Best Practice Company Experiences with Annual Financial Planning and Budgeting:

➤ At **AGFA** S&OP has become the basis for all long term manufacturing capacity and manpower planning. It is also the starting point for the annual budgeting process. With S&OP, there has been a significant reduction (especially within the manufacturing organization) in the time needed to develop annual budgets and plans. S&OP provides not only the starting point for the annual planning exercise, but also a basis for making key "sanity checks " to validate future plans.

➤ At **Danfoss** S&OP has strong links to the business plan, updated twice a year in the strategic planning process. The S&OP plans are directly derived from the strategic plans, and the budget is based on the S&OP plans. Monthly budget comparisons and "expected-to-realize" calculations are made during the global S&OP Meeting.

➤ At **EMS** S&OP ties together the entire business planning process. The detailed operating plans and other financial plans for the business are based on the initial annual plan that becomes the starting point for the monthly S&OP review cycle. These plans are revised as a part of the monthly S&OP review cycle

S&OP's Role in Capital Planning and Investment Decisions

"In the past, our manufacturing groups were typically in a reactive mode as they responded to customer orders. Now, we view our forecast and capacity a year into the future. We can better manage our resources. We can better plan our capital needs." John F. Deininger, Vice President, Operations, **Norse Dairy Systems**

A vital factor in any business's success is deciding how to invest for the future. This could involve replacing resources that have grown old or inefficient, adding additional resources to support volume growth or product line additions, or adding completely new resources to support new product initiatives or different lines of business.

Many of these capital investments are needed to support specific product volumes that are part of either current or future demand and supply plans. Where this is the case, it's an easy and obvious step to base the capital planning and justification process on S&OP's constantly updated demand and supply plans, ensuring that all capital decisions and plans consider the latest, most reliable product volume plans. And it adds one more reason why everyone in the organization should be working towards keeping the S&OP plans as realistic as possible.

No fancy system integration is normally required here. It's simply a matter of setting company guidelines to insist that all product volumes used in the capital appropriation request process be taken directly from S&OP, and updated whenever changed by S&OP.

Basing capital decisions on S&OP represents a major time savings across the organization. Instead of having to develop new future product volume estimates whenever a capital appropriation request is being prepared, the numbers can be taken directly from the S&OP plans. Then capital investments will be based on the same projections as the annual financial planning and budgeting, and the day-to-day execution of demand and supply plans.

A Best Practice Example:
S&OP and Capital Planning at *Pyosa*

Pyosa does **Rough Cut *Capital* Planning** as part of their monthly S&OP process, even before the forecasts or production plans are finalized. This is a company that has limited availability of working capital, where even the ability to borrow money has limitations (capital availability in Mexico is much tighter than in the US).

So each month, they take the preliminary forecast, involve purchasing to determine the raw material investment required to support it, and then decide whether the current capital availability in the company can support all such forecasts. If you will, they adjust or "constrain" the forecast to match how management wishes to allocate the available capital.

In this way they avoid cash constraints, planning around them, rather than getting caught at the last minute and not being able to satisfy the customer. So for *Pyosa* S&OP is the main monthly mechanism to:

➤ manage sales, revenue, production and inventory, in kilograms, Mexican pesos and US dollars

➤ identify cash requirements and communicate them to corporate management

➤ compare performance to budget and make the appropriate adjustments in the individual functional, and/or business unit portions of the budget

Another Best Practice Example of S&OP and Capital Planning at *Eli Lilly*

➤ For a seven year horizon, 130 sales affiliate teams and over twenty Global Marketing Product Teams maintain a forecast for each key product.

➤ As part of their quarterly global S&OP process, they identify when production responsibility for existing or new products can be shifted from an overloaded to an underloaded site, thus avoiding unneeded plant expansion and capital spending.

➤ In some cases, older products coming off patent protection are outsourced to third party manufacturers, rather than investing capital in new plant capacity.

➤ The seven year planning horizon gives them plenty of lead time to make and execute these decisions, without incurring extra costs.

➤ Through the visibility and decision-making forum created by their global S&OP process, *Lilly* was able to defer or cancel over $80 million in proposed capital investments during the past two years, while still supporting all product demand for existing and new products.

S&OP's Role in Managing Cash Flow

In many cases, significant inventory reductions are the result of a good S&OP process. Therefore, whenever management has a need for improving cash flow and reducing inventories, S&OP should be one of the first places to look. Ensuring that demand and supply are balanced at the aggregate level is a prerequisite to fine tuning smaller slices of inventory.

Since S&OP is a powerful tool for managing inventory levels, it can be seen as a key "cash manager". For example, both *AGFA* and *UMC* reduced their finished inventories by 67% (to 1/3 of the original total). They both attribute much of this to S&OP, since it provides a clear and effective mechanism to communicate inventory targets to the entire organization, and to ensure that the sales and production plans being pursued will support those targets.

Summary

S&OP is a key tool for developing, monitoring (each month) and adjusting financial plans, budgets and capital plans.

By ensuring that all plans are looked at concurrently, it helps avoid product line, functional or regional sub-optimization.

The constant comparison and reconciliation between operating and financial plans in the S&OP process results in a clear and integrated direction, so that sales, marketing, manufacturing, supply chain management, planning, purchasing and product development can adjust tactics and resources to better meet the financial objectives, and the overall business and strategic ones as well.

Chapter 12

Looking Forward

"There are many methods for predicting the future. For example, you can read horoscopes, tea leaves, tarot cards, or crystal balls. Collectively, these methods are known as "nutty methods". Or you can put well-researched facts into sophisticated computer models, more commonly referred to as "a complete waste of time." Scott Adams, American cartoonist (Dilbert)

Where will S&OP go in the next twenty years?

In the end, no one really knows for sure. But we have some opinions about what has and is happening with S&OP, and in what ways S&OP *might* evolve. This is what we'd like to share with you.

First and foremost, we feel strongly that sales and operations planning will continue to be an important part of professional manufacturing and supply chain management. In twenty years, manufacturing and distribution companies will still be managing their supply chains using this method and it will still be recognizable as S&OP.

Application vs. Operation

Increasingly S&OP has helped deal with new and changing business issues such as:

➤ improving cash management in companies in competitive or financial distress

➤ transitioning from "supply-driven" to "demand driven"

➤ managing outsourced and offshore manufacturing

➤ integrating different organizations into one competitive supply chain

➤ or even just integrating different organizations into a single company, as an industry consolidates and restructures

We believe that the use of S&OP to deal with these types of issues will continue and expand.

But one thing that we have observed, in twenty odd years of its application, is that the core processes that make up S&OP really haven't changed much at all.

What has changed during that time is the degree to which different parts of organizations **participate** in the S&OP process, and the degree to which S&OP is **integrated with other business processes**.

Participation and Integration

In the beginning was "production planning". Isolated, a manufacturing/materials only activity, it got little if any top management attention. Sales and marketing involvement was a dream that only the most optimistic ever thought would come true. Finance and accounting were the same - ditto for quality management, HR, and engineering.

As for its integration with key business processes - well, let's put it this way - if you couldn't get sales and marketing interested in the overall process, how much chance was there that it was well integrated with the demand planning processes of the company? Or that business planning and budgeting would be connected to S&OP? Or that new product introductions would be linked to it?

Yet in the period between 1987 and the present, participation in S&OP has expanded to include sales and marketing, finance, executive management, quality, HR, design and development, and product and process engineering. During the same period, as is apparent from the best practices companies, S&OP became increasingly integrated with processes for demand planning, budgeting and business planning, supply chain and distribution management, quality planning, hiring and training activities, new product introduction, and other business improvement processes.[23]

And Next?

We think, that in this case, the past is the best predictor of the future.

We believe that S&OP will get increased attention as companies recognize they really aren't doing it at all, or aren't doing it well. More companies will implement or re-implement S&OP, and more companies will use it well.

Another safe bet is that the lessons from the best practice companies will be applied more widely. Examples would include:

---

[23] The changes made in our model companies paralleled the evolution of S&OP, and are described throughout this book, especially in chapters 3, 6 through 11, and summarized in chapter 5 - Lessons Learned.

➤ S&OP processes will be more efficient, with cycles that end earlier in the month.

➤ There will be more applications of S&OP across extended or global supply chains, principally because of outsourcing and "off-shoring", and the continued flattening of manufacturing organizations.

➤ Contingency planning to handle long supply lead times, principally because of Asian sourcing, will improve.

➤ High/low volume planning to handle volatile demand patterns and short customer lead times will become more widespread and common.

➤ S&OP will better integrate with underlying resource planning systems and the enterprise's supply chain data, and it will have improved access to real demand data captured at the point of sale or point of use. Improved access to data will support faster S&OP cycles with more real time "what-if" decision-making and more rapid response to change.

➤ S&OP will be standard operating procedure for lean manufacturers - helping with the major limitation in Lean: adding distance vision to a nearsighted process.

And we think that the same kinds of improved technology and communication tools - like teleconferencing and video conferencing - that made effective S&OP more accessible to global companies over the last twenty years, will be improved even further. This will bring S&OP across a globally coordinated supply chain to even the smallest organizations.

And as S&OP evolves further, we believe it will most likely be along similar lines - expanded participation and improved integration with other business processes, without fundamental changes in the core S&OP process. For example:

➤ Is it possible that a company's Board of Directors might participate in S&OP in a meaningful way?

➤ Might an innovative company push the decision-making processes of S&OP even further away from the executive suite, to perhaps field sales people or production workers or supply chain partners?

➤ Could S&OP be better integrated with "business strategy"?

➤ Could it integrate business processes across an extended supply chain where multiple corporations participate and operate together as a single synchronized unit - directed by a single S&OP demand and supply planning process?

➤ With more and more production being outsourced, will S&OP integrate further into new product development and introduction?

The Future

Will S&OP still be used in the future? We think it's guaranteed. As long as there's a need to plan resources and volumes longer term, there will be a need for S&OP. When we look back twenty years from now on professional manufacturing and distribution management, we expect to see S&OP as a key component.

Will S&OP still be called "S&OP" in the future? We don't know. But we do hope that whatever it's called, it's used to gain competitive advantage in the great global game of manufacturing. And we hope that you are able to match or even surpass the improvements achieved by the best practice companies described in this book.

Good luck in your own journey.

Part III

Company Profiles

Chapter 13

AGFA US HealthCare
A Division of AGFA Corporation

Greenville, South Carolina, USA

Medical Imaging Products

Why would a mature business with steadily declining market demand for its base products continue emphasizing S&OP for eleven years?

Can S&OP help with:
    1) Significant product rationalization?
    2) The introduction of an entirely new product technology that will gradually
       cannibalize the base business?
    3) Two acquisitions?
    4) Two plant shutdowns?

AGFA Gevaert N.V ("AGFA") is a global giant in the imaging business, based in Belgium. The US Healthcare division produces and distributes radiology and information systems for medical imaging. It is experiencing major changes as the technology shifts from traditional silver halide film images to digital imaging.

What's Unique?

Companies, processes, technology and people evolve. As always, the fittest survive.

➤ In 1996 Du Pont sold its medical imaging division to private venture capitalists, and the company was renamed Sterling Diagnostic Imaging - SDI. The new owners accelerated and completed the implementation of better management controls through enterprise resource planning (ERP), with S&OP as the linchpin.

➤ In 1999, the business was acquired by AGFA

    o New digital technology and an expanded line of digital equipment was introduced.

    o The pre-existing AGFA product lines were integrated and reconciled with the products produced at the old DuPont plants.

o   Existing AGFA plants took over for the original Du Pont plants and warehouses, which closed.

Not surprisingly, the management team also evolved through continuous improvements in their management processes and skills. Many of the key managers stayed with the company through all these changes, while increasing their responsibilities.

Company Characteristics

Size:

➤ Revenue of 4.2 billion Euros for AGFA globally, 1.4 billion Euros for US Healthcare

➤ 17,000 employees for AGFA worldwide, 1,000 for US Healthcare

➤ Sales of over 100,000,000 square meters of film per year, in over ten million boxes

➤ Thousands of pieces of processing equipment installed across North America

Products:

➤ Conventional (film-based) products

    o   Films, processing equipment, and screens and cassettes (frames to hold the film as it is inserted in the equipment)

    o   Four families, one hundred sub-families, and one thousand equipment SKU's, five hundred film SKU's, and two thousand screen and cassette SKU's

➤ Digital products (an emerging technology)

    o   Three thousand possible SKU's

    o   Twenty major typical units forecasted and planned

    o   Various options planned by historical percentages

The Demand Side:

➢ Within the NAFTA market, sales and technical support personnel work with customers to place equipment on a contract basis. Once the conventional equipment is sold, the customers order film and screens and cassettes through a network of dealers and distributors supplied by AGFA. The sales effort goes into placing the equipment, not selling the film.

➢ This is a mature market gradually being replaced by digital radiography. All films and conventional equipment are maintained in finished good stock, since superior customer service is required by a demanding marketplace.

➢ Major customers:

   o Group Purchasing Organizations (GPO's) - hospital buying groups such as Premier, HPG, etc.

   o Integrated Dealer Networks (IDN's)

   o Imaging centers

   o Individual dealers (for radiology and consumable products only)

   o The US Department of Defense (AGFA is the preferred supplier of digital equipment.)

The Supply Side:

➢ All manufacturing activities are part of the global AGFA Manufacturing group. However, the planning, scheduling, and inventory management for North America is controlled by the North American supply chain management group.

➢ The logistics, warehousing, transportation, human resources, information systems, research and development, and finance functions are provided through the global organization.

➢ A high-volume, process approach to manufacturing film is employed:

   o Plastic film is "cast" (liquid petro-chemicals are mixed, dried and hardened) in 6-foot wide rolls.

   o These rolls are then coated with photographic emulsions on devoted coating lines in AGFA's mother plant in Mortsel, Belgium (six week lead time to the US). They are shipped to the US along with most of the high volume packaging materials.

o Two to three weeks of safety stock are maintained on these master coated rolls in the finishing plant in S. Carolina, to accommodate short term changes to their production schedule.

o The film is slit, chopped and packaged into various sized boxes to maintain finished inventory in S. Carolina and California warehouses. Lead time for this process is less than one week.

➤ Conventional (non-digital) equipment is assembled in one week or less in a plant in Germany. These products are shipped to the New Jersey distribution center, which holds about one month of finished goods inventory and ships directly to customers in North America

➤ Also in New Jersey, digital imaging equipment is assembled to customer order using the modules, components, and software specified by the customer. The lead time here is one to six weeks, depending on the product and options specified.

o High technology modules and components are purchased from companies such as Dell™, HP™, EMC™, Sun™ and IBM™.

o Proprietary software for the digital IMPAX® product line is developed in Ontario, Canada.

➤ Overcapacity exists in the industry and causes continual price erosion. As a result, there is a constant focus on cost reduction and cash flow management.

Other Tools Employed

➤ Supplier partnering.

➤ Collaborative forecasting with customers.

The S&OP Process

"The trick is to get things done as early as you can. S&OP is not a meeting or meetings, it's a process. By the time the meetings are held, most issues are fixed!" Malcolm Jaggard, Director Supply Chain Management

The Mechanics for Conventional Products

➤ Five families and one hundred sub-families - eighteen month horizon.

➤ Film planned in equivalent square meters, despite varying saleable dimensions.

➤ Standard S&OP spreadsheets for each sub-family are reviewed:
  o sales vs. forecast vs. budget
  o actual production vs. plan
  o actual inventory vs. plan, + # of turns
  o number of units for equipment
  o square meters for finished film and master rolls of semi-finished film

➤ KPI's are reviewed:
  o forecast accuracy at subfamily level - four month rolling average
  o on-time delivery in full to customers
  o product availability for customers
  o inventory record accuracy
  o the Inventory Efficiency Index (IEI), which measures aging, excess and obsolete inventory, with a goal to avoid it, rather than report and write it off
  o on-time delivery from manufacturing to warehouse locations
  o current backlog of deliveries to the warehouse
  o manufacturing production plan performance
  o all manufacturing schedule compliance
  o supplier on-time deliveries in full

Because digital imaging equipment is a new product line with separate people and resources devoted to it, overall product line performance is reviewed in a separate monthly meeting. Improvements in precision, and lengthening of the planning horizon is being instituted to improve the S&OP process on this new product line.

Demand Planning

➢ Sales and marketing own the forecast

➢ Supply chain management inventory planners manage the statistical forecast (maintained eighteen months out by subfamily and six weeks out by SKU)

   o They review actual sales, previous forecasts, system-suggested forecast changes, and other demand data on all one hundred subfamilies.

   o They monitor the forecast accuracy at the SKU level, highlight exception situations and suggest changes (family volumes and mix factors by SKU), for the review and approval of marketing product managers.

   o Roughly 10% of the one hundred subfamilies are adjusted in any given month. This reflects that film in general has very stable demand patterns, with over 25% of the volume coming from a single SKU, 38% from the top two.

➢ Analysis of the financial impact of critical changes vs. the business plan is done by financial personnel two to three times a year, and then fed to the executive S&OP meeting.

AGFA plans to improve forecasting through better sales input on equipment forecasts, and more automation, with less reliance on individual intervention and the manual integration of disconnected systems.

AGFA sees forecasting as a continuous process, with occasional updates. Management trusts the process and the people executing it. They review the forecast by exception only in the partnership or executive S&OP meetings.

Supply Planning

➢ Several times per year, production plans may be reallocated between regions and divisions of AGFA based on:

   o regional capacity utilization and demand

   o cost and global performance

   o decisions made in global S&OP meetings in Europe, involving global supply chain management and global marketing, based on inputs from the regional partnership meetings.

➢ The North American Supply Chain Manager proposes production plan changes (or alternative scenarios) prior to the partnership meeting. In virtually all cases, the changes are accepted as proposed.

➢ Rough cut capacity planning is used to validate production plans by major resources.

➢ Master scheduling by end item is done weekly in the US, used to drive material requirements planning (MRP), so that replenishment orders for wide stock film and packaging material can be placed on the Mortsel, Belgium mother plant.

➢ Digital equipment has constant design changes and a long customer backlog that varies in size. Strategic suppliers hold safety stock, and most provide parts and equipment in two to four weeks. This production plan is basically a reflection of the customer backlog and component availability.

➢ No senior management approval is required for changes in the production plan. They are reviewed at the executive meetings, but management trusts the process and the people to make adjustments during the month as needed.

Partnership Meeting

On the second Wednesday of every month, these 90-minute meetings are held in the Greenville, South Carolina North American headquarters, with local people in attendance, and others conference calling from both North America and Europe. Because data is available on a timely basis, most of the detail review is done daily or weekly prior to the meetings, often cross-functionally resolved at the same time, and passed as an issue to the meeting only if critical or unresolved.

Attendees:

Director of Supply Chain Management	Production Planners
	Customer Service Manager
Product Managers	European Plant Planning Managers
Planning Manager	Production Director
Director of Marketing (as needed)	Global AGFA Manufacturing Manager
Inventory Planners	Finance Manager
Marketing Managers	

At the end of each meeting, a packet of quantitative data, minutes and source data is published to the attendees and selected others. Each functional leader is responsible for the communication of critical issues and decisions to their teams.

The Executive Meeting - "Just give me the bad news!"

During the third week of each month, the President, Bob Pryor, personally leads this monthly executive staff meeting, of which the thirty minute S&OP executive review is a critical part. At the start, the S&OP executive meeting was a stand-alone meeting, lasting over an hour. But as it became efficient, focused and institutionalized, it was folded into the executive staff meeting as the first agenda item.

No time is spent reviewing sales and revenue performance if it meets the plan. Every issue, KPI, target, etc. is color-coded: red means "a problem"; yellow indicates "progress but not to target"; or green says "everything is okay". Only reds and yellows are reviewed in this meeting. They can't remember the last time they had a red issue!

The company has moved to this exception based management process, based on management's trust in the process, the teams, and the people doing the work. This has evolved over the last eleven years of continual improvement to the S&OP process.

Global S&OP

AGFA's sales and operations planning in the North American region feeds a global S&OP process for the entire AGFA Healthcare business. Other regions also send their S&OP results into the global process. Monthly global S&OP meetings at the corporate headquarters in Mortsel, Belgium are conducted to balance forecasts and production capacities at regional sites and globally. The S&OP process is used as a rough cut tool to balance loads both locally and globally. Occasionally it is used to allocate large customer orders (often government tender orders) to the region that can best accommodate them.

Hard Benefits

The impact of S&OP in terms of balancing prudent cash flow management, cost, and Class A customer service levels has been enormous, as our metrics will attest." Bob Pryor, President, ***AGFA Healthcare, Americas***

➤ Even while closing plants and transferring production:

　o Customer service was continually improved.

　o Total inventory was reduced from **one hundred twenty days** to **forty days** over the last three years (including fifteen to twenty days of intransit inventory from Europe). Finished goods averages twelve to thirteen days in total, with two to three days supply of the top two items (which represent 38% of total sales).

➢ Other business improvement initiatives, including product rationalization, plant and warehouse consolidation, and various cost reduction programs, also played a part in achieving these benefits.

Soft Benefits

➢ The S&OP process helped to very quickly complete the product rationalizations and phase out of the old US manufacturing plants, with virtually no impact on customer service.

➢ Subsequently, improved customer service - caused in part by S&OP - led to better customer relations and the widespread perception that AGFA was a truly reliable supplier.

➢ The process has fostered accurate data, consistent processes, and empowered, reliable people.

➢ S&OP has become the basis for all long term manufacturing capacity and manpower planning, and for the annual budgeting process. There has been a significant reduction (especially within the manufacturing organization) in the time needed to develop annual budgets and plans.

➢ S&OP provides a basis for making key "sanity checks" to validate future plans.

➢ S&OP ties together decision-making processes such as forecasting, master scheduling and customer order management. This insures that consistent, timely decisions are made on a daily basis at the lowest possible level in the organization, where knowledge of the detail is strongest.

➢ Manufacturing, supply chain management, sales and marketing, and finance work together with very little finger-pointing, having overcome historical resistance to change by the plants, and to any form of cross functional teamwork.

➢ S&OP is key in managing product rationalizations, plant and warehouse closings, and all forms of inventory reduction programs.

➢ AGFA's strong belief is that further benefits will be forthcoming. Continuous improvement is embedded in the S&OP process, and continuous improvement cannot be maximized without S&OP.

➢ *"The seamless integration from Du Pont to SDI into AGFA, with minimal impact on customer service, cost containment and inventory management, would have been impossible without the business processes with S&OP at their core."* Malcolm Jaggard, Director Supply Chain Management

*Go to Chapter 4 to read more about **Benefits***

Lessons Learned

➤ S&OP can lead to an organization-wide "management by exception" approach. But be careful, you can't start out that way!

➤ You have to stick with it, it takes time.

➤ S&OP is a process, not a series of meetings. It requires discipline and commitment at all levels (especially the top) to succeed.

➤ S&OP would have never worked well without "fixing the holes in our systems." But without S&OP, AGFA may never have fixed those holes or improved the accuracy and timeliness of data.

➤ S&OP can survive ownership, organization and personnel changes. In fact, it can be a key process to help manage those changes.

*Go to Chapter 5 to read more about **Lessons Learned***

Consultant's Summary

"Originally manufacturing resisted S&OP, but the effort was sustained because top management began to see results in lowered inventory, better customer service, a better manufacturing plan, and better visibility to manage the business. They insisted that it be perpetuated through the various organizational and business changes over the last eleven years.

S&OP evolved, but it never wavered. It has grown in both efficiency and effectiveness.

AGFA acquired this business to gain North American market share and manufacturing sites. The unexpected bonus was a set of excellent business processes with S&OP at their core, which AGFA was willing to embrace in their pursuit of continuous improvement, building on the strength of their new acquisition.

Thus S&OP has attracted the participation of other units within AGFA. Today there is a robust global Healthcare planning process, based in Europe, with a vigorous partnership meeting providing key

inputs to decision-making at the executive level." John R. Dougherty, Consultant

AGFA, the AGFA rhombus, and IMPAX are trademarks of AGFA Gevaert N.V, Belgium or its affiliates. All other trademarks are held by their respective owners and are used in an editorial fashion only, with no intention of infringement.

Chapter 14

Amcor Limited
Flexible Packaging Division

Moorabbin, Victoria, Australia

Packaging for Consumer Goods

Why would a small Australian site of an international packaging manufacturer need S&OP for planning products unique to each customer?

Amcor Flexibles manufactures specialty flexible polyethylene packaging, in both plain and printed versions. These products go to customers who produce and sell consumer goods into key retail outlets. For example, Amcor supplies bags to major bread manufacturers who sell their finished products directly to major Australian retail companies and to other customers through distributors. Other retail products using Amcor packaging include frozen foods, snack foods and rice.

What's Unique?

In this extremely price sensitive industry, Amcor's customers hold only small inventories and demand short lead times. The customers advise Amcor of major changes in requirements on very short notice, since they announce their product promotions as late as possible to avoid tipping off their competitors.

The desire for long manufacturing runs in specific sequences to keep costs low, contrasts with pressures from the market place for short lead times and flexible response. It also can result in large work-in-process (WIP) inventory levels.

Company Characteristics

Size:

➢ sales of $75 million (Australian dollars)

➤ 220 employees

➤ 35 machines

Products:

➤ Printed and plain polyethylene packaging: bags and flat sheet

➤ 30% make-to-order, 70% make-to-stock by sales volume

➤ Virtually all product designs are customer specific, with finished goods inventories carried for the customer on approximately 55% of the products

➤ Approximately 1400 finished good items

The Demand Side:

➤ For Amcor's customers the average life of a product is only six months. Safety stock at the finished good level is generally not viewed as a viable option because of the unpredictable lifetime of the products, the potential perishability of many of them, and the resulting possible obsolescence costs. Because of this, Amcor is subject to the unpredictability of many product launches and pipeline fills, as well as constant promotional and counter promotional activity.

➤ Amcor's Sales Account Managers are located close to the customers. The majority of Amcor's business is won by bidding on large customer contracts, which are typically decided on cost. But incumbent suppliers have an advantage if they have been providing excellent service, which may enable the retention of business at a premium equal to the value placed on the superior service by the customer.

➤ KPI's tracked for major customers include:

   o On-time delivery in-full with all items complete

   o Forecast accuracy

   o New item lead times

   o Short lead time requests

   o Quality data

The Supply Side:

➤ The flexible packaging business is a classic process industry: few raw materials yielding many finished products.

➤ The first stage of the manufacturing process is to extrude the polyethylene film using tiny beads of polyethylene mixed with specific additives. The end product from this stage is a large roll of "film", a meter wide and *nine kilometers long* (that's 5.4 miles)!

➤ The second stage is the printing of the film with customer specific graphics.

➤ The third stage is fabrication, which takes the printed film and converts it into a format that is specific to the customer's filling process. It could be a bag (for bread) or it could be rolls of product suitable for a "for-fill and seal" process (for vegetables).

➤ The fourth stage occurs on some products, when more complex structures require lamination of different types of film delivering different packaging properties.

➤ Ninety-eight percent of production is done in house, with some products sent outside for the 4th stage.

➤ Since long set-up times and process waste are significant to the product cost, advantageous manufacturing sequencing is critical to keeping costs low. The different manufacturing stages sequence on different criteria, leading to high WIP inventory between stages.

➤ Product lead times are one to five weeks, depending on the number of manufacturing stages required.

➤ Many of the raw materials purchased from overseas are subject to significant lead times and cost penalties for small purchase quantities.

Other Tools Employed

➤ Amcor manages with a well integrated, closed-loop resource planning and control process (ERP or MRPII). They achieved Class A MRPII[24] accreditation in December 2003.

---

[24] MRPII was the name used most frequently in the 1970's through the 1990's to describe an integrated, cross-functional resource planning and control process. Some companies were certified "Class A" in recognition of their complete and intensive use of all the tools to produce superior business results. It is similar to the term "World Class".

➤ Supply chain management approaches are being pursued with some major customers providing Amcor with weekly requirements updated monthly.

The S&OP Process

"Sales and operations planning is not just a set of meetings - it's the way we run our business." Graeme Hazeldine, General Manager, Flexible Division

The S&OP process is the main tactical planning and communication tool for the company. Specific reasons for Amcor adopting S&OP, which was started in June 2000, include:

➤ Delivery performance "propped up" by lots of chronic fire-fighting and "crashing" the plan

➤ Too much of the wrong items resulting in inventory write-offs

➤ No structured, regular forecasting process

➤ No medium-term planning resulting in:

- o Capacity issues being discovered too late

- o Big variations in plant loading leading to costly overtime

- o Extra costs due to outsourcing work at the last minute because of capacity overloads

Demand Planning

"Everyone knows what the customer takes, why can't we just use history?"

When Amcor started the S&OP process there was very little formal forecasting. What was done was without sales participation. The information that was used for manufacturing and capacity planning was not tightly linked to the customers' plans.

The Sales Account Managers saw their markets as having fairly smooth demand patterns with a couple of retail promotions a year, and a Christmas close down. On the other hand, planning saw waves of coinciding, unexpected demand, often conflicting with maintenance or shutdown plans.

Sales felt that "No extra value would be gained from forecasting at the item level". At first, family level forecasting was tried, but it quickly became apparent that item / customer level forecasts were needed to identify potential mix sensitive capacity and material problems. And the decision to create the position of Demand Analyst to coordinate the process became key to improving forecasting.

The forecasting process includes:

➢ A time horizon of usually twelve months (twenty months at budget time)

➢ Forecasts done at the item level (most of which are customer specific), in weekly buckets

➢ Some customers sending in a refreshed forecast (supplier or vendor schedules indicating requirements into the future) for the required horizon, in weekly buckets. Here only a sensibility check is required, preferably with the customer.

➢ For those customers not providing a forecast, Amcor generates a forecast and seeks customer agreement. For two major customers, a statistical forecast is generated and then collaboratively finalized with the customer in a formal meeting.

➢ For major customers a formal meeting is an ongoing activity. Smaller customers may require as little as a telephone call.

➢ The process culminates in a demand management review meeting, held on approximately the 25th of each month, with the following attendees:

-Demand Analyst   -Supply Chain Manager
-Key Account Coordinator   -Account Managers
-Sales and Marketing Manager

➢ Senior sales and marketing executives approve the final sales forecasts.

Supply Planning

"Good collaborative planning is essential to react to the volatility of demand with a minimum amount of safety stock." Peter Were, General Manager Supply Chain, Flexible Division

Production planning takes place after sales forecasts have been finalized, with rough cut capacity planning providing information on resource issues. The plans are developed at the item level using detailed master scheduling logic to take into account current inventories, customer backlogs, schedules in process, etc. Material requirements planning provides the demand supply review for work-in-progress and purchased items. The resulting aggregate family production plan used in the SOP process has been built up from the item level.

Key personnel involved in preparing and evaluating production plans are:

-Master Scheduler   -Technical Manager
-Manufacturing Manager   -Customer Service Manager

Partnership Meeting

There is no formal partnership meeting/step in the Amcor process, which is not unusual in a smaller, relatively flat organization. Typically, the people in a partnership meeting are largely department managers, while most of those in the executive S&OP meeting report directly to the president/general manager. At this Amcor site, as in most smaller companies, these two groups are one and the same. Hence the need for the partnership meeting goes away.

On the other hand, this is not the case in larger organizations, where many issues should be addressed by a layer of middle managers who do not attend the executive S&OP meeting. Here a partnership meeting would be required to gain consensus among the various functions and to reduce the amount of time required at the executive meeting.

The Executive Meeting

➢ takes place on the fifth working day of the month

➢ is chaired by the General Manager

➢ takes about two hours

➢ includes a review of supply, demand and inventory positions, and key performance measures by product family and major customers (who often comprise separate families)

➢ is the major communication meeting of the business

➢ has replaced the previously held "monthly management meeting"

➢ the following members of the GM's staff attend:

-Operations Manager   -Master Scheduler
-Supply Chain Manager.   -Demand Analyst
-Commercial Manager   -Factory Department Managers
-Sales and Marketing Manager

➢ Agenda:

  o A review of specific manufacturing issues such as: safety, project status, capital requirements, quality, etc. - these were formerly covered in a separate operations meeting.

  o The second part of the meeting covers the traditional S&OP supply, demand, inventory and planning agenda items. Some people (for example, the Demand Analyst) attend only this part of the meeting.

The combining of the operations meeting and the S&OP meeting came about because of the improvement in both the process and the data, as well as planning's ability to present a final set of plans with almost all issues resolved beforehand. Amcor is able to do this because they have a small, flat management structure. In other organizations, a separate operations review meeting might be required.

Amcor's environment can change so quickly that an executive meeting only once per month has proven to be inadequate. Thus a shortened weekly review of key short term issues with the appropriate executives is also held. This is not an executive S&OP meeting, but rather is focused close in and gives high-level direction to demand shifts, production resequencing, and so forth.

Hard Benefits

"It is our belief that balancing supply with demand puts you at the point of least cost. This includes overtime, distribution, and factory efficiency. S&OP's main intention is to balance supply with demand and so is one very important variable in the total product cost." Graeme Hazeldine, General Manager, Flexible Division

Since June 2000, the following improvements have been achieved through the use of MRPII, with S&OP as the key management control mechanism:

➢ Inventory has fallen by 40%

➢ DIFOT (Delivered In Full On Time or customer service) rose by 10%

➢ Distribution cost fell by 30 %

➤ Improved customer retention

➤ Reduced obsolescence

Soft Benefits

➤ Increased customer satisfaction

➤ Improved labor planning leading to:

- o balanced supply and demand that keeps Amcor at the point of least cost

- o reasonable levels of overtime

- o the direct labor workforce having a balance between work and home. An improved, stable shut down plan at Christmas has been just one of the benefits delivered through good planning. This is considered very important by management and is appreciated by all the workers.

➤ Improved introduction of new business/ new products ensuring effective communication across functions, with less disruption and higher customer satisfaction

➤ Improved confidence in the data presented, and in the decisions taken, as supporting data and processes from other areas of the business also improved

➤ Less tension and more teamwork between functions, with wide cross-functional agreement on the strategy and plan going forward

➤ Better clarity for both the timing and type of major capital investment decisions

➤ Better understanding of the role of the supply chain and its value to the business

➤ S&OP is a vehicle for the review of supply chain performance measurements

Go to Chapter 4 to read more about **Benefits**

Lessons Learned

➢ Linkage to item level planning thru ERP / MRPII is critical to maximizing the results.

➢ The implementation of a collaborative forecasting process with key customers was essential to improving forecast accuracy. The Demand Analyst was vital in improving the process.

➢ Without accurate data, the plans presented in the S&OP process are not valid, so senior management placed a heavy emphasis on data accuracy.

➢ New product development and finance must be intrinsically linked to the process. Without their involvement, integrated business management would be impossible.

➢ The monthly meeting is the major communication meeting of the business.

*Go to Chapter 5 to read more about **Lessons Learned***

Consultant's Summary

*"This division of Amcor is now being impressively managed utilizing S&OP as both a translator for higher level planning processes, as well as an excellent communication and decision-making process. The behavior within the company reminds me of the saying: **'If you take on a proactive initiative, you remove the need for reactive responses'**.*

Management came to realize that through S&OP they could achieve high levels of customer satisfaction from a position of least cost. Other substantial benefits have also been realized because planning stability has enabled effort to be spent on further value creation opportunities. An example of this would be anticipating large customer orders which may have been outsourced due to a lack of capacity, thus eroding margins. With enough notice, they now have the opportunity to find the necessary capacity in house, or to let their competitors lose money on the sale instead of them.

*S&OP is a tool that can be used **to achieve outstanding business results!** The way in which Amcor uses the S&OP process is indicative of their approach to 'running the business with an integrated set of management processes providing one set of numbers throughout the organization'".* Phil Heenan, Consultant

Chapter 15

Cast-Fab Technologies, Inc.

Cincinnati, Ohio

Castings and Metal Fabrications

Why would a small, privately-held foundry and fabrication shop, producing strictly to customer order, consider their ten year old S&OP process key to managing their business?

Cast-Fab Technologies supplies original equipment manufacturers (OEM's) of plastics machinery, machine tools, automated teller machines, security equipment, and others.

Cast-Fab was spun off from Cincinnati Milacron (now known as Milacron Inc.), where it was the company's captive foundry and fabrication shop, supplying its machine tool and injection molding machine businesses. When Jim Bushman acquired what became Cast-Fab, Milacron was 100% of the customer base. Over the years, pursuing a deliberate strategy, Cast-Fab has been able to diversify its customer base greatly. S&OP has helped in acquiring and retaining significant new customers.

What's Unique?

Cast-Fab is at the extreme outer end of the overall supply chain: its products are used by machinery manufacturers whose products are sold to producers of other products, which may go directly to an end consumer or, in many cases, are sold to other manufacturers.

For example, a Cast-Fab casting might go to a machine tool manufacturer whose product is sold to a Tier 2 automotive supplier, who in turn sells to a Tier 1 supplier, who supplies an auto assembly plant, which produces and ships cars to dealers, who deliver them to people like you and I.

As such, Cast-Fab is "far away" from the final marketplace. The ups and downs of the business cycle tend to be amplified as they move backward in the supply chain; thus the demand streams coming to Cast-Fab tend to be highly variable and erratic.

The problems caused by this variability motivated Cast-Fab to implement sales and operations planning in 1995. Company executives credit S&OP with helping them deal with oscillations in demand, giving them simultaneously more rapid response capability for changes in demand and, at the same time, more stability in production.

Company Characteristics

Size:

➢ Approximately $37 million in annual sales

➢ 265 people

Products:

➢ Highly engineered gray iron and ductile iron castings:

- o between 200 and 80,000 lbs each

- o with annual volumes for each part ranging between 5 and 800 pieces

- o 2004 product volumes:

    -2,139 large castings, with the average shipment size between one and three pieces
    -10,431 medium castings, with the average shipment size between six and ten pieces
    -3,672 small castings, with the average shipment size between six and ten pieces

➢ Highly engineered plate and sheet metal fabrications, such as housings, cabinets, covers, and components for ATM's:

- o Product size, cost, and volumes vary greatly, for example:

    -Shipped 918 pieces to Siemens Energy and Automation in 2004 representing over $2 million in sales
    -Shipped 428,000 pieces of bank equipment components to Security Systems Equipment in 2004, representing about $3.5 million in sales

➢ All of their products are custom designed for each customer, with about 15% of their sales each year generated by new products. Most new products result in repeat business from the customer over a two to five year horizon.

The Demand Side:

➢ Markets and customers:

- o Plastic injection molding machinery: Milacron, Demag, Engel, Husky

- o Wind energy: General Electric, SKF, ClipperWind

- o Air conditioning and refrigeration: Carrier

- o Banking equipment: Security Systems Equipment (sister division)

- o Power conversion and mining: Siemens Energy and Automation, Hitachi Construction Equipment (formerly Euclid-Hitachi), Komatsu

- o Water control products: Coldwell-Wilcox Technologies, Inc. (sister division)

➢ All shipments are direct to the customer or to their outsourced machine shops

➢ There are three outside sales people, two service people, and another who is 1/4 outside sales and 3/4 service. The service people primarily perform internal sales functions.

➢ The Production Control Managers and Planners are also in close contact with the customers.

➢ Cast-Fab's goal is to maintain most of their customer order backlog in the four week range, with the large castings (over 30,000 lbs.) in the five to six week range. And they almost always succeed in doing so by using S&OP:

- o to identify when working hours need to be adjusted (often between forty and sixty hours plant wide)

- o to increase or decrease inventory levels of finished product held for key customers

The Supply Side:

➢ All products are produced in-house at the same site as the general office, with the foundry and the fabrication shop in separate parts of the plant.

➢ The foundry is divided into three main departments: large, medium and small. Within the departments, the processes are:

   -Core
       -Mold
            - Pour
                  -Shake-out
                        - Clean

➢ The foundry produces 67% of the revenues

➢ The capabilities of the fabrication shop, which makes metal fabrications, are divided into heavy, light, and machining areas.

➢ Production cycle times are generally about one week, with larger castings at two weeks due to the time required to cool and solidify.

➢ Customer lead times are two to four weeks, with smaller products having shorter lead times. This stands in sharp contrast to foundry lead times of years ago: ten to thirty weeks and sometimes beyond!

➢ Speed, cost, and manufacturing capabilities are their key competitive variables. *"Our design and manufacturing expertise is actually 'our product'. It's what we sell. And S&OP is an important tool in our tool kit."* - Jim Bushman, Chairman and CEO

Other Tools Employed

➢ They use a manufacturing resource planning (MRPII) process, primarily master scheduling and MRP

➢ Several lean manufacturing efforts have been pursued: *"We cut some batch sizes, did some 5S[25] and did some work on balancing load."* Ross Bushman, President and COO.

The S&OP Process

"S&OP allows us (& forces us) to lift our heads up and look out into the future!" Ross Bushman, President and COO

---

[25] 5S is a methodology for organizing the manufacturing workplace for cleanliness, safety, ergonomics and efficiency

➢ The elapsed time for the entire monthly S&OP cycle is about one and a half weeks.

➢ Planning horizon: six to twelve months for sales; six months for production.

     o   The short production planning horizon is due to lots of labor flexibility

     o   Cross training is a major strategic initiative, with managers reviewed on the number of people they move to the 'well qualified' or 'qualified' categories. Hourly employees score higher in performance reviews if they have learned new operational tasks.

     o   It takes about sixty days to hire a new employee and get her/him down the learning curve

     o   However, beyond a certain point, capacity can only be increased with significant commitments or costs. A firm business agreement with the customer is needed to commit to these levels.

➢ Four product families:

-Large castings
-Medium castings
-Small castings

-Heavy and light fabrications +
  machined parts

➢ This is an example of product families *exactly matching resources*. The sales department thinks in the same terms as manufacturing, which is rare. Sales groups the customer data into the families used in S&OP.

➢ No formal sub-families exist, but major customers serve as sub-families

Demand Planning

➢ A twelve month forecast is developed jointly by the sales people, the VP of Sales and the two Production Planners, based on customer knowledge and experience:

     o   most forecasts are done in aggregate with detail existing only close in

     o   forecasts are done in units, which gets translated to dollars

     o   there is a concentration on the 20% of customers that make up 85% of the business

➢ A demand planning meeting includes:

-VP of Sales and Service (chair)   -Foundry Production Control
-Sales Administration Manager   -Fab Shop Production Control
-Sales Representatives

➢ New products are totally customer dependent and are handled as a normal part of forecasting the business

➢ Cast-Fab's future focus is on getting more forecast information from customers, and as a part of that, getting contact at higher levels within the customer's company. The real goal is to track customer performance to the *customer's* plans. To help take the "edge off" with customers regarding the dreaded "forecasting" word, Cast-Fab sometimes uses the term "sales tracking" instead.

Supply Planning

➢ The six month production plan horizon is based on the accurate portion of the forecast submitted by the customers

➢ The production plan can be projected further in the future (when needed for long term planning) by repeating the numbers for the first six months, adjusted by the addition or subtraction of known projects or items.

➢ There is no one formal supply planning meeting; but it's really a process involving foundry and fabrication shop production control people with several steps:

   o translate the output from the demand planning meeting into capacity terms

   o smooth it using standard rough cut capacity planning

   o discuss the situation with the department managers

   o do this separately for both the foundry and the fabrication shop

➢ The results of this process are reviewed with the President and COO, who has responsibility for operations, prior to the executive S&OP meeting

➢ Material planning and acquisition is not a major issue - MRP is used for raw material replenishment

➢ Cast-Fab is actively developing stocking programs for key customers:

- o   To help support last minute changes in requirements

- o   To help smooth production loads at Cast-Fab

- o   For example, they supply one key customer "just-in-time", in one week's lead time, but are able to support abrupt changes in demand by mutually holding one week of inventory on key products

Partnership Meeting

There is no formal partnership meeting (although the demand planning meeting is referred to as "the Pre-SOP" meeting). Not having a separate partnership meeting is typical for companies of this size.

The Executive Meeting

➢   This sixty minute (or less) meeting occurs around the first of the month, covering the upcoming month and beyond.

➢   This means that all of the preparatory SOP activities occur before the end of the prior month. Cast-Fab is comfortable with this because the customer order situation for the upcoming month changes very little during the last week of a month.

➢   Units and dollars are viewed and discussed

➢   Attendees include:
-CEO	-VP Human Resources
-President and COO	-Foundry Manager
-CFO	-Fab Shop Manager
-VP of Sales (Chair)	-two Production Control Managers

➢   The CFO uses S&OP numbers for revising budgets, projecting cash flow, etc. In effect, the sales and operations plans become the *new* budget each month.

Hard Benefits

➢   When S&OP indicated that foundry volume was beginning to significantly increase in 2004 over the prior slow years:

- o   previously laid off people were called back and retrained

- o   new employees were hired and trained from scratch

- o   a 40% volume increase was supported

- o   all customer commitments were met

➤ Impressively, Cast-Fab realized a productivity increase of 2% on the year despite all of the hiring, training, retraining, and new people on the job. This is yet another example of how S&OP provides a "window into the future," allowing companies to get a head start on volume shifts.

Soft Benefits

➤ More rapid response to shifts in demand

➤ More stability in the plant

➤ Fewer and less severe layoffs

➤ Much better communication with the customers

➤ A more fact-based relationship with the customers

➤ S&OP has helped Cast-Fab stay lean and efficient while growing

Go to Chapter 4 to read more about **Benefits**

Lessons Learned

➤ Seeing demand twelve months out, and knowing what capacity limits are, gives sufficient visibility to run the business well

➤ Decision-making can be moved to lower levels in the organization

➤ The S&OP process serves as an "early warning system"

➤ SOP is an effective process for companies that are:

o   small

o   privately-held

o   100% make-to-order

o   at the very beginning of the supply chain

o   experience cyclical, drastic shifts in demand

o   foundries and metal workers

*Go to Chapter 5 to read more about **Lessons Learned***

Consultant's Summary

"Cast-Fab is an excellent, if somewhat atypical, S&OP user, operating in a pure make-to-order environment. They've been at it for over ten years and remain enthusiastic and committed to the process. They're obviously believers; they're putting S&OP into their other, newly acquired businesses.

The company survived a very difficult period during the early 2000's with only a moderate decline in business, while a number of their competitors went belly up. This is a very well run business and S&OP is one of their key management tools." Tom Wallace, Consultant

Chapter 16

Coca-Cola Midi (CCM)

Toulon, France

Beverage and Juice Products

They manufacture thousands of tons of products for their "captive", intra-company customers. In most cases, they are the sole supplier. So do they really need S&OP to balance demand and supply, deliver on time, and keep the inventories low?

Coca-Cola Midi (CCM) is one of the major Coca-Cola concentrate plants in the Americas, Europe, Asia and Africa, manufacturing concentrates and beverage bases, and either sourcing or supplying juice products for customers in Europe, Asia, and Africa.

What's Unique?

CCM started as a green field operation in the Cote d'Azur region of southern France, specifically designed as a mega-plant for production of the company's highest volume concentrates. During its fifteen year history its product mix has evolved from a high-volume, low-mix profile, to a low- to medium-volume, high-mix profile.

Today, a sizable portion of the volumes covered by this organization's S&OP process is *not even manufactured by them.* Fully 72% of the product volume for Coca-Cola Midi never sees the inside of their plant. For these products CCM provides sourcing, specialized analytical testing of juice samples prior to shipment, and logistics coordination services for delivery of juices from juice processors directly to Coca-Cola bottling operations, third-party packers and other customer locations.

Company Characteristics

Size:

➤ 220 associates

➤ 79,000 tons shipped, of which approximately 72% is juice products

Products and Services:

➢ About 700 SKU's shipped to over 65 locations in 54 countries.

➢ The principal ingredients for many well-known brands made by The Coca-Cola Company, including Coca-Cola™, Coca-Cola Classic™, Diet Coke™, Sprite™, Fanta™ and Minute Maid™

➢ CCM's product and services portfolio includes five major components, all of which are coordinated by the S&OP process:

1. Concentrate and beverage base manufacturing

Here CCM sources ingredients, packaging materials and juices which are processed, blended and packaged in the plant, and then shipped on to customers in Europe, Asia, and Africa. Today, the volumes of concentrate (liquids) are substantially smaller than what the plant was originally designed for, while the beverage base (dry parts) volumes are higher and more varied. However, the customers continue to be canning and bottling plants of the Coca-Cola network of companies.

2. New product development and introduction

Part of CCM's charter is to develop new products that will eventually be produced elsewhere. They have specific expertise in taking a product concept and initial formulation, then bringing it out for its initial launch. Once the product reaches sufficient volume for full commercialization it will be transferred to another concentrate plant.

3. Direct Product Supply (DPS) of juice and flavors

This covers the sourcing and supply of flavors and juices to canning and bottling customers principally in Europe. In this business, CCM coordinates the direct delivery of juices (high volume) to the customers. They also produce and ship smaller volumes of strategic ingredients manufactured from key flavors that they purchase and process.

CCM has control of the entire supply chain for an extensive juice supplier network. It coordinates all planning, scheduling, inventory management, and transportation resources for this Direct Product Supply process. The activities encompass three major areas:

> o Quality assurance and supplier development including juice testing and release, packaging compatibility testing, supplier auditing, and trouble shooting

    o   Strategic procurement including supplier selection, value analysis, contract negotiation and demand management

    o   Supply chain management covering materials management, co-packer coordination, transportation and warehouse management

4. Finished product supply chain management

CCM's combined expertise in logistics management, materials and manufacturing management, and direct ingredient supply is offered as a service to other companies.

For example, in their "Chilled Finished Product" supply chain, on behalf of a sister company, CCM coordinates multiple suppliers and a third party manufacturer (a "co-packer"), as well as the distribution channel activities provided by still another company. They schedule ingredient and packaging deliveries, schedule production, and plan and control distribution. In fact, in this entire supply chain, only the retail activities are not managed by Coca-Cola Midi.

Similarly in their "Immediate Consumption" supply chain, CCM manages the manufacturing activities of a "co-packer", and all the subsequent logistics and distribution activities for a fast-foods company.

5. Technical services (analytical testing, juice expertise)

As Coca-Cola's European "Center for Juice Expertise", CCM provides services to other Coca-Cola facilities including:

    o   Authenticity testing
    o   Pesticide testing
    o   Juice substitution
    o   Trouble shooting
    o   Juice co-packer audits
    o   Juice handling training

The Demand Side:

The customers are principally Coca-Cola bottling operations, formulators, and distributors in over 67 locations in 57 countries on three continents. For the "finished product supply chain management" activities there are six customer companies in five European countries.

Order fulfillment strategies are:

➢ Make-to-order: 4% of volume, 28% of the SKUs, four week lead times

➢ Make-to-stock: 24% of volume, 50% the of SKUs, five to ten day lead times

➢ Direct Product Supply (DPS) - juices: 72% of volume, 22 % of the SKUs

The Supply Side - Plants, Suppliers and Co-Producers:

➢ There is one plant, located in Signes, France, organized by process type: liquid mixing, liquid blending, liquid filling, dry parts dosage and filling, with dedicated mixing areas for major product families. Actual batch production time is typically about four hours mixing plus two hours filling, with a quarantine time of five to ten days.

➢ Several "co-packers" (for the "finished product supply chain management" business)

➢ About one hundred and fifty suppliers of around five hundred materials and components, with eight weeks' lead time on average

Other Tools Employed

➢ A manufacturing resource planning process (MRPII), driven by S&OP, has been key in dealing with competitive challenges in the rapidly changing nature of CCM's business. CCM achieved Class A MRPII[26] certification ten months after the site was opened in 1990 and has maintained that level of excellence for over fifteen years. They are one of thirteen concentrate plants in the company who achieved this certification (three in North America, one in South America, three in Europe, one in Africa and five in Asia) from independent third-party assessments.

➢ The Coca-Cola Company in general, and Coca-Cola Midi specifically, has an extensive contingency planning process for dealing with natural disasters and business interruptions. Part of their internal Class A assessment process is to evaluate disaster preparedness including capacity availability, plans for transferring key company information and data, ability to respond to a business interruption, etc. The company consciously loads to only a portion of their theoretical capacity so as to be able to absorb production volumes from other sites if required. Obviously this planning process is a key component of S&OP as well.

---

[26] MRPII was the name used most frequently in the 1970's through the 1990's to describe an integrated, cross-functional resource planning and control process. Some companies were certified "Class A" in recognition of their complete and intensive use of all the tools to produce superior business results. It is similar to the term "World Class".

➤ "The Coca-Cola Quality System" (TCCQS) is a corporate initiative of The Coca-Cola Company. It encompasses all the quality management activities of TQM and ISO 9001/ISO 2000. TCCQS is a key element of the integrated management system that CCM employs. In fact, diagrams of their management system generally depict quality management as the underlying element to everything else including MRPII, GMP ("good manufacturing practices"), security, safety, environmental controls, and laboratory methods.

The S&OP Process

Demand Planning

The monthly S&OP cycle starts two weeks prior to the end of the month. "Preliminary" results are used up to the actual closing, then actual results are used once they are available. In the concentrate business, most of the volume is shipped from stock and the company has very close relations and communication with the customers. "End of the month" demand variability tends to be manageable and fairly predictable.

The benefits of starting early are significant. CCM has now gotten to the point where they can complete the process and approve new sales and operations plans *four days into the new month*. This allows them to make realistic rate and volume changes to the current month. In many companies the final S&OP meeting ends up being in the third or fourth week of the month. This makes current month volume adjustments difficult if not impossible, if they must be first approved at the executive meeting.

Key people involved in the initial steps of the demand planning process are the:

    -Customer Service Manager
    -Planning Manager
    -Customer Service Representatives
    -Direct Product Supply Manager
    -Planners

The steps are as follows:

➤ The demand planning cycle begins with a "pre-meeting" to review month-to-date performance and estimate end of month performance numbers.

➤ This is followed by an upload of forecasts from the key stakeholders in the forecasting process. This upload typically happens three days prior to month end.

➢ Customers and bottlers provide forecasts one to three months out. These numbers come from bottling plans based on country or regional activities reflecting current demands.

➢ CCM management provides forecasts four to eighteen month out. These numbers reflect marketing activities planned by Coca-Cola Corporate, such as promotions, advertising, etc. They may also reflect financial goals.

➢ Customer service and planning teams meet to analyze, validate and consolidate the various streams of demand into a blended "final forecast", around the month close date.

➢ This synthesis of demand - validation of volumes, significant trends and events by country is shared with customers - in some cases face-to-face - as part of the CCM demand planning and S&OP process.

➢ Final forecast figures are approved by the financial managers of The Coca-Cola Company Division in the Atlanta, Georgia headquarters, or sent back for modification.

Supply Planning

➢ The supply plan developed and reviewed in the S&OP process is really a byproduct of the master production scheduling process, which responds to demand changes as the forecast is adjusted, based on capacity availability. The totaled MPS becomes the family supply plan. The master scheduler has strict guidelines including timing rules that prevent him or her from creating plans that are not do-able. This work is reviewed every month in the partnership and executive meetings.

➢ The final adjustment and approval of the supply plan happens in the partnership meeting. This is possible because, generally speaking, the capacity of the plant is very flexible. Fairly large changes can be accommodated within the current month.

➢ The rough cut capacity planning process insures that the plans properly reflect:

   o   manufacturing resources (labor and equipment)
   o   available warehouse space
   o   laboratory equipment
   o   maintenance activity
   o   quality assurance requirements
   o   other operational activities in the warehouse and laboratories

Partnership Meeting

➢ This meeting is held either on the day of month end closing, or one day afterwards. It sets production rates and finalizes the sales and operations plans to be presented to the executive group. Attendees include:

-Production Managers
-Warehouse Manager
-Planners and Planning Manager
-Purchasing Manager
-Laboratory Manager
-Pilot Operators
-Plant Manager
-A vendor scheduler or buyer representing each DPS juice supplier
-Financial analysts (to develop financial results and projections)

➢ In the vast majority of cases, all S&OP plans are finalized in this meeting and subject only to executive review. As noted above, CCM has a great deal of manufacturing flexibility, and if component materials and ingredients are available, most production rate adjustments can be accommodated quickly. Because of strategic stocking policies for most non-juice ingredients, components will usually be available.

➢ Topics discussed in the partnership and executive S&OP meetings include:

o Last meeting minutes and action items under investigation
o MRPII "Vital Signs" (KPI's) including detailed and aggregate forecast accuracy, aggregate supply plan performance, MPS on-time performance, customer service performance (service defect rates), MPS stability, exception trends and data accuracy
o Actual sales and forecasts (significant assumptions and variance analysis)
o Supply plans and master schedules (short, medium and long term)
o Warehouse and inventory levels
o Capacity analysis (rough cut, labor and process times)
o Preventative maintenance plans
o New product launches
o Manpower plans
o Training programs

➢ The agenda for all meetings is issued in advance of the meeting, and documented minutes are distributed two days following the meeting.

The Executive Meeting

This meeting, led by the General Manager, has the mission of validating the plans by challenging the assumptions that went into them, looking for areas of improvement (especially with respect to KPI's), and finally approving the plans, including the financial projections. It normally lasts around ninety minutes.

➤ Attendees:

> -General Manager
> -Plant Manager
> -Managers or Directors from: HR, Commercial, Legal, IS, DPS, Production, Warehouse, Maintenance, Customer Service, QA, Budget, and Safety and Environment

➤ Executive management is issued a packet of S&OP data including volume information about total liquid products, total dry parts, and DPS juice products. Detailed information by family is available but rarely consulted.

➤ The pre-published agenda is as listed above under the partnership meeting, with documented minutes distributed two days following the meeting.

Other S&OP Activities

➤ Monthly "Operational Meetings with Suppliers" occur *after* the final executive S&OP meeting. Face-to-face meetings cover four suppliers representing 71% of total juice volume. Volume changes are implemented based upon agreed limits within select time frames.

In addition to S&OP volume issues, the agenda for these meetings includes:
  o Inventory and demand management issues
  o Product in QA quarantine
  o Service defect rates and corrective actions
  o Improvements planned and requested

➤ All the steps in the S&OP process are carefully guided by a written S&OP policy, which is frequently reviewed and adjusted as needed, to improve the process. It includes a carefully worded "emergency provision" that insures that appropriate short term, mid-month plan changes outside of the defined monthly S&OP cycle, are reviewed and approved within set guidelines by company management.

For example, if demand in a given family of concentrates surges by more than X% in a given month, should the supply plan be adjusted? What if demand drops by more than Y%? Or suppose inventory drops below some pre-established limit because of a combination of demand increases and production problems?

Currently the emergency provision requires that an emergency meeting of the management team approve any mid-month S&OP adjustments.

Hard Benefits

The people at Coca-Cola Midi believe strongly that an effective S&OP process is essential to achieving first-rate results. The following improvements over the previous year were documented in their last formal audit (2003):

➤ Superior customer service: service defects reduced from 4.3% to 2.5% of customer shipments. This measurement includes incorrect paperwork, defective packaging, damage in shipping, and general customer complaints on any subject, as well as missed deliveries.

➤ Inventory write-offs reduced by 56%

➤ Forecast accuracy improved by 9.7%

➤ Trucking costs reduced by 5%

➤ 52% reduction in costs from transportation providers for loading and unloading delays (demurrage)

Over the past fifteen years, through approximately seven external assessments, CCM has demonstrated that S&OP drives continuous improvements year after year in customer service, inventory and cost. They see S&OP as a key driver for future improvement as well.

Soft Benefits

➤ S&OP is the backbone of all planning, manufacturing, and supply chain logistics activities for Coca-Cola Midi

➤ It provides a common language and set of measurements

➤ It has created a disciplined and formalized set of communications across the entire organization

➢ S&OP metrics have helped associates focus on improvements on an ongoing basis

Go to Chapter 4 to read more about **Benefits**

Lessons Learned

➢ S&OP can be a key controlling process to manage external supply chains, including third party manufacturers

➢ S&OP and rough cut capacity planning (RCCP) helps manage support activities like QA and warehousing

➢ The Coca-Cola S&OP success formula: local ownership of the process, with support, high expectations and high standards of performance provided by Corporate

➢ Education is key: both an intensive initial program for all employees, and an on-going program to insure continuous improvement

Go to Chapter 5 to read more about **Lessons Learned**

Consultant's Summary

"Over the past fourteen years, S&OP has been continuously expanded, improved and used to manage beyond just manufacturing. S&OP today covers internal manufacturing as well as the extended external supply chain for juice, where it has been integrated with suppliers and customers. And S&OP and RCCP are used to manage resources that are both traditional (mixing and blending labor and equipment) and non-traditional (analytical lab capacity, warehouse and cold storage space)." Chris Gray, Consultant

Chapter 17

Danfoss Commercial Compressors (DCC)

a division of The Danfoss Group

Trevoux, France

Compressors for commercial air-conditioning and refrigeration applications

Why is S&OP so important to a family-owned Danish company focused on global growth - one utilizing lean manufacturing, supply chain management, and a postponement (finish-to-order) strategy for customer order fulfillment?

Danfoss was founded by Mads Clausen in 1933 in the attic of a farmhouse, as a local Danish manufacturer of a line of valves and other industrial controls. Since then, the Danfoss Group purchased the Maneurop Compressor Company and several compressor-technology licences from Trane in the 1990's to serve as the basis of its entry into the air-conditioning and refrigeration business.

Today, only twenty years later, Danfoss Commercial Compressors operates across the world. It's become a major supplier of compressors to a wide variety of customers who themselves make and install air-conditioning and refrigeration equipment.

What's Unique?

The construction of a worldwide supply chain (including Europe, North America, China and the Far East) to manufacture and deliver highly technical commercial compressors required creating a robust sales and operations planning process to optimize it.

The order fulfilment strategy is generally assemble-to-order (postponement) since demand is highly variable and the factory cannot produce in advance of customer orders, yet customers require short delivery lead times. To support this, lean manufacturing initiatives are being pursued at all manufacturing locations.

Company Characteristics

Size:

➤ Revenue of 230 million Euros

➤ 1100 employees worldwide

➤ DCC is one of the business units of the Danfoss Group, third largest industrial group in Denmark with sales of 2+ billion Euros, and 17,000 employees worldwide

Products:

➤ Three main product lines:
  o Piston or reciprocating compressors, sold under the brand name of Maneurop
  o Scroll compressors, sold under the brand name of Performer
  o Condensing groups, sold under the name of Blue Star

➤ Products have many different possible configurations and are sold to a wide variety of customers. For example, reciprocating compressors offer a total of around 1200 possible configurations, of which around 600 are actually ordered in a year, sometimes only one compressor in a particular configuration.

The Demand Side:

➤ Danfoss sells direct to major OEM customers and to others via worldwide Danfoss sales affiliates, organized into separate regions for Europe, Asia, and North and South America

➤ Major distribution centers are in Denmark, the U.S., Latin America, China, and Singapore

➤ Markets include:
  o Light commercial and commercial air-conditioning
  o Commercial refrigeration
  o Wholesale refrigeration
  o Food retail industry

➤ Major OEM customers are Carrier, Trane, York, Lennox and CIAT

➤ Flexibility and customer responsiveness are key competitive variables in the face of sudden shifts in customer demand.

The Supply Side:

➤ For most of its compressors, DCC uses a postponement strategy, with modularized bills of material. The modules themselves are built or purchased in advance, held in minimum "lineside" inventories, and are pulled out for final assembly when customer orders are received.

➤ All finished goods, and between 40% and 70% of the component volume is produced in house.

➤ Typical product lead times:
  o one to sixteen weeks for purchasing
  o one to two weeks for fabrication (formerly one to two months, before lean manufacturing)
  o twelve to forty-eight hours for assembly
  o one week for transportation to the customer.
  o The customer "sees" only the assembly and transportation lead times at the end of the process.

Two plants are located in France, as well as one each in the U.S. and China. They machine the major components, and assemble and test the finished compressors.

Other Tools Employed

An ERP package is used to do MRPII, providing detailed information (demand, supply, and inventory) which is extracted and totalled to family levels for S&OP.

Many major lean manufacturing initiatives have either been implemented or are underway, focusing on value-stream mapping, takt time development, cycle time reduction, quick changeover, kanban, total preventive maintenance, and small group improvement activities.

The S&OP Process

➤ Implemented three years ago, with a written S&OP policy

➤ A monthly process with an eighteen month horizon, connected to a complementary biannual business planning process that goes out five years

➤ Currently fifteen product families are reviewed

➤ Data is reviewed in spreadsheet or graphical form, including:
   o Unit of measures in physical units, with a second set of reports in euros
   o Financial comparison to current year's business plan or budget
   o Previous to latest forecast
   o Future vs. projected backlog
   o Latest to previous production plan
   o Projected to actual inventory
   o Inventory turns vs. target
   o Average actual customer lead time to target
   o Impact of new products noted separately

➤ The key customer service measurements are "reliability" (delivery to negotiated or confirmed customer delivery dates) and "availability" (delivery to customer request dates).

Demand Planning

Years ago, DCC Headquarters forecasted everything, and regional sales affiliates sent in orders. Today, customer purchase programs are actively sought for the OEM demand segment, and forecasting responsibility for high volume products has been transferred to the sales affiliates. Headquarter's role is to now complete the forecast for low-volume compressors (at the family level only), making sure that the total is reasonable. The total forecast and the budget don't have to be equal; the differences just have to be explained.

➤ Little or no statistical forecasting is used over the first eighteen months

➤ OEM programs and "Best-Seller" forecasts comprise a large part of forecasted demand, and the rest is estimated

➤ Detailed forecasts by module are developed and totalled to the family level for S&OP over the first six to twelve months

➤ Over the remainder of the S&OP horizon, the forecast is done directly at the family level

➤ All large deviations or "abnormal" demands are challenged before being introduced into the demand plan

➤ Main participants:
  o The Global Logistics Director (DCC)
  o The Customer Service Manager
  o The Corporate Global Sales Manager
  o Demand Planners (from the sales organizations for each region)
  o Global Account Managers (from the sales organizations for each region)
  o The President is actively involved, too

➤ On a monthly basis, the Corporate Global Sales Manager and the Global Demand Manager review and approve the forecast by region before it is used further in the S&OP process

Supply Planning

➤ For production and capacity planning, monthly meetings are held at the plant level, with the following attendees:
  o Global Logistics Director
  o Global Demand Manager
  o Global Supplier Logistic Manager
  o Factory Manager
  o Factory Logistic Manager
  o Local Purchasing manager
  o Master Scheduler

➤ These capacity meetings feed into a regional S&OP Process, which then feeds the global level.

➤ Based on the updated module forecasts, the master schedule is developed and aggregated into family S&OP production plans using spread sheets.

➤ Rough cut material requirements for major components are developed by multiplying production plans by a resource bill of material, using product mix percentages.

➤ The master schedule is used to drive detailed material and capacity requirements.

➤ Operational takt time - the units of production required per unit of time - derived from the S&OP production plan, is now being implemented to govern the Lean production processes in the factories.

Partnership ("Regional Consolidation") Meetings

➤ Attendees at the Regional Consolidation S&OP Meetings include:
- o Global Logistics Director (DCC)
- o Global Demand Manager (DCC)
- o Global Supplier Logistic Manager (DCC)
- o Factory Manager (DCC)
- o Factory Logistics Manager (DCC)
- o Local Purchasing Manager (DCC)
- o Demand Planners (from the sales organizations for each region)
- o Global Account Managers (from the sales organizations for each region)

➤ Regional meetings are about one to two hours long and are held by video-conferencing

➤ Demand, supply, inventory and customer service issues for the customers and markets in each respective region are discussed and resolved in these four meetings

The Executive Meeting

➤ This global S&OP meeting is held at DCC Headquarters, after the regional meetings

➤ Attendees:
- o DCC President
- o Vice President for Global Operations
- o Global Logistics Director
- o Vice President of Finance
- o Vice President of Product Development
- o Regional Presidents (through video teleconferencing)

➤ The meeting lasts one hour, less than the four hours it took at the beginning of the process three years ago

Hard Benefits

➤ Market share on Scroll compressors is up 9 % mainly due to improved sales and operations planning and demand management, as well as shortened production lead times from implementing Lean techniques.

➤ Customer service increased from 60% to 90%+ mainly due to improved S&OP, and better execution of all processes, which were supported by a company-wide education program covering both MRPII and Lean.

➢ Better balancing of regional inventories avoiding high inter-regional shipping costs

Soft Benefits

➢ Better inventory visibility through the whole supply chain

➢ Better supply demand alignment

➢ Improved new product introduction

➢ More decisive, and earlier decision-making on regional sourcing and capacity planning

➢ Better visibility of problems, issues and opportunities for top management

Go to Chapter 4 to read more about **Benefits**

Lessons Learned

➢ Forecasting can be improved by using customer and regional sales input

➢ A successful S&OP process must be driven by top management

➢ S&OP identifies problems in detailed planning systems

➢ S&OP governs lean manufacturing plant processes

➢ S&OP can guide the design and implementation of a supply chain management network

Go to Chapter 5 to read more about **Lessons Learned**

Consultant's Summary

"For a division of a medium-sized Danish company headquartered on the outskirts of Lyon, France, Danfoss Commercial Compressors has a remarkable worldwide supply chain. It manages compressor sales in Asia, with parts coming from Europe and the U.S. With globalization, this could flip-flop in the future, but Danfoss will be able to manage the transition better because of its powerful S&OP process.

The Danfoss Commercial Compressor Company needed to improve its customer service in order to meet its ambitious growth objectives. Instead of taking a short term approach, the company took the larger view of its entire supply chain and then prioritized improvement actions. The first area was sales and operations planning and demand management worldwide.

The company's worldwide expansion is now focusing on reconfiguring the back end or upstream portion of the supply chain, to better integrate suppliers and to logically structure worldwide product flows.

The hallmarks of DCC's success have been excellent internal communications, a young and dynamic management group, and strong participation from sales and marketing to keep the entire Lean supply chain management effort focused on the customer. S&OP is a key process fostering all of this."

Bill Belt, Consultant

Chapter 18

Eclipse, Inc.

Rockford, Illinois

Industrial Process Heating Equipment

Why would a relatively small, family-owned business that is transforming itself with lean manufacturing, re-engineer its ten year old S&OP process?

Eclipse, Inc. is a design, fabrication, and assembly company that serves the glass, automotive, metals, food, building products and other markets around the world.

What's Unique

Eclipse has a strong presence in the markets it serves. The company is nearly one hundred years old, and is operated by the third generation of the family.

Eclipse has four divisions: Americas and Asia, Europe, "Algas-SDI", and "Exothermics". While one executive team at the corporate level leads them all, each division has its own general manager with a full supporting staff. R&D and administrative support are centralized.

They have drastically improved lead times and efficiencies through lean manufacturing.

Company Characteristics

Size:

➤ About 500 employees with over $90 million in sales

Products:

➤ From individual piece parts all the way to complex systems - including burners, control systems and support services.

➤ Both high and low volume products, made from standard parts and assemblies

➤ Over 18,100 different line items were sold over a recent three year period

The Demand Side:

➤ Sales are made directly to major customers (including: Ford, Timken, Owens Corning, U.S. Gypsum and Nabisco) and through independent sales representatives to all others.

➤ Product is shipped out of manufacturing or supply centers in:
Rockford, Illinois   Puna, India
Gouda, The Netherlands   Barcelona, Spain
Suzhou, China

➤ Key Competitive Variables include:

    o   Flexibility

    o   Application experience

    o   Technical field service capability

    o   Worldwide presence

    o   Beyond hardware functionality, providing more 'value added' services than the competition, especially technical product design services

The Supply Side:

➤ Make-to-stock products: 5% of the total

➤ Assemble-to-order products: 60% of the total, with lead times of one to two weeks

➤ Make-to-order products: 13% of the total, with lead times of two to four weeks

➤ Engineer-to-order products: 22% of the total, with lead times of eight to twelve weeks

Most of the products are produced in-house, but some of the primary machining operations are beginning to be outsourced to India and China.

Eclipse does heavy machining, fabrication, and assembly operations in:

-Rockford, Illinois
-Gouda, The Netherlands
-Suzhou, China

-Puna, India
-Barcelona, Spain

Other Tools Employed

Eclipse has been a user of ERP/MRPII for fifteen years. In spite of having implemented MRPII with fairly good results, the company wanted to further improve customer satisfaction and operating efficiencies. Using the Deming philosophy of "plan-do-check-act" to manage improvements, they began lean manufacturing activities in 1999, due to competitive pressures on cost and lead time.

The S&OP Process

Their initial ERP efforts included something called "S&OP", but it was far from what it needed to be. It required sales to develop forecasts at a SKU level, which they found to be too detailed and inevitably less accurate than for a family grouping. Therefore, there was very little sales and marketing participation, and their "S&OP" was fundamentally a production planning process that guided the master scheduling activities. Additionally, the numbers were aggregated for product families grouped by common manufacturing processes. This even further disengaged the sales and marketing team.

They also experienced difficulty in getting, storing and displaying good, clean data in a timely fashion. And as their business went through growth spurts, they could not seem to hold the sales increases over time.

Lach Perks, the President and Jeff Townsend, the Director of Operations initiated and led an effort to upgrade and improve their ten year old S&OP process. This effort was supported and sponsored by Doug Perks, the CEO.

Demand Planning

➤ Each month, the demand planning process begins with analyzing and understanding forecast performance through "waterfall" charts. These charts are their primary audit tool, showing the rolling forecast as it is changed, month-by-month, over time. Since this makes it easy to see demand variations and potential forecast bias over time, when management is hesitant to trust the forecast, they check the waterfall charts.

➤ Then a new statistical forecast is generated for twenty+ sub-families (products, spares, systems, etc.) for a rolling twenty-four months, using 'best fit forecasting' software.

➤ Market managers then consider any new market, customer, or competitive knowledge or information, and review the last forecast vs. actual sales, and the new statistical forecast.

➤ Last month's "management forecast" for the sub-families is then changed as appropriate, with new documented assumptions and actions.

➤ This is then aggregated to seven S&OP families (four of which are the bulk of the volume) which are aligned with the market place.

➤ A formal meeting is conducted to finalize the new management forecast, with the entire process overseen by the VP of Sales, and the Marketing Managers.

➤ A person acting as Demand Manager handles the data intensive parts of the process.

➤ The forecast is also disaggregated to an end item level for the next four to six months.

Supply Planning

➤ Each month there is a formal meeting to do the supply planning.

➤ It is chaired by the Plant Manager and includes the:

-Purchasing Manager   -Engineering Manager
-Manufacturing Manager   -Master Scheduler

➤ Based on historical mix percentages and some simplifying assumptions, the forecast for market oriented families is converted to families that are manufacturing oriented.

➤ Once the agreed upon family production plan is established, it becomes the framework for doing master scheduling.

➤ Through load profiles containing reasonable assumptions, rough cut capacity and rough cut material planning is performed to validate and adjust the plans. This information is plotted on graphs that compare demonstrated past performance to current planned capacity to required capacity.

Partnership Meeting

➤ During the implementation of S&OP, Eclipse senior management combined the partnership and the executive meetings into one meeting because:

   o They were a relatively small company, with a flat organization structure, and many people initially wore multiple hats, serving as both doers and leaders. Until they got the "number two" person in each functional area up the learning curve, they held one meeting.

   o Senior management needed to lead the culture change, which started at the partnership meeting.

   o Senior management needed to be "hands-on" until they mastered the process improvement themselves.

➤ Once these objectives were accomplished, a separate partnership meeting (which they called the "pre-S&OP meeting") was established to allow middle management to make more of the decisions and grow in experience. It is:

   o chaired by the S&OP process owner (a person dedicated to this process and other similar processes and projects)

   o held a day in advance of the executive meeting

   o attended by: the Manufacturing Manager, the Procurement Manager, the Sales/Marketing Product Managers, the Financial Analyst, and the Process Facilitator

   o focused on making tactical decisions about balancing demand and supply within the framework of existing policy, strategy, and the annual business plan

The Executive Meeting

This meeting is held late in the third week of the month. The key demand, supply and finance people, along with all functional executives attend it. Although the President is the leader, this two hour meeting is facilitated by the S&OP process owner. The agenda includes:

- ➤ Departmental/functional summaries of what's new, including a macro discussion of the economy and key business influence factors such as energy supply and costs, cost of money, GDP growth, etc. (this takes about one half hour)

- ➤ A demand/supply review summary on each family, focusing on those with issues

- ➤ Policy, strategy, or risk avoidance decisions, made as appropriate

- ➤ Any changes to the annual business plan, made if and when appropriate

- ➤ The review of action meeting minutes to be published

Hard Benefits

- ➤ Customer order delinquencies have been greatly reduced, while on-time shipping performance has remained steadily high. These service levels are considered the best in their industry.

- ➤ Due in part to their ability to anticipate and plan for increased customer demand, Eclipse has experienced a 39% increase in sales volume over a recent twenty month period.

- ➤ With earlier visibility of increases in business, Eclipse is able to add sufficient production staff gradually to meet the increased demand without extending lead times.

- ➤ Net profitability has jumped several percentage points.

Soft Benefits

- ➤ Greatly improved company-wide communication, coordination, and decision-making:

  - o based on good data

  - o allowing proactive timing

  - o bringing discipline through a defined executive process that has become an important part of running the business o becoming the main communications vehicle between departments, keeping them aligned

➢ S&OP identifies the need to add capacity in key "bottleneck" areas, such as engineering and manufacturing, helping to maintain customer satisfaction during growth.

➢ It provides enough forward vision to allow long lead time decisions to made and implemented in a way that allows profit levels to be maintained through the peaks and valleys of sales.

➢ S&OP has changed how the company negotiates delivery dates with their customers so that loads on key resources are leveled, and all customer commitments are met. And with the visibility S&OP provides, they know when to turn down business when they cannot support the customer's requirements economically.

➢ S&OP has now taken on the role of being the "monthly update to the annual business plan", when things have changed.

➢ S&OP nicely compliments their lean manufacturing efforts and has become the "launch pad" for several other improvement efforts throughout the company, such as postponement.

➢ *"S&OP has allowed us to integrate, simplify and solidify our combined organization structure (value-streams on the supply side and customer industries on the demand side). It's amazing how we look differently at the business today because of this orientation. This is one of the keys to our growth and profitability!"* Lach Perks, President

Go to Chapter 4 to read more about **Benefits**

Lessons Learned

➢ Even if an initial implementation of S&OP yields disappointing results, re-engineering the process based on the proven success factors can lead to significant operating improvements.

➢ Management needs to take the time to get into a sufficient level of detail to design the process, and use it to make good decisions.

➢ If leadership understands and embraces S&OP, it applies to any environment, including privately owned and operated businesses, large or small.

➤ Today, powerful tools to organize and manage data are affordable to not only large companies, but to small ones as well.

➤ The S&OP process can be effectively used to lead change and improvement on many fronts.

Go to Chapter 5 to read more about **Lessons Learned**

Consultant's Summary

"One of the big challenges in making S&OP work better at Eclipse was convincing people that it was not at all like what they were currently doing and calling S&OP. But since management was becoming increasingly disappointed with executive communication and decision-making, they decided they had to overcome the inertia, and develop a more effective process.

To kick start the process, Eclipse leadership sought a credible source of guidance ("Sales & Operations Planning: The How-To Handbook", by Tom Wallace), and then immersed themselves in sufficient detail to understand and embrace the proper approach to S&OP. They then commissioned a change project, which not only had a substantial positive impact on balancing demand and supply, but also brought about a culture of change and improvement throughout the organization. Many other improvement initiatives, such as postponement/finish-to-order, have been spawned by the work done in S&OP." Bob Stahl, Consultant

Chapter 19

Eli Lilly & Company

Indianapolis, Indiana

Pharmaceutical and Animal Health Products

How does a pharmaceutical company use S&OP to help launch five times as many new products as the industry average, all while adding manufacturing sites?

Eli Lilly specializes in Neuroscience, Oncology, Diabetes, Primary Care and Woman's Health. They have had one of the best new product pipelines in the industry; and their focus is on growth via new product innovation rather than through mergers and acquisitions.

What's Unique?

Customer service levels are expected to be near 100% (particularly in life saving medicines). In an industry where gross margins are relatively high, the cost of a lost sale is significantly greater than the cost of holding inventory.

The pharmaceutical industry has strict regulatory requirements for product approval, including approval of a simple manufacturing process parameter, a raw material change or a change of site sourcing for manufacturing the product.

Significant amounts of time and resources are devoted to new product launches. Managing each new drug through its life cycle: clinical trial testing, FDA submission, new product launch, volume growth and patent expiration, is critical.

Eli Lilly launched ten new products from 2001 through 2005, a rate over *five times higher* than the pharmaceutical industry average. Further, Lilly can bring products to market *faster*, averaging less than eleven years from product concept to market, versus an industry average of over fourteen years.

Lilly has also added new manufacturing sites, and outsourced products for both capacity increases and the offloading of late life cycle products to make room for new products. Many of these sourcing changes and product development projects have highly variable conditions and timing. This has resulted in a great dependence upon supply chain principles, organization and processes to effectively manage it all, with S&OP providing a forum to manage, approve and communicate change effectively.

Company Characteristics

Size:

➢ over $12 billion in sales, with 43,000 employees in 146 countries, and global inventory of $1.7 billion

Products: 65 products are sold in different strengths and packaging or delivery devices. A total of 8,000 SKU's are sold in 146 countries. The number of key products (all those on patent control) have grown from eight in the 1990's to twenty in 2005, with the number of older, "legacy" products (those that have generic competition) shrinking from over forty to five or less.

The Demand Side:

Lilly markets its products globally through 130 Lilly sales affiliates[27] to wholesalers (like McKesson), large retail pharmacy chains (Walgreen's, CVS, and Wal-Mart), other pharmaceutical partners, hospitals and government agencies.

➢ Each sales affiliate is responsible for their forecasting and finished goods inventory (most of which is country specific, due to unique packaging languages and regulatory requirements).

➢ The affiliates report to regional Sales Vice Presidents, who report to the President of Sales/Marketing.

➢ Order fulfillment strategies are:

    o Make-to-order : 10% (usually government tender offers with thirteen to eighteen week lead time)

    o Make-to-stock : 90%

➢ Four regional Demand Management Centers operate the demand management processes and tools, and coordinate demand plans and signals between sales affiliates and manufacturing sites. They distribute to over sixty local

---

[27] Lilly local, regional or country-specific internal sales organizations, staffed with Lilly employees

distribution centers (both internal and third party) who manage inventory and customer orders.

The Supply Side:

- ➤ 90% of the products are manufactured at twenty-one Lilly global manufacturing sites (plus three new sites being built in 2004 through 2006) in twelve countries, organized in four global "Network" groups, each with different manufacturing technology and type of product.

    - o Most products go through at least three manufacturing sites in its supply chain path. Examples are:
        - ▪ Bulk (fermentation, recovery, active chemical syntheses or biosynthesis)
        - ▪ Liquid form-filling (in vials, cartridges, etc.) and dry products (capsules, tablets, etc.)
        - ▪ Packaging (in bottles, blister packs, other devices, etc.)

    - o Eighty third party manufacturers in thirty-three countries are used:
        - ▪ many are managed as part of two "hubs" in North America and Europe, which have their own manufacturing S&OP processes
        - ▪ the others are incorporated into the S&OP processes of the local plant site that coordinates their activities

    - o Total product lead times through all the steps vary from ninety to two hundred seventy days

- ➤ Approximately 10% of the products have a manufacturing process that includes significant outsourcing, which is usually tied to technology or licensed innovation provided by the supplier.

Other Tools Employed

- ➤ The principles of supply chain management have been used with a strong emphasis on the life cycle stages of a product through development, to launch, and eventually to legacy status (where there is generic competition):

    - o A corporate supply chain organization guides the planning processes of four networks of plants producing various stages of product lines sold by many affiliates.

    - o The principles and tools of MRPII / ERP, incorporated with company goals, objectives and metrics, are used as part of documented business processes.

> ➤ Distribution resource planning (DRP) is used by sales affiliates and monitored by the Global Demand Management Centers, to assure the effective replenishment of finished product inventories throughout the network.

> ➤ An advanced planning system (APS) is used as an integrated tool within their MRPII / ERP system, to schedule their manufacturing sites in a way that avoids overloads, and minimizes inventories and lead times.

> ➤ A formal new product development and launch process is rigorously followed, with capacity additions and sourcing decisions made when the probability of success of a product launch is still only 20 to 40%.

> ➤ Lean manufacturing / 6 Sigma in all areas of the company is in the early stages of education and certification of internal "black/green belt" experts, with specific project identification and rollout of implementation activities just beginning.

The S&OP Process

"S&OP is a universal business process at Lilly. It is hard to move throughout the company and not have a large contingent of people who understand it, support it and are responsible for some element of its success." Jon Rucker, Director of Supply Chain Operations

Figure 19-1

Sales & Operations Planning at Eli Lilly: *A four step process to match demand and supply globally across a product family or molecule*

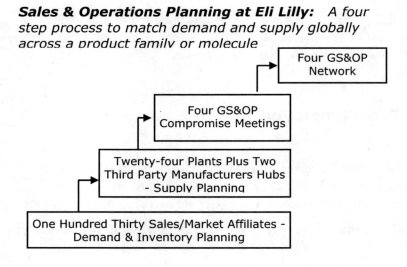

As shown in the figure above, Lilly's S&OP process has four steps originating with the affiliates.

➤ Each of Lilly's 130 sales affiliates maintains forecast and inventory replenishment orders over a twenty-four month horizon.

➤ Then Lilly's twenty-four manufacturing sites and key third-party manufacturers update twenty-four month production plans that consider capacities, inventories, cost and customer service.

➤ For the four quarterly global S&OP (GS&OP) "Compromise" meetings, the affiliate and manufacturing site plans for the next two years are extended to seven years. This process looks by molecule or supply chain family to support product launches, product outsourcing, and strategic facility expansions. It insures that the worldwide production plans will satisfy the worldwide demand plans in a way that minimizes customer service problems, inventories and supply-chain costs, well best taking advantage of the capabilities and capacities of Lilly's internal plants as well as their third party manufacturing partners.

➤ Four management-level GS&OP "Network" review meetings are held quarterly.

➤ All of the S&OP steps follow a formal documented process, with templates to assure consistency in data gathering, review and decision-making.

➤ Each of the steps provides visibility into issues and opportunities that drive contingency planning and action plans to meet the market demands, and mitigate as much of the risk as affordable.

➤ The annual business plan can be modified on a quarterly basis based on changes identified in the S&OP process.

➤ The corporate supply chain management organization has one person responsible for the overall S&OP business process, although several people actively coordinate and facilitate its execution at all sales, manufacturing and corporate sites.

Demand Planning

➤ Each sales affiliate, over the first five days of the month, updates their forecast, and assures it is aligned with supply capabilities over the next two years. This is particularly important during global launches of the many new products. It includes:

    o formal documentation, with clearly defined roles and responsibilities, including approval of each monthly forecast by the senior sales affiliate executive

- o software support and data templates including statistical forecasting software, but with adjustment capability by product managers and marketing personnel

- o forecasts out two years at the SKU level, for all marketed products and new product launches in the next two years (including samples and clinical trials), with an intense focus on the top twenty products that represent 83% of the sales volume globally

- o quarterly comparison of these affiliate unit forecasts to the financial forecasts (business plans), with reconciliation and explanation required if the difference is greater than 5%

- o quarterly regional consolidation and review of the unit and financial forecasts versus the business plans

- o a review of KPI's including on-time shipments to customers within twenty-four hours, affiliate forecast accuracy, distribution center inventory levels, and slow-moving, obsolete and written-off inventory

- o a formal monthly meeting at each affiliate location, with minutes published

➤ A Global Demand Management Center (15 people in four locations: part of the supply chain management organization) consolidates, validates and measures the completeness and accuracy of the affiliate forecasts (by SKU, family and affiliate total). They ensure that robust forecasting processes are in place, while providing a communications link between the affiliates and plant sites. They also monitor the alignment of new product launches and "exits" (product discontinuations) at each affiliate as compared to the global plans.

➤ Forecasting and replenishment resides in one global system. Affiliates are responsible for maintaining forecasts in the system and running the replenishment process (DRP) that drives requirements to manufacturing.

➤ Forecast completeness and monthly accuracy (generally about 95 to 100% for completeness and 80% for accuracy) are reviewed by the Marketing Executive Committee monthly.

➤ For years three to seven, over twenty Global Marketing Product Teams maintain a forecast for each key product. These forecasts are approved quarterly by key executives throughout the organization, with special emphasis during the bi-annual long-range planning review process.

(Plant Site) Supply Planning

A formal, documented production planning process occurs over the second five days of the month at each plant site, ensuring that plant people take appropriate capacity actions within a two-year planning horizon. This process encompasses:

- ➤ a four step approach:

    - ○ demands are consolidated by family, from the replenishment processes of each of the sales/market affiliates

    - ○ then dependent demands from other manufacturing sites in the supply chain are considered, along with any internal demands, such as product testing

    - ○ plans are updated including "what-if" planning to determine the potential impact on resources and materials

    - ○ "S&OP" meetings are held at each plant for decision-making, approvals and accountability

- ➤ software support including a formal S&OP "workbook" drawn from the ERP system that shows:

    - ○ forecasts out two years at the family level
    - ○ monthly production plans two years out, compared to past plans and the business plan
    - ○ inventory results and projections
    - ○ capacity implications of the smoothed plans

- ➤ input from Global Demand Managers representing all sales and marketing organizations, covering significant changes in demand

- ➤ a ""resource and operations planning" - R&OP process used at the bulk manufacturing and filling plants, based on the dependent requirements driven by the production plans of the upstream plants

- ➤ a review of key metrics including on-time shipments to distribution centers and both internal and external customers, by line item, and on complete orders

- ➤ minutes from each of the meetings at each plant site, and the North American and European "Hubs" managing the key third party manufacturers

(Global) Supply Planning

The global supply chain management organization:

- ➤ aggregates and reviews worldwide demand from all affiliates and regions by product family. The demand has already been validated in the local and regional demand planning activities for the first two years of the horizon. The demand for years three through seven is brought in from the Lilly Market Research group and includes new product developments, line extensions and product deletions within that timeframe. It is added together here so the networks can look at the total set of demands worldwide, plan their capacities globally and alert sales if there is a global supply problem.

➢ works with manufacturing plants to gain commitments to support "high side" forecasts that are often twice the base demand.

➢ extends production plans out seven years to meet the global demand by molecule. Cost, customer service, inventory and capacity are considered as these plans are generated.

➢ establishes inventory targets and safety stock levels, by product, with manufacturing and shipping lot sizes negotiated between the affiliates and the plants.

➢ enables global decisions to be made that best meet the needs of the customers, while synchronizing the supply chains within a "network".

➢ identifies when production responsibility for a product can be shifted from an overloaded to an underloaded site, thus avoiding unneeded plant expansion and capital spending.

➢ uses advanced planning system (APS) software to help with "what if" scenarios that might identify different allocations of capacity, to adjust the sources of supply, and where necessary, to give feedback to affiliates to adjust the timing of new product launches.

("Global") Partnership Meetings

These quarterly meetings are called "Global Sales and Operations Planning (GS&OP) Compromise" meetings, and are held for each of the four global networks. They are led by each Network Supply Chain Steward with the corporate supply chain management staff and the respective plant site Supply Chain Leaders to:

➢ review demand, supply and inventory product summaries, with special attention to major changes and issues

➢ create a single, doable plan that optimizes customer service, capacity utilization, and working capital investment while supporting product launches, product outsourcing, and strategic facility expansions

➢ review multiple "what if " scenarios for proactive contingency plans, and agree on actions to be taken

➢ review key metrics

➢ review and approve written action plans

➢ document and communicate demand, capacity and other assumptions, production plan issues, decisions, and recommendations, to ensure they are incorporated into plant and affiliate plans

➢ agree on the agenda for the subsequent "network" meetings

The (Global) Executive Meetings

Four quarterly "GS&OP Network" meetings are held, led by the four Network Leaders:

➢ Attendees include:

o   Network Lead Team:
   -heads of each plant site in that network
   -production engineering
   -representatives for the third party manufacturers
   -HR representatives
   -demand management representatives (representing the sales affiliates)
   -plant site Supply Chain Leaders, if needed
   -IT representatives
   -Manufacturing Science and Technology representatives
   -Quality/Regulatory representatives

o   Supply Chain Stewards for each product group

o   Director of Supply Chain Operations

o   Strategic Facilities Planning Analyst

o   R&D Technical Leader

➢ The agenda includes:

o   a high level review of the "compromise" meeting, including major changes in demand and the underlying assumptions and root causes for these changes

o   a review of product plans with issues, including approving action plans

> o   a review of key product and network indicators

> o   a review of the status of the previous network action plans

Hard Benefits

➤ *"In times of unpredictable demand (especially new product launches) and high manufacturing asset utilization, S&OP activities have allowed global customer service levels to remain very close to 100%."* Ken Thomas, Manager of MSSC Capabilities

➤ S&OP has facilitated optimizing the use of network capacity while controlling risk, and avoiding costs, loss of sales and delays in the launch of new products. Through the visibility and decision-making forum created by the GS&OP process, Lilly was able to defer and or cancel over $80 million in proposed capital investments during the past two years.

➤ *"In the past three years we have launched ten new products and met all demand despite two products that sold significantly above the high-side forecast. Without global sales and operations planning, we would have been driven to reaction mode, which could have resulted in an increase in investment in new assets, a slow down in our launch plans, and/or missed demand opportunities."* Dan Gehring, Supply Chain Steward for the Eli Lilly "DPN" Network

➤ Over $19 million dollars in inventory reductions were realized through effective management of the supply chains within the past twelve months.

➤ *"The value of S&OP at Lilly has been the ability to launch all of our products in a very complex environment without adding significant cost, resources or inventories. We have managed a strong customer service performance metric while controlling our growth in assets. The benefits are not cost reductions, but revenue generation at the most affordable and optimal cost!"* Stephan Bancel, Executive Director of Manufacturing Strategy and Supply Chain.

Soft Benefits

➤ S&OP is a powerful management process for a global company with complex supply chains, an extensive sales network, and aggressive new product development plans.

➤ It increased the clarity and speed of clearly aligned decisions and action plans.

➤ The S&OP process enhanced the accountability in the sales affiliates for managing their demands and understanding how the accuracy of those forecasts and demands can impact manufacturing.

➤ S&OP is an integral part of a robust supply chain management approach, leading to an improved understanding of the value of supply chain management and the need for the timely execution of roles and responsibilities.

➤ It dramatically widened the range of options considered regarding inventory risk, capacity actions and so forth. Instead of just adding capacity or increasing cost, the process provides the forward visibility and thus sufficient time to offload work, while balancing network cost, utilization and inventory.

➤ S&OP helped tom integrate third party manufacturing and technical resources in product planning decisions.

Go to Chapter 4 to read more about **Benefits**

Lessons Learned

➤ *"The organizational capability of our people is our greatest asset and a foundation for our S&OP processes. We also have excellent documentation, defined roles and responsibilities, education and training programs to support and sustain the processes."* Ron Bohl, Global Supply Chain Advisor

➤ S&OP requires education of key stakeholders and decision makers. It also requires full understanding of all the tools used in the process.

➤ A supply planning process won't work well without a disciplined demand planning process. Supply and demand planning processes need to be monitored and guided by subsequent steps in the S&OP process to help motivate accuracy, and insure supply demand balance.

➤ Metrics need to be understood, accepted and governed on a regular frequency.

➤ Analytical tools and master data management for accessing local and global data with accuracy and trust, are needed to identify issues and opportunities.

➤ Organizational responsibilities need to be defined, and the process must be monitored until established well enough to sustain itself.

Go to Chapter 5 to read more about **Lessons Learned**

Consultant's Summary

"Lilly has made major improvements in its internal communications, and planning and decision-making processes. The development of the global sales and operations planning processes has been a key factor in this improvement. The demand side of the organization now accepts its responsibilities to provide accurate and timely demand information for the supply side to plan its resources.

There is also more trust between plants and suppliers in the supply chains. There is less reason to carry safety inventories because the plants generate more accurate and stable plans throughout the supply chain, including to their suppliers. Consequently, the suppliers adhere more closely to their plans.

Plant performance is still important, but now supply chain performance is also important. S&OP helps set guidelines for managing inventories and capacities in the supply chains. It is easier to measure true performance in execution now that the plans are more accurate, stable and doable.

Through their central supply chain management group, the Demand Managers speak for the multitude of sales organizations that sell products produced in multiple supply chains, networks, and plants, without overburdening the sales people with hundreds of meetings to attend. They then participate in the global S&OP process to help navigate the complex organizational maze and contribute to decisions incorporating the viewpoints of top management, the supply chain, the resources across the network of plants and third party manufacturers, and each individual plant.

Lilly was once a company of many individual plans that generated a final result often more costly than management wanted, or surprising in its outcome. It is now driven by a global plan that considers the possibilities of demand, and the limitations of its resources. The global plan sets boundaries for the individual plans, and results are pre-determined, expected, and most often delivered. The evolution of S&OP and its success at Lilly has brought more teamwork, coordination, and control to the supply chains, the overall business processes and the operating results of this fine company." Jack Gips, Consultant

Chapter 20

Engineered Materials Solutions, Inc. (EMS)

Attleboro, Massachusetts

Clad Metal Components for Industrial Equipment

Why would a metals processor, with a low volume, high mix, seasonal product line, need S&OP as well as Lean manufacturing to survive a venture capital-backed leveraged buy-out (LBO)?

Engineers throughout the world turn to EMS for innovative, cost-effective solutions - to problems involving thermal, electrical, mechanical, chemical or magnetic performance. EMS produces bimetals, clad materials and electrical contacts for industries as diverse as automotive, heavy truck, industrial controls, cookware, electrical distribution, electronics, home ventilation and air conditioning, appliances, and telecommunications.

What's Unique

Formerly the Clad Metals division of Texas Instruments (TI), EMS was spun-off via a venture capital backed LBO in 2000. Until then, the emphasis was on helping to reduce TI product development lead times. Thus, large inventories were never an issue. After the LBO, emphasis on cash flow and profitability increased, as did the pressures resulting from being a stand-alone business.

For example, bank loan covenants demanded low year-end inventories. This was in direct conflict with their practice of building inventories in the 4th quarter to support heavy seasonal, 1st half demand from their automotive customers. This was further complicated by a volatile metals marketplace that had a significant impact on product cost and pricing.

And, since many of their major OEM customers were moving manufacturing to low cost countries in Asia for lower labor costs, EMS was driven to relocate some portion of its manufacturing to China, to stay close to the customers' manufacturing sites.

EMS quickly decided they needed to pursue lean manufacturing to minimize costs, lead times and inventories. And just as quickly, they realized they needed to broaden their existing S&OP process that initially focused on forecasting. It needed to become a responsive, cross-functional management control mechanism to guide them through the ocean of change they were navigating.

Company Characteristics

Size:

➤ $100 million sales with 400 employees

➤ 450,000 square feet of fully integrated manufacturing that includes an array of roll-bonding processes, high speed stamping and custom assembly in Attleboro, MA.

Products:

EMS is the largest producer of clad metals in North America. The cladding process is one in which two or more metals are bonded together under extremely high pressures to form a consolidated strip of metal.

➤ Examples of products from their two major lines include:

   o CMS products (using non-precious metals):

     Clad inserts for automotive welding uses
     Cable shielding material
     Catalytic converter substrate
     Selfbrazing materials
     Bimetal thermostat material
     RF room shielding material
     Clad materials for automotive trim, CRT's, batteries and cookware

   o ECS products (using precious metals such as gold and silver primarily for electrical contacts):

     Welded or brazed contact assemblies
     Toplay contact material
     Custom contact materials
     Welding tapes
     Inlay, button, terminal, composite and solid rivet contacts

➤ 7 product families

- ➤ 23 Sub-families

- ➤ 1400 SKU's

- ➤ 1300 Different product configurations manufactured in a typical year

The Demand Side:

The company sales representatives sell directly to their NAFTA, Asian, and European customers. Shipments are made directly from EMS.

Major customers include:

Texas Instruments	Emerson Electric
ThermODisc	General Cable Corp.
Delphi Automotive	General Electric
Square D Company	General Motors
BorgWarner	Honeywell
Chrysler Corporation	

Order Fulfillment strategies are:

- ➤ Make-to-stock: 60 "A" items (high volume, consistent demand items) with finished goods inventory allowing flexibility to smooth fluctuations in customer demand, anticipate seasonal surges and level production volume in the factory

- ➤ Finish-to-order: 1100 items with semi-finished goods inventory held to accommodate the minimum run sizes on the bonding lines

- ➤ Make-to-order: 60 items

The Supply Side:

- ➤ The Attleboro, Massachusetts manufacturing facility contains both continuous processes along with some functional (job shop) operations. The relatively large equipment used in some of their processing requires fairly long runs.

- ➤ New manufacturing facilities are being developed in China.

- ➤ Most products start as purchased coils of metal alloys, which are then:
  - o bonded into multi layered coils

- o heat treated to consolidate the bond
- o rolled to gauge
- o slit to width
- o much product is shipped to the customer in coil form
- o some products, such as the contacts, are stamped into parts
- o a few assemblies are built in house

➤ EMS has slowly evolved from a low mix, high volume, to a high mix, low volume business. This is supported by basically the same equipment that was purchased for the high volume environment.

➤ Clad material production has been re-engineered by lean manufacturing into the "Clad value-streams;" these have lead times of about four weeks in production, with overall inventory turns of about 7.

➤ The Bi Metal value-streams, not yet fully re-engineered, currently have a lead time of eight weeks, down from thirteen weeks. The goal is four weeks. Inventory turns are below 4.

➤ Raw material lead times range from eight to twenty-two weeks.

Other Tools Employed

➤ Lean manufacturing efforts over the past two years have had the highest priority

➤ There also has been a significant effort to integrate supply chain partners into both lean manufacturing and Product Development processes.

➤ EMS has taken a value-stream mapping approach to the implementation of Lean, implementing one product family at a time.

➤ The initial families, as defined by Lean, matched fairly well with the S&OP groupings, making it easy for S&OP to set Takt times and guide demand management within each value-stream. .

➤ 6 Sigma/TQM was implemented across all areas of the plant when Texas Instruments owned the business. It is still an important part of the management process.

➤ 5S (a methodology for organizing the manufacturing workplace for cleanliness, safety, ergonomics and efficiency) and Total Productive Maintenance techniques are implemented and practiced.

The S&OP Process

"Coupled with the effectiveness of lean manufacturing, S&OP has transformed our job shop, customer order-by-order approach to one where we anticipate changes in market dynamics, with the production ability to respond. As a result, we've become the service leader in many of our markets, even though inventories (which many of our competitors view is the only way to service the market) have been reduced by over 60%." Kevin Stevick, CEO

The monthly S&OP cycle, implemented in 2001, with a twelve month horizon, encompasses roughly sixteen days.

Demand Planning

➢ The twelve month forecast is done mainly at the aggregate level, then decomposed by percent into the SKU level.

➢ Forecasting is a blend of statistical and extrinsic inputs, coming from both the sales force and directly from the customer.

➢ A Demand Manager provides sales forecast information for both the S&OP process by family, as well as by SKU for detailed planning. There is a process in place to make sure these match.

➢ The steps are as follows:

   o Days 1-2: Demand Manager publishes actual sales, backlog and forecast accuracy data

   o Days 3-5: Product Managers update demand spreadsheets, and document summary comments and action items. Inputs include:
      ▪ Global insights data
      ▪ Statistical forecasts by sub-family
      ▪ Requested demand history
      ▪ Customer feedback and requirements

   o Day 5: demand meeting - marketing and planning review the forecasts and finalize the plan o Days 6-7: the Demand Manager, with corrections from Product Managers, updates the demand files, along with at least quarterly updates to the Financial Forecast.

- As a program of customer collaborative planning expands, there will be a movement away from statistical forecasts and more reliance on customer demand projections rather than internal forecasts.

Supply Planning

➢ On day 7 of the S&OP cycle, the Demand Manager updates the forecasts in the production plan model.

➢ On days 8-11 the production plans are developed by the Value-stream Planners, using an Excel-based tool that adjusts the plans to match the latest forecasts, customer backlogs, inventory positions, and management targets. Excel-based rough cut capacity planning is then used to level load the plant.

➢ All of the following must buy into the plan and agree on the actions required to balance supply and demand:

Supply Chain Manager	Mfg. Supervisors
Value-stream Managers	Operations Managers
Planning Manager	Demand Manager

➢ On days 15-16 (after the executive meeting), the planners utilize S&OP data to set rates (takt times) for lean manufacturing. and material purchases. Some material requirements are calculated directly by the family production plans using historic percentages and cycle times (rough cut material Planning).

➢ EMS has recently begun to more tightly integrate a few key suppliers into the future planning process.

Partnership Meeting

This day 13 meeting lasts two to three hours and includes:

Demand Manager
Value-stream Managers
Operations Managers

Data reviewed includes:

➤ The current sales plan in dollars compared to the business plan and budget at both the family and aggregate level

➤ The future backlog of customer orders compared in pounds and dollars to the previously projected backlog

➤ Average actual customer lead time versus target by value-stream

➤ Projected inventory versus actual production at the family level

➤ Projected inventory versus actual inventory turns at the family level.

To monitor inventory performance during the month, EMS has applied TQM and SPC "x-bar" techniques:

o   the initial inventory target for the current S&OP period is set as the median

o   the upper and lower limits are based on normal demand variation experienced by each value-stream

o   reaching an upper or lower limit within an S&OP cycle indicates an extraordinary event is occurring that needs immediate review

The Executive Meeting

➤ Attendees:

President	VP Business Development
CFO	Value-stream Mgrs. (as needed)
COO	Operations Mgrs. (as needed)
VP Sales and Marketing	

➤ The president leads this one to two hour meeting and ensures that the plans are supporting the corporate objectives.

➤ Unusually, a fairly fine level of detail is reviewed, such as lead times for key suppliers and forecast accuracy by family. Overall, the participants are happy with the meeting contents, although there is also a feeling that more content could be covered in summary.

➤ S&OP spreadsheets, updated information and key metrics are reviewed. Pending issues are resolved.

➤ Finance is a very active user of the results of the process and has tied several of their planning processes to S&OP.

Hard Benefits

"S&OP has been a cornerstone in our strategic plan. It has allowed us to provide world-class service on a global level." Dom Archino, VP Business Development (until recently the VP of Sales and Marketing), one of the prime drivers of S&OP at the company.

Benefits jointly produced by S&OP, lean manufacturing and better supply chain management with both customers and suppliers over the last two and a half years include:

➤ Customer service improved to between 85% and 97%, by product.

➤ Inventory reduced by 62%, allowing for a significant improvement in cash flow to meet the tighter targets set to support the LBO, while still meeting customer on-time delivery expectations.

➤ Forecast error was cut by 90% with each subfamily having a forecast accuracy goal that fits the actual profile of demand for that subfamily.

➤ Increased process and operational speed and flexibility was attained.

Soft Benefits

➤ Improved teamwork between working groups: sales, marketing, operations and supply chain functions

➤ Improved collaboration with customers on forecasts and EMS performance

➤ S&OP is a key tool to reduce inventory and manage cash flow. For EMS, this was vital to support their transition in ownership.

Go to Chapter 4 to read more about **Benefits**

Lessons Learned

➢ The VP of Sales and Marketing driving the process was a key success factor.

➢ Field sales should be involved from the start.

➢ Continually focus on making the forecast more accurate and more usable. This includes tailoring the forecasting process to provide information that is relevant to each product and market.

➢ Robust tools for supply planning, including rough cut capacity planning (RCCP), are needed.

➢ S&OP is needed to manage and focus lean manufacturing and supply chain management improvement efforts.

➢ Insure that supply plan rates drive takt times, S&OP inventory plans match Lean scheduling rules, and RCCP is used to validate plans based on the current lean manufacturing set-up.

Go to Chapter 5 to read more about **Lessons Learned**

Consultant's Summary

Before lean manufacturing concepts were introduced, the focus of S&OP was mainly on the sales portion of the business. As the need to coordinate all the various functions became more apparent, the process naturally began to expand to encompass the operations side of the business. As the S&OP planning process and Lean concepts took hold in manufacturing, and the inventory levels and lead times were reduced, the value-streams began to gain speed and flexibility.

The result was a simultaneous reduction in inventory and an increase in on-time delivery to the customer. The company has learned that a small amount of strategically placed inventory is far more beneficial than lots of inventory in the wrong places, especially when the large inventories are in the form of queues in front of key processes. Such inventories add nothing but waste and cost, a primary target for the Lean effort, and are the culprit behind long lead times to the customer.

Lean techniques typically focus on short term action and long term thinking, with an overriding approach of making continuous improvement to the process each day. The S&OP process, with its long to medium term horizon, has a primary objective of deploying the correct resources to execute the business plan. This fits nicely around Lean concepts such as leveling volume and mix for a value-stream, and using inventory as a strategic buffer for customer service. As management's steering wheel for the business, it serves as the logical starting point for any Lean transformation.

Bill Kerber, Consultant

Chapter 21

Interbake Foods, LLC
A division of Weston Foods, USA

Richmond, VA

Cookies, crackers, and ice cream wafers

Why and how would a contract manufacturing food processor do sales and operations planning to support its highly seasonal business?

Interbake is a consumer food processing company that supplies large bakeries and ice cream dairies.

What's Unique

Interbake is an industry leader because they specialize in selling products, programs, and services in non-branded niches, uncontested by national branded companies. They command market share by being a "worry free", high quality, low cost producer through the use of automation, statistical process control, and excellent planning and scheduling tools.

Interbake is under Food and Drug Administration (FDA) control for ingredients and packaging. Since some of their products are kosher, some of their manufacturing processes and lines must be periodically verified by a rabbi to ensure they conform to Jewish dietary law. Also, when using nuts, milk, eggs and the like, they must also ensure an effective allergen clean up upon completion. These clean up activities have a major impact on capacities and schedules.

Company Characteristics

Size: 1700 employees, with annual sales of $340 million (of which $165 million comes from their Norse Dairy Systems subsidiary, see chapter xx on Norse Dairy Systems)

Products: over 275 products for four market segments:

> ➢ Retail: twelve different private label specialty cookies and crackers with unique packaging for each customer

> ➢ Fund raising: One of only two manufacturers that produce six million cases of eight different varieties of Girl Scout cookies in the USA.

> ➢ Contract manufacturing: fifty-five baked ingredients and end products sold in retail grocery stores in US

> ➢ Dairy: over two hundred stock keeping units (SKU's) of baked ingredients (ice cream wafers, cones, crunches)

The Demand Side:

> ➢ There are dedicated sales people for each of these markets and major customers:
>   - o Retail: Dollar General, Wal-Mart, Family Dollar and others in the US and Canada
>   - o Fund Raising: 330 US Girl Scout councils.
>   - o Contract: other large baking manufacturers
>   - o Dairy: all major us manufacturers (including Unilever, Dean's Food, Nestle, Schwans, Well's, M&M Mars, ICS and Kroger) plus many in Canada, and South and Central America

> ➢ Distribution Channels:
>   - o Retail: customer warehouses
>   - o Fund Raising: Girl Scout council locations through 130 local agents for storage and delivery, plus several distribution centers and floating stock warehouses
>   - o Contract: through the large baking companies' own channels
>   - o Dairy: shipped direct to customer or customer warehouses

The Supply Side:

> ➢ Plants and distribution centers at

Richmond, Virginia
North Sioux City, South Dakota
Elizabeth, New Jersey

➢ These plants are organized with a synchronized flow from mixing through baking to packaging, and are in a just-in-time mode with their common raw material suppliers

➢ They produce products for the four business units on common production lines

➢ Order fulfillment strategies and product lead times:

   o Retail: 24-hour shipments from finished goods inventory on core private label items, all other items are baked-to-order in ten days

   o Fund raising: customer shipping schedules drive shipments out of finished goods inventory by 5 PM the next day, with lead time for initial orders between three and fifteen days

   o Contract: very little finished goods inventory, mostly baked-to-order in three weeks

   o Dairy: some items have twenty-four hour deliveries out of finished inventory, others are baked-to-order in two to four weeks

Other Tools Employed

➢ Interbake has a very strong total quality management (TQM) system called Integrated Process Management (IPM) using statistical process control (SPC) and team problem solving

➢ The company is certified under ISO 9001:2000, only one of a handful of baking companies in North America to be designated as such.

➢ Interbake has been certified Class A in manufacturing resource planning (MRPII)[28], in three of their manufacturing plants, four business segments, and Enterprise-wide.

➢ The Design Control Initiation Process (DCIP) is used to formally introduce new products, change the existing products or processes, transfer existing products from line to line or plant to plant, then pass the information to the S&OP process.

---

[28] MRPII was the name used most frequently in the 1970's through the 1990's to describe an integrated, cross-functional resource planning and control process. Some companies were certified "Class A" in recognition of their complete and intensive use of all the tools to produce superior business results. It is similar to the term "World Class".

➢ A balanced scorecard process is used company wide, with the key performance criteria set from S&OP, and reviewed at each step in the S&OP process.

The S&OP Process

Interbake decided to implement sales and operations planning in 1990 because of communication gaps between the demand and supply groups. Highlighting the need to implement S&OP was a major demand drop, which resulted in a severe cutback at two plants, while the workforce was reduced and several lines were shut down for an extended period.

Because of poor forecasting and capacity planning, they were experiencing frequent product and people shortages. Plus, there were a number of conflicts between the business segments over which customers should get priority. They seemed to be frequently in crisis mode. Major obstacles included:

➢ Inadequate communication and trust between sales and manufacturing

➢ Senior management's focus, which was very short term and reactive, with little visibility into the future

➢ The tendency of various departments to pad their numbers versus developing a common game plan they all believed in and were committed to execute

The goals were:

➢ reductions in customer complaints, cost, labor, downtime, and scrap and rework

➢ improvements in process productivity and capacity utilization

Demand Planning

Participants: Vice Presidents of Sales/Marketing and Demand Managers from each business segment, sales personnel, regional Business Managers

Mechanics:

➢ the sales/marketing people for each business segment review customer demand and forecast tracking information

➤ Norse Dairy, an Interbake subsidiary, provides a forecast for the wafers produced for them at the Elizabeth, NJ and Richmond, VA Interbake plants

➤ for the Contract, Retail, and Dairy business segments, a revised, rolling eighteen month "core" forecast of items and families is generated after doing a root cause analysis on the reasons for forecast error, with discussions on corrective actions.

➤ retail forecasts are done only at a family level

➤ "big events" or promotional forecasts are made on individual items and are added to the core forecast for each business segment, both of which are tracked and adjusted each period

➤ feedback from the sales force, the demand managers, and the master schedulers is sometimes used to adjust the future forecast.

➤ Fund Raising generates a shipping schedule, based on the highly seasonal demand for Girl Scout cookies

Prior to sending it to operations, the Sales/Marketing Vice President for each business segment reviews and approves the forecast that in turn becomes the "sales plan"

Supply Planning

For Retail, Contract and Dairy, the plants:

o maintain a weekly production schedule by item for two to eight weeks out, depending on the plant, with a weekly master production schedule covering out through twenty-six weeks

o use customer backlog, individual item forecasts, where available, and for all other items, a family planning bill of material to derive the item mix from the family forecast

o in some cases, convert the family level forecast to an eighteen month family production plan, which drives long range material requirements, crewing, and line capacity for months 3 through 18. The other plants generate a monthly production plan for each end item to drive their material and capacity requirements.

Packaging items are planned with a min/max for high volume and repetitive items, with the rest buy-to-order

In the Fund Raising business unit, the Girl Scout cookie shipping schedule is back scheduled into a production schedule.

There is a weekly production schedule with minimums and maximums that is adjusted each month throughout the Girl Scout Cookie season.

Capacity is planned to the maximum while raw materials and packaging are planned to the minimum, and adjusted when required. This provides flexibility to increase the schedule quickly if the Girl Scout demand suddenly increases, since people and equipment capacity isn't easily increased, while much of the raw material is common across multiple products and easily procured, and packaging material can be quickly purchased.

Rough cut capacity planning for both crewing and the lines takes place, while detailed capacity requirements planning is only done for those few production lines that are considered critical.

After consensus is reached in the partnership meetings on the demand and supply plans, the detailed master schedule is finalized and rolled up to the family production plan for review in the executive S&OP meeting

Partnership Meetings

Separate "partnership" meetings are held for each of the four market segments, with attendees from each plant supplying product to that business. The Dairy meeting has active participation by sales and marketing people from Interbake's subsidiary, Norse Dairy[29], for whom they make wafers.

Each three to four hour meeting has a pre-published agenda covering the 20% of the demand, supply, and business issues that are causing 80% of the problems. The data to be reviewed in the meeting is distributed prior to the meeting

The focus is on the top twenty-five stocked items which represent about 80% of the total sales volume.

The partnership teams are responsible for recommending demand and supply plans to executive management for their final review and approval.

These groups are responsible for reviewing and acting upon:

---

[29] See Chapter 22 on Norse Dairy Systems, a subsidiary of Interbake Foods

quality
customer service performance and issues
inventory levels
demand and supply issues and gaps
production rates and goals

on time production performance
capacity planning (crewing and line) issues
both short and long term supplier issues

Meeting action items are assigned with completion dates for resolution of the root causes of issues, and are tracked until resolved. If not resolved within a given time period (usually two months), they are sent to the Executive S&OP meeting to be discussed and resolved.

The meetings are routinely conducted using videoconferencing, but the groups meet in person at least once a quarter at each plant

Attendees include:
- Demand Managers
- Customer Service Managers
- Master Schedulers
- Plant Managers
- Operations Managers
- Purchasing Managers
- Financial Managers
- Quality Managers

- Distribution Managers
- Norse Dairy sales personnel
- Customer Service and demand management personnel
- R&D personnel are on call if there are any new product introduction issues

The Executive Meeting

This meeting is chaired by the President and includes these attendees:

- Senior Executive VP, Norse Dairy Systems
- Senior VP Sales/Marketing, Fund Raising/Retail
- Director Sales/Marketing, Contract
- Senior VP of Operations
- VP Research and Development
- Information Technology Director
- Director of Engineering
- Three (3) VP/ General Managers from the plants
- Director of Purchasing
- Vice President Organizational Development
- Chief Financial Officer
- VP Marketing Norse Dairy Systems
- VP Sales Norse Dairy Systems
- VP Operations Norse Dairy Systems
- Plus some partnership meeting attendees, primarily from sales and marketing

This five hour monthly meeting addresses the key business issues and financial objectives. It is broken down into four separate sections:
➤ Performance, problems, root cause and corrective actions review of:
  o only the top twenty-five Interbake/Norse products that do 80% of the business
  o proposed corrective actions and recommendations from the partnership groups, by exception. This includes only the 15 - 20% of the supply and/or demand issues that are not resolved by these groups, or issues they do not have the authority to resolve.
  o problems are always presented with a root cause analysis, recommended corrective actions, solutions, and a risk analysis.
➤ A capacity planning review:
  o by the Capacity Steering Team comprised of VP / General Managers from the plants, Sr. VP Operations, VP Commercialization, VP R&D, VP Engineering, and Sr. Executive VP Norse Dairy Systems
  o of facilities, plant, line, and crewing capacity issues, plans, corrective actions and increases
  o of new product development and transfer of products from one plant to another plant
➤ An R&D and Engineering review:

- o with sales and marketing people from each business segment in attendance
- o discussing the status of new products, including cost and feasibility studies
- o authorizing and prioritizing new products as agreed to with the business segments, along with approval of R&D capacity requirements
➤ The final S&OP Review where all proposed plans and financial objectives are reviewed and agreed upon, including capacity changes as agreed to and presented by the Capacity Steering Team

Hard Benefits

Interbake feels strongly that improvements listed below are the result of the integrated operation of all of their business processes. This includes continuous improvement through IPM (their version of TQM), detailed resource planning and management through MRPII, and especially sales and operations planning. It's S&OP which is used to the drive all their desired business improvements, and to get participation, ownership and buy-in throughout the organization.

➤ Compliance to customer orders has improved to 97-8%, up from 90% in 1993.

➤ Inventories have been lowered by 12% and finished goods inventories are much better managed

➤ Manufacturing downtime has been reduced from 10% to 8%, since 1993

➤ Output per man-hour has increased by 33% since 1993

➤ Individual package overfills or overweights reduced from 7% to 1.5% since 1993

➤ Significant reduction of process variability by 28%

➤ Total continuous improvement savings of $ 41.3 million.

Soft Benefits

➤ Good teamwork and communication are common

➤ The S&OP process drove the implementation of ISO and continuous improvement

➤ There is more efficient planning and capacity conflicts are very rare

➢ Manufacturing facilities spend less time firefighting, and have more time to devote to true improvement efforts

➢ S&OP provides an opportunity to share information in a much more meaningful way, with the visibility and understanding gained helping to assure alignment between sales/marketing and production

➢ S&OP is used to understand where they are and to identify where they need to improve, with a constant focus on continuous improvement, even in the areas where benefits have already been achieved

➢ S&OP is an effective regulating process for managing inventory builds, capacity allocation and responsive customer service in a highly seasonal, contract manufacturing business

➢ S&OP works well in a line flow process environment and for different market channels

*Go to Chapter 4 to read more about **Benefits***

Lessons Learned

"I think the S&OP process has proved to be our best communication tool. It allows everyone with a stake in the way the company operates to have input at the appropriate level of concern and give feedback on achievement against established goals for their area and for the company. No major problem should go unchallenged for more than four weeks." Scott Fullbright, Senior Executive VP, Norse Dairy Systems and facilitator for S&OP at Interbake (a former VP / General Manager at Interbake who was promoted to the top management position at Norse)

➢ No longer can there be multiple individual plans from the functional areas in the company - there must be a single company game plan that everyone agrees to execute

➢ People are more focused on managing the business plan and less focused on optimizing their function's performance at the expense of the overall business

➢ Partnership meetings are excellent communication and action-oriented meetings when they focus on solutions, not symptoms. Many issues previously brought to senior management are now resolved at this level.

*Go to Chapter 5 to read more about **Lessons Learned***

Consultant's Summary

*"Senior Management delegates to the partnership team, the responsibility for defining the strategies, implementation plans, balanced scorecard performance measurements, and expected results and involvement on all improvement efforts. This avoids making people feel that change is just "forced" on them. Senior Management is only involved in the decision-making on 10 to 15% of the issues, when consensus can't be reached or cross-functional buy-in doesn't exist at the partnership level. The end result is a **vertical partnership** between operating management and senior management regarding a single company game plan.*

*This approach, successful because of the management style of company president Ray Baxter, has helped break down the traditional vertical silos of functional excellence, resulting in a **horizontal partnership** between the functional areas of the business that are responsible for achieving the business plans and financial results."* John Civerolo, Consultant

EPILOGUE

In March, 2005, Interbake announced the reconfiguration of their manufacturing assets, with plans to close the Elizabeth, NJ and Richmond, VA bakeries over the next twelve to eighteen months. Both were over seventy years old and no longer cost competitive. The products and production lines will be relocated to a new bakery, with modern cost competitive assets, in Front Royal, VA, and to an existing Interbake facility in North Sioux City, SD.

Interbake used the S&OP process to help make these tough business decisions and to communicate the decisions, plans and implementation schedules to the rest of the company. They have found S&OP to be an extremely effective process for analyzing and monitoring progress on decisions such as plant closings, new plant startups, product rationalization, and the transfer of products and production lines, to ensure that all the changes are done on time, and in a cost efficient and productive manner.

Chapter 22

Norse Dairy Systems
A division of Interbake Foods[30], LLC

Columbus, Ohio

Filling and packaging equipment, and baked dairy products for the ice cream industry

How does S&OP operate in a company that

1. *makes high volume consumable products in a process environment*
2. *at the other end of the spectrum, makes custom designed, assembled-to-order equipment in a functional, machine-shop environment*
3. *has a direct ship business supplied by contract manufacturers and their parent company*

Purchased by Interbake[1] in May of 2000, Norse Dairy Systems serves customers in the ice cream cone, wafer and novelty businesses. Norse focuses on market niches where innovation and operational excellence are the primary determinants of success.

What's Unique

A major part of Norse's product line is food and, as such, the company is under the purview of the Food and Drug Administration (FDA). Further, some of Norse's food products are kosher and thus some of their manufacturing processes must be verified by a rabbi to ensure their conformance to Jewish dietary law.

At the other end of the manufacturing spectrum, Norse designs, fabricates and assembles ice cream filling and packaging equipment in a job shop, metal-working, make-to-order environment.

Company Characteristics

Size: $165 million in sales, 400 employees

---

[30] See chapter 21 on Interbake Foods, LLC.

Products:

➢ **Baked Commodity** Products. These include ice cream cones (17% of total sales) and wafers (54% of total sales): three hundred items, with seventy-five bake-to-stock and two hundred twenty-five bake-to-order with two to four week lead times

➢ The **Equipment** Product Line contains assemble-to-order products with many unique options and attachments, and an engineer-to-order line with products built to customer supplied specifications. There is an extensive aftermarket business in service and spare parts.

Seventy-five or more machines are produced each year, with thousands of options and attachments, many of them unique to the customer.

The Demand Side: The market is major dairy companies, with 88% of sales in the U.S. Customers include Unilever, Dean's Food, Nestle, Dreyers, Schwans, Wells, Good Humor, M&M Mars, ICS, and Kroger, with most products shipped directly to the customer's location

The Supply Side:

Norse **Baked Commodity** plants are located in Los Angeles CA, Somerset PA, Green Bay WI, and San Jose, Costa Rica. These plants are process oriented, with a synchronized flow from mixing through baking to packaging.

Norse wafers are made at Interbake plants in Richmond VA and Elizabeth NJ. Thus the Interbake S&OP process must recognize the Norse demand that is placed on these two plants. (See page xxx.)

Twenty-nine percent of total sales comes from fifteen third-party (contract manufacturer) plants producing and shipping 1,000 different lids and cups shipped directly to select Norse customers.

The plant at Columbus, Ohio manufactures and services the custom designed, ice cream filling and packaging products (**Equipment**) for dairies to produce frozen novelties. Characteristics include:

➢ Engineering design lead times ranging from four to one hundred weeks, based on the complexity

➤ A substantial service parts business with unit volumes of 3,400 different items per year representing annual sales of about $1.3 million

Other Tools Employed

➤ Norse achieved Class A certification in their use of manufacturing resource planning (MRPII)[31], with S&OP numbers driving the operational and financial plans

➤ Driven by S&OP, there is a strong continuous improvement focus on reduction of customer complaints, cost, waste, and labor, using Kepner-Tregoe problem solving and decision-making tools, to find the root causes of problems and develop corrective actions.

➤ Norse utilizes a company-wide balanced scorecard that is reviewed at all the Norse and Interbake S&OP meetings. Objectives include:

   o continuous improvement, learning, growth

   o financial, customer centric, selling process improvements

   o improved R& D service to internal and external customers

➤ Norse has implemented lean manufacturing in all of their US plants with outstanding results, including: increased capacity utilization, less inventory in queue and the stockroom, shorter manufacturing lead times and improved manufacturing flow

➤ All plants are implementing People Empowerment and delegation of authority and responsibility to process owners (operators) for on time and quality products

➤ Norse has a quality management system called Integrated Process Management (IPM), which has led to significant improvement in quality and reduction in customer complaints. Quality is reviewed in each step in the S&OP process

➤ There is a separate Design Control Initiation Process (DCIP), for managing new product introductions and changes to products, processes and plants

---

[31] MRPII was the name used most frequently in the 1970's through the 1990's to describe an integrated, cross-functional resource planning and control process. Some companies were certified "Class A" in recognition of their complete and intensive use of all the tools to produce superior business results. It is similar to the term "World Class".

The S&OP Process

Norse implemented S&OP in 2000 for the **Commodity Products**, mostly within only ninety days of the acquisition by Interbake, leveraging on Interbake's experience with S&OP.

S&OP was extended to the **Equipment** product line, the Design Engineering department and the Equipment Plant over the next one hundred eighty days, the longer time reflecting the greater complexity of the **Equipment** product, and related design and manufacturing processes.

The four-week S&OP cycle ends in a Norse Executive S&OP meeting, followed by the final Interbake Foods S&OP meeting which includes Norse executives.

The S&OP numbers are converted into an updated financial plan each month for both Interbake and Norse. Because of this, the focus is on ensuring that the numbers are valid and not inflated or unrealistic. If the financial plan changes by more than +/- 5% over eighteen months, the reasons must be explained, reconciled and then the financial plan is sent to Weston Corporation.

Demand Planning

➢ For **Commodity Products**:

- o a statistical forecast is generated for all three hundred products and is then adjusted by feedback from the sales force, demand managers and the corporate master scheduler

- o on the 20% of the items that represent 90% of sales, root cause analysis is performed on forecast errors or changes, and corrective actions are discussed and assigned with clear accountability to improve forecast accuracy

- o The Commodity Products Group locks down the item forecast, going forward eighteen months, during their Dairy sales planning meeting whose attendees include the Vice President of Marketing of Dairy Products and the Demand Manager.

➢ An **Equipment** sales planning meeting, including the V.P. Sales, the Director of Field Service and the Equipment Demand Manager, is held each month to:

- o review and update customer order slotting for plant capacity allocation

- o review and adjust the Equipment forecast for fifteen models eighteen months into the future, based on input from field sales people about their specific customers

- o using over two hundred modular planning bills of material to forecast two thousand options and attachments

➤ the forecasts are finalized into a formal "sales plan" when senior sales and marketing executives review and approve the forecasts for both **Commodity Products** and **Equipment**.

Supply Planning

For **Commodity Products,** the Corporate Master Scheduler uses the item forecast to create a monthly production plan by family for each plant. Then each plant scheduler uses the item-level forecast to create a twelve week master schedule, which is aggregated and reconciled to the monthly production plan.

Rough cut capacity planning is used to validate these plans for crewing and line capacity in each plant

The Master Scheduler for **Equipment** plans production by family based on the forecasts for fifteen models for the next eighteen months, with two thousand options and attachments.

- o A planning bill of material is used to calculate the material requirements and capacity plans for critical resources

- o This process also manages, schedules, and allocates Engineering's time: the engineering department is planned and scheduled in a manner similar to a production work center.

  Engineering on-time performance on drawings, material specifications, and bills of material is monitored, with defined root causes for any issues or problems used to plan the appropriate corrective actions

  A capacity plan for each engineer is tracked for actual hours vs. a plan based on the design complexity and actual hours spent on previous orders

- o The culminating part of Norse's supply planning phase is what they call the "Plant Demand and Operations Planning" (D&OP) meetings. These meetings, approximately two hours each, are held at each plant with key plant operating personnel, that:

Analyze performance to the Production Plans, Master Schedules, Shop Schedules, Vendor Schedules and Shipping Plans, among others

Identify and resolve future capacity problems including overloads, underloads, overtime and the use of temporary labor in crewing and line capacity

Identify issues that need to be elevated to the Corporate D&OP and/or to the partnership meetings

A 1.5 hour meeting that Norse calls the "Corporate D&OP" meeting takes place after the plant meetings, attended by Plant Managers, the Corporate Master Scheduler, and Plant Planners. Demand issues, plant performance, capacity issues, staffing changes, and in some cases, shifting product from plant to plant are discussed and resolved

This step demands that each plant commits to the material, capacity and inventory necessary to support their production plan, ensuring buy-in to the corporate production plan. Any unresolved issues are sent to partnership meetings.

Partnership Meetings

The cross-functional "partnership" teams approve the supply and demand plans at five **partnership** meetings, making extensive use of videoconferencing. An agenda and the appropriate data are in the attendees' hands prior to each meeting. Action items are tracked to ensure all outstanding issues are settled or, if unresolved after two months, sent to the **executive S&OP** meeting to be discussed and acted upon. The five meetings are:

o A one hour partnership meeting for **Equipment**, where engineering capacity, missed deliverables and performance issues are examined for root causes and corrective actions. Attended by: equipment operations management, R&D, engineering, planning, purchasing, marketing, and the VP of Operations.

o a four hour partnership meeting for **Commodity Products** attended by: domestic and international sales, the Corporate Master Scheduler, the Manufacturing Directors, the Demand Manager, the Controller, purchasing and customer service

o Two 1.5 to 2 hour **Interbake** Richmond, VA and Elizabeth, NJ **plant partnership** meetings with both Norse and Interbake attendees. These meetings are seen as crucial to the proper communication and prioritization of Norse requirements from their sister Interbake plants.

o a thirty minute **third party Manufacturer, "Direct Ship partnership"** meeting attended by: customer service, the Demand Manager, the Controller, the

Purchasing Manager, international sales, and the Export Manager

The Executive Meeting

➤ The Senior Executive VP of Norse Dairy Systems (their top operating executive) chairs this three hour meeting where:

- o open issues on demand, inventory and supply for **Commodity Products, Equipment, Service Parts, and Third Party-Direct Ship** are discussed and resolved

- o customer service on-time performance, demand ,supply, and inventory plans, and financial objectives are reviewed, occasionally modified, and approved

- o new product projects, along with engineering capacity, manpower needs and overtime are approved and prioritized

- o the meeting focuses on less than 20% of the items that represent more than 85% of the sales dollars, with all other issues handled at the **partnership** meetings

- o any major Norse issues that are not resolved are taken to the final **Interbake executive S&OP** meeting

➤ the attendees in person or through videoconferencing include:

Vice President of Marketing	Production/Inventory Control Mgr.
Controller	2 Purchasing Managers
Vice President of Operations	Director of Manufacturing,
Vice President of Sales	Engineering and Paper Packaging
Director of International Operations	(Equipment)
Integration Manager	Administrative Assistant to the Senior
Director of Customer Service	Vice President
Director of Bakery and Tube Mfg.	

➤ twice a year, each of the twelve sales people attends to see how their forecasts are being used to drive the business plans

Hard Benefits

"With S&OP, we are better planners and much more efficient. In the past, it took us twelve to sixteen weeks to build a filling machine and we now have a standard lead time of six weeks and the machine configuration does not matter." Jeff Crawford, Director of Manufacturing, Engineering and Packaging

The **Equipment** Group achieved:

> reduction in design time by 27% with a 30% improvement in efficiency

> reduction in customer machine order configuration time from forty-five days to four days

> 98% on time performance for completion of drawings, specifications and BOM's

> service parts inventory turns improved by 22% with a $ 600,000 inventory reduction from 2004 to 2005

For **Commodity** products:

> downtime reduced 51%

> scrap reduced 55%

> overweights reduced 38%

> all wafers, cones and packaging materials from the third party manufacturers ship 98% on time

Soft Benefits

"The S&OP process provides a great way to routinely review company performance, critical issues and opportunities. It keeps all of us on the same page and provides a great forum to keep critical issues and action plans at task." Nick Kosanovich, VP Sales High volume, process flow consumer products and low-volume, complex, highly engineered machinery (ETO, MTO, engineering capacity constrained) can be well managed through S&OP

A more thorough understanding of managing production capacity and materials to meet the forecasted demand. The traditional manufacturing "reactive" mode process has been replaced by a future planning approach to managing resources and capital needs based on actual capabilities

The S&OP meetings got engineering, sales, marketing, master scheduling, and manufacturing working together, getting to the root causes of problems. Reaching consensus on proposed solutions has resulted in less conflict and finger pointing between the functional areas, because of objective performance measurements.

Engineering document accuracy has significantly improved

Every engineer knows their work for each day. They are not constantly jerked around, allowing them to look for opportunities to eliminate waste and increase capacity.

Better visibility to allocate engineers to customer orders, or to look at alternatives such as scheduling overtime or contract engineering, so costs can be controlled.

Better communications between Manufacturing and Engineering have led to a better understanding of each others' issues and requirements. The silos between them have been broken down. They now work together as a team.

"Our team members at all levels of the organization have a better understanding of our performance and capabilities through involvement in DOP, partnership, and S&OP. Solutions to problems take place whenever possible by individuals that are closest to the processes." John F. Deininger, Vice President, Operations, **Norse Dairy Systems**

Go to Chapter 4 to read more about **Benefits**

Lessons Learned

➢ The leadership of Senior Management was instrumental in ensuring that all functional areas embraced the new S&OP process

➢ Educating and integrating sales and marketing, manufacturing (equipment and dairy products), finance, distribution, direct ship, customer service, IT, service parts, R&D, and engineering from the start was key to their quick success

➢ Requirements from third party direct ship suppliers (contract manufacturers), and from sister plants can be managed through S&OP

➢ S&OP works well with, and is required by, lean manufacturing

➢ S&OP is a key process to monitor, adjust and achieve financial plans

➢ S&OP can be successfully used to plan, monitor and manage engineering resources for new product development and engineer-to-order products

➢ *"The key is providing the correct planning tools, empowering the individuals using these tools and* <u>*strong*</u> *support from the senior management team."* Jeff Crawford, Director of Manufacturing, Engineering and Packaging

Go to Chapter 5 to read more about **Lessons Learned**

Consultant's Summary

"*When Interbake purchased Norse and appointed Scott Fullbright Senior Vice President, he wanted to get an S&OP process started immediately. This was because Interbake's S&OP process was a tremendous success, and because Scott had played a major role in designing and leading the process at Interbake.*

After S&OP education for the Norse operating personnel, they started to design and implement a traditional five step S&OP process based on the Interbake model, with just one partnership meeting. But because of their different types of products and an Engineering Department integral to the Equipment business, they quickly discovered they needed a more robust process. Within several months they instituted six separate supply planning (D&OP) meetings, and five partnership meetings for each business segment, as well as the executive review meeting. This was to ensure they got the required focused involvement, communications, consensus and ownership in each meeting, for each plant and market segment.

Since a "command and control" management structure did not fit the leadership style of the Norse executive group, they delegated authority and ownership to the partnership teams to resolve business decisions without executive approval, where possible. If there are any unresolved problems or issues, the partnership teams must present a recommended solution for executive approval.

The Norse S&OP process has been extremely successful in setting achievable business plans and getting bottom line results. Plus having a master schedule and capacity plan for each engineer has allowed Norse to prioritize projects based on available capacity, while improving overall engineering performance.

Most of the success of the Norse S&OP process is directly attributed to their partnership meetings."
John Civerolo, Consultant

Chapter 23

PYOSA S.A. DE C.V.
Colors Division

Monterrey, Mexico

Industrial Dyestuffs and Pigments

How does a small, batch chemical division of a family-owned Mexican company use S&OP to manage their business?

Pyosa, one of the country's largest domestically owned companies, is the leading manufacturer of inorganic pigments in México, produced from internally developed technology. The Colors division also produces dyestuffs. Three other specialty chemical divisions of Pyosa are jointly owned with Asian and European companies.

What's Unique

➤ This competitive marketplace demands high quality, but is driven by low prices. It is increasingly affected by competition from Asia, regulated in the use of certain of its products, and hindered by worldwide shortages of certain raw materials.

➤ Further, Pyosa has limited availability of working capital.

Company Characteristics

Size: $35 million (US Dollars) in sales, 300 employees.

Products:

➤ Pigments (18 families and 194 end products)

   Inorganic

Organic   Preparations
Phtalocyanine

➢ Dyes (12 families and 155 end products)

Solvents   Dispersions
Direct
Basic

The Demand Side:

➢ The markets include:

Paint   Dyes production
Inks   Fragrances
Cleaning products   Plastics
Textiles   Anticorrosive coverings
Fuels

➢ 75% direct sales to customers:

45% in Mexico
15% in the U.S.
15% in South America

➢ Pyosa Distribution Center locations (and the # of products stocked there):

Monterrey, Mexico (340)
Mexico City, Mexico (340)
Guadalajara, Mexico (30)
New Jersey, USA (2)
California, USA (2)
South America (10)

➢ 25% of sales through distributors:

2 in Mexico
15 in South America
each stocking about ten products

➢ Major Customers:

Comex BASF   Octel

Sherwin Williams	Telas Y Tintas
Berel	Toyo Ink
Q. Rana	Flint
FMC	Johnson Controls

➢ Dyestuffs: 60% are just-in-time items stocked in the Mexico City warehouse with 24-hour delivery

➢ Pigments:

80% are stocked commodity items = 70% of sales
20 % are items stocked for specific customers = 30% of sales

The Supply Side:

➢ 88% (307) of the items are produced by Pyosa in their three plants in Monterrey

89.0 % batch process
9.3 % mixing and blending
1.6 % toll manufacturing
equipment arranged both functionally and in product line fashion
lead time = fifteen to thirty days

➢ 12% (42 items) are purchased complete from China, India or the U.S.

➢ Competition:

United States
Africa
Argentina
Asia - especially China (formerly, just raw materials and semi-finished products, now finished products with forty-five to sixty day lead times at low cost)

➢ Suppliers:

Some suppliers with very inflexible capacity and forty-five to sixty day lead times

Semi-finished products going into 25% of the product line are purchased from China and India

One critical raw material on allocation from the supplier, who is given a rolling three-month forecast but maintains a six-day delivery lead time

Lead times = 2 to 75 days

Other Tools Employed

➤ First "Class A" manufacturing resource planning (MRPII)[32] user in México, linking management strategies through S&OP plans to detailed manufacturing and supplier schedules, all to support the business plan and target objectives

➤ Distribution resource planning (DRP) is used to manage regional forecasts, demands and inventories through the network of six Pyosa distribution centers in North and South America

➤ Pyosa has implemented TQM company-wide. It is used to identify process variation and waste, along with the root causes of problems, by helping everyone look at things in a "process management" manner, driving improvements in all other business processes, including planning, execution and data accuracy

The S&OP Process

"With the S&OP process we get to speak the same language and use the same numbers between all departments, helping us to make decisions more intelligently and effectively." Emilio Assam, President

➤ In 1987 S&OP was implemented to:

    ○ better support the business plan
    ○ have a better overview of the demand plan
    ○ figure problems out "before they occurred"

➤ The implementation methodology included:

    ○ "signed internal contracts" by all the participants
    ○ clear understanding of "internal suppliers and customers"

---

[32] MRPII was the name used most frequently in the 1970's through the 1990's to describe an integrated, cross-functional resource planning and control process. Some companies were certified "Class A" in recognition of their complete and intensive use of all the tools to produce superior business results. It is similar to the term "World Class".

- o well defined deliverables
- o carefully established project control points
- o clearly defined business measurements

➤ Now, S&OP is the main monthly mechanism to:

- o manage sales, revenue, production and inventory, in kilograms, Mexican pesos and US dollars
- o identify cash requirements and communicate them to corporate management
- o compare performance to budget and make the appropriate adjustments in the individual functional, and/or business unit portions of the budget

➤ There is an eighteen day S&OP cycle, beginning in the LAST week of the previous month

Demand Planning

➤ Key people involved in the demand planning process are the:

      -Sales people who have issues or input from their customers
      -Demand Managers from both Pigments and Dyestuffs (who input the
          forecast transactions)
      -Sales Assistant
      -Sales Manager
      -Director of Sales
      -Master Scheduler

➤ The forecasts are:

- o Based on a statistical projection from the previous two years' history (day # 1)

- o Adjusted by salesmen based on visits to the client (by day # 2)

- o Done by customer, family, and major items for twelve months out

- o Are checked for major changes by purchasing and treasury personnel for the impact on cash flow and meeting revenue goals, by downloading family forecasts from the ERP system to spreadsheets for rough cut analysis (days # 2-4)

  - ▪ Compared to budgets
  - ▪ Supplier payment terms are considered

- Customer payment terms are considered
- Time commitment to the customer may be adjusted based on cash availability

o Adjusted by sales management, in a two hour demand planning meeting, based on cash flow availability for raw materials and inventories (day # 5)

o Updated by the start of each month, for a rolling three months, with about 50% of the numbers changed in each month (day # 6)

Supply Planning

➤ Participants include:

Master Scheduler	Buyers
Material Planners	Plant Manager
Purchasing Manager	Area Manufacturing Managers

➤ This process steps are:

o The monthly production plan and thirteen week master schedule is adjusted (day # 6) based on the new forecast, with minimal changes in the current month considering:

The capacity of key manufacturing resources, especially in the inorganic processes (based on rough cut capacity planning done off-line using a spreadsheet)

Availability of key raw materials

Production performance capability as monitored in a weekly KPI review meeting

o The new master schedule (sequenced by item, by manufacturing resource) is exploded through the material requirements planning program (days # 6-7)

Validated in a one hour meeting of the master scheduler, the purchasing manager, and the buyers, who review the detailed output of MRP planning for every supplier and every item, with roughly 25% of the items requiring some change to the master schedule

o The master schedule (adjusted for material availability) is re-exploded through the material requirements planning program (days # 7-8)

Validated in a one hour meeting with the plant manager, area manufacturing managers and the master scheduler, based on capacity, quality and inventory considerations using rough cut capacity planning tools

There are very few adjustments

Manufacturing commitment is gained in this meeting

o   Purchasing and production work to the new schedules

Partnership Meeting

➤   This one hour meeting with sales is held on day # 10 in person, by telephone or videoconferencing, with these attendees:

Demand Managers from both Pigments and Dyestuffs
Sales Assistant
Sales Manager
Director of Sales
Master Scheduler

Manager of Customer Service
Purchasing Manager (for problem situations only)
Plant Manager (if big reschedules are required)

➤   All plans are finalized for the executive S&OP meeting with very few changes made from previous steps

➤   Note that there are four separate meetings (described above) prior to the executive S&OP meeting:

o   No one meeting includes all functions. Due to the size of this company, the typical attendees in a traditional "partnership" meeting all attend the executive meeting.

o   Each function meets with the master scheduler consecutively.

o   They are held over a seven-day time span.

The Executive Meeting

➤ This 1.5 hour meeting, normally on the 2nd Friday of each month (day # 12 to 14) includes:

President (the ultimate decision-maker on issues not resolved earlier)
Vice President of Finance
Treasurer
Directors of each business unit
Sales Managers

Demand Managers
Master Scheduler
Vice President of Operations
Plant Manager
Purchasing Manager
Two Buyers

➤ The meeting dates are set a year in advance with reminders sent out one week prior to the meeting.

➤ The executive S&OP meeting:
  o reviews overall sales and production performance
  o gets into detail only on
    ▪ supply/demand exceptions or problems
    ▪ customer issues
    ▪ production or capacity problems
  o approves and/or decides on questions involving the allocation of:
    ▪ cash
    ▪ critical capacity
    ▪ scarce material resources
    ▪ capital
  o forwards critical cross functional issues (such as new products, etc.) to the monthly directors meeting
  o forwards critical customer, sales and marketing issues (such as market share, etc.) to the separate monthly business unit meetings (where all key business KPI's are monitored)
  o forwards critical business issues to the bimonthly Board of Directors meeting

Hard Benefits

➤ *"By managing our S&OP we achieved a common language in our team, with clear plans and goals for the period. All of this translates directly to lower inventories and better customer service."* Jose Fernandez, Vice President of Operations

➤ Despite more and more customers requiring 24-hour lead time, customer service rose from 80 to 92% in 2004

➤ Without S&OP, inventories would be twice as high

➤ Profitability and ROI have increased significantly with the careful use of S&OP to optimally allocate scarce capital to the appropriate products and customers

Soft Benefits

➤ Improved communication between all business areas and functions (sales, marketing, manufacturing, purchasing, finance, and human resources)

➤ Better, more accurate and more specific information available quickly

➤ Fewer surprises and a more effective ability to cope with change

➤ An established "plan of battle" for the future, understood and followed by all, and with many critical issues solved before the meetings

➤ TQM drives continuous improvement, with S&OP facilitating this by providing information and a management communication and decision-making structure, guiding everyone's participation

➤ S&OP is a very effective way to allocate scarce capital to the appropriate product line and/or customer

➤ S&OP works well in a privately-held Mexican Company

➤ S&OP works well in a low margin, competitive chemical industry

Go to Chapter 4 to read more about **Benefits**

Lessons Learned

➤ *If you don't manage the daily and weekly steps that maintain accurate information and execute the plans, then you will lose the potential benefits of the S&OP process."* Hector Gil, Vice President, Finance, IT and HR

➤ Senior management, especially the Business Directors, must accept accountability for the outcome. During times of organizational restructuring or new management, if senior management's participation wanes, the process suffers.

➢ Don't institutionalize the status quo. Based on everyone understanding the markets and customers, challenge your business strategies, such as make-to-stock vs. make-to-order.

➢ Pyosa had sharply reduced their planning horizon from twelve months down to three, doing so due to a lack of confidence in their forecasts. This shortened horizon has been shown not to work well for them. The company is in the process of expanding their planning horizon back to its original twelve months, to enable an enhanced focus and attention on understanding the customers and the marketplace. This, we believe is the proper response: make the forecast better to support the longer horizon, rather than to shorten the horizon because of the poor forecasts.

➢ Keys to the implementation of S&OP:

  o Education of all functions
  o Top management leadership
  o Process design by a cross-functional team

➢ *"If we do something uniquely or in a different way, I worry!"* Hector Gil, Vice President, Finance, IT and HR

Go to Chapter 5 to read more about **Lessons Learned**

Consultant's Summary

"What are the chances that a small, family-owned Mexican business would embrace and devote the time, money, management attention and organizational persistence required to properly incorporate World Class methodologies like TQM, ERP/MPPII, DRP and S&OP?

Well when it comes to a well-managed, hard-working group of people like those of Pyosa, the chances were quite good. And the results have been great!

These process management approaches were a perfect match for the Pyosa management culture of openness, respect and a constant search for improvement. S&OP driving an effective detailed resource planning process, proved to be just what Pyosa needed to survive in its cost sensitive, specialty chemical, process environment of global customers, suppliers and competitors.

Pyosa's unique use of S&OP to proactively manage cash flow and dynamically allocate scarce capital to the appropriate product really pays dividends for them.

In the words of their former President and current Chairman, Alberto Fernandez: 'El secreto esta en **pegarse**' *or 'The secret is* **sticking to it**!'"

John R. Dougherty, Consultant

Chapter 24

The Scotts Company

North American Consumer Products

Marysville, Ohio

Lawn and Garden Products

How is S&OP used in a highly seasonal company that has almost doubled its size through acquisitions and internal growth over the last fifteen years?

Approaching Marysville, Ohio, one sees an exit sign stating "Scottslawn Road 1 Mile." It's appropriately green. This leads to the corporate offices of The Scotts Miracle-Gro Company, along with their R&D facility and one of three major plants.

Scotts has had quite a run, growing both internally and through acquisitions: Grace-Sierra, Miracle-Gro, Ortho, and RoundUp. These product lines complement and enhance Scott's traditional business of Turf Builder and related lawn products.

Scotts has received vendor of the year awards from, alphabetically: Ace Hardware, Costco, Home Depot, Sam's Club, and Wal-Mart.

What's Unique

This business unit has highly concentrated sales volume. It sells mainly to relatively few immediate customers: home centers (Lowe's, Home Depot), mass merchandisers (Wal-Mart, K-Mart), clubs (Sam's, Costco), and hardware co-ops (Ace, Pro). These customers can be challenging.

Another challenge is with the extreme seasonality of the business. For lawn products, the main selling season lasts about thirteen weeks: over ninety percent of the sales occur in 25% of the year (see the graph below).

Figure 24-1

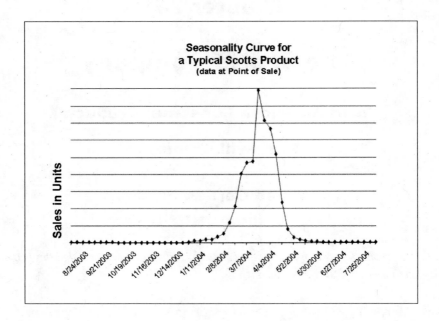

There is also a regulatory aspect to this business. The company products come under review by the U.S. Environmental Protection Agency and its state-level counterparts.

Company Characteristics

Size:

➤ $2 billion in annual sales for the corporation, with the North American business accounting for about $1.7 billion

➤ about 4,000 employees in North America

Products:

➤ Four main product lines, called *brands*:
  - o Lawn Products, including the Turfbuilder line
  - o Miracle-Gro
  - o Ortho
  - o RoundUp

➤ About 1500 SKU's

The Demand Side:

➤ 11 distribution centers

➤ The Order fulfillment strategy is almost entirely make-to-stock

➤ Competitive variables:

   o   Product performance: Scotts' products deliver what they promise; they work.

   o   Brand strength: Scotts brands dominate this industry with a very high market share, and this gives them substantial advertising clout

The Supply Side:

➤ Three plants:

   o   Marysville Ohio: dry fertilizer (mixing, blending and packaging)

   o   Ft. Madison Iowa: Ortho, RoundUp, liquid fertilizer (mixing, blending and packaging)

   o   Temecula California: spreaders and sprayers (fabrication and assembly)

➤ 80% of the products produced in house. Virtually all of the Miracle-Gro products are fully outsourced, reflecting the history of that company.

➤ Typical lead times:

   o   Production: several hours to several days

   o   Purchasing: four to six weeks

Other Tools Employed:

- ➢ Manufacturing resource planning process (MRPII):

  - o Demand management

  - o Master scheduling

  - o MRP

- ➢ Some lean manufacturing and supply chain management efforts:

  - o At the spreader/sprayer plant in California

  - o Just-in-time with suppliers of packaging materials, for example bottles from a key supplier located near the Iowa plant

- ➢ 6 Sigma: efforts in process for about a year

The S&OP Process

- ➢ S&OP was implemented in 1995, following attendance by three key players in a S&OP seminar at Ohio State taught by Tom Wallace

- ➢ Major obstacles were:

  - o Inadequate top management buy-in early in the process

  - o Information had to be drawn from the multiple legacy systems resulting from acquisitions

- ➢ S&OP is done monthly

  - o The current forward planning horizon ranges from eight to eighteen months, depending on the time of year.   They plan to change that to a rolling fifteen months.

  - o 15-20 product families, with a brand focus, but with a good bit of detail on major SKU's because of the predominance of relatively few customers.

o   New product requirements are made highly visible in S&OP to allow for planning capacity in the plants or at suppliers, not only for production but also earlier for line trials.

o   "Gates" for new product launch - product registration, packaging, etc. - are reviewed at the S&OP meetings to check for viability of the plan.

o   The process has migrated from a more or less standard four-step process into what's described below, with an intense focus on the demand side of the business, given the nature of Scott's business (seasonality, mass merchandisers). The process is somewhat unconventional but works well.

Demand Planning

This is a very robust activity at Scotts and represents a majority of the work involved in the entire S&OP planning cycle. It encompasses:

➤   A "consensus" meeting by the business development teams (BDT'S), which are cross-functional groups based on the ground at Wal-Mart, Home Depot, Lowe's, etc.

   o   Includes sales and marketing people, and supply chain individuals who work on the major chains listed above

   o   Led by a director-level person with a sales and marketing background

   o   Generates the POS (Point-of-Sale) forecast (retail demand at the stores) plus the resultant projected replenishment demand from Scotts to the chains, based on pipeline inventory - at stores, DC's etc.

   o   About 80% of the total volume is to customers serviced by Scotts BDT's.

➤   Also generated, back at the home office, is a "non-POS forecast" reflecting customers who don't have a close relationship with Scotts:

   o   A statistical projection based on history, from a standard forecasting software package

   o   Adjusted based on marketing judgment

   o   This is added to the replenishment demand developed by the BDT's

➤ These planned demands are aggregated and reviewed at "Brand Consensus Meetings" for each of the basic business units: Lawn Products, Miracle-Gro, Ortho, and Round Up

o The head of each brand is a Vice President

o This meeting takes four to six hours because it operates largely at an SKU level

Supply Planning

➤ Some initial rough cut capacity planning occurs at the BDT Consensus meetings

➤ "Unsmoothed production plans" (actually shipping plans), by month, are given to the suppliers following each step of the S&OP cycle. If the suppliers want to produce early they're free to do so. But they will be expected to ship in the pattern of the final adjusted production plan from Scotts

➤ SKU production plans are updated based on the latest demand plans from the BDT meetings and the "non-POS" forecasts

➤ Inventory swings, supplier constraints, the need to add a shift or equipment etc., are considered, and production plans are adjusted by Manufacturing and/or Supply Chain Managers to optimize performance

➤ At the Brand Consensus Meeting, there is another rough cut capacity check. Scotts is rarely capacity constrained, maybe once or twice per year across the entire business. They can almost always say "yes", but they do need to know when they have to say no.

Partnership Meetings

There's another set of meetings called "S&OP" both at the BDT (Business Development Team) level and the Brand level:

➤ These sessions deal less with the forecast and more with supply side issues including new products, special promotions, performance data, etc.

➤ Significant production plan change decisions that involve outsourcing, adding major capital equipment or other major impacts are ratified at this meeting.

➤ The Brand S&OP Meeting is attended by the VP in charge of the brand and the Directors of:

Planning
Marketing
Finance
Portfolio Management (new products)
Manufacturing
Purchasing
Customer Service

➤ Metrics are reviewed, problems discussed, and decisions are made

➤ This overall process is unusual; it's a bit like a partnership meeting held *after* the executive S&OP meeting, which at Scotts is the Corporate Consensus Meeting.

The Executive Meeting:

➤ The Corporate Consensus Meeting:

   o The revenue forecasts for all brands across the North American business unit, preliminarily validated for doability, are reviewed from a financial viewpoint as compared to previous forecasts published to Wall Street

   o The output is fed to the corporate staff for financial roll-up data to be reviewed at this Corporate Consensus Meeting, from which revenue projections for Wall Street calls are made.

➤ This series of consensus meetings are mainly focused on forecasting, in both units and dollars, with capacity checks along the way.

➤ Plans for the future include the implementation of S&OP into the European businesses.

Hard Benefits

➤ *"During the last four years, almost half of the company's increase in earnings has come from supply chain savings: inventory down, manufacturing efficiency up, purchase and transportation costs down. All of these are due to improved planning."* Ken Reiff, Vice President, Product Planning

➤ From 2000 to 2003, order fill increased from 91% to 97.8%, virtually all of this due to improved planning made possible by S&OP. Order fill to Lowe's = 99.4%.

➤ During the same period, total inventories (raw, wip and finished goods) dropped 33% - a decrease of $100 million

➤ Reduced the number of warehouses by 2/3.   Some were overlapping legacies from the acquisitions. Most were no longer needed due to better tools for managing the supply chain and to better transportation.

Soft Benefits

➤ *"S&OP is the forum to rally people around a specific issue."* Marilee Cameron, Director, Ortho/RoundUp Planning

➤ Enhanced communications, which Scotts considers the most important benefit because it gets everyone on the same page

➤ A higher level of teamwork

➤ Clarified roles: S&OP taught people who they needed to talk to, why, and when

➤ Much improved new product introductions

➤ S&OP is a vital management process to support a highly seasonal, consumer goods, make-to-stock business

➤ *"S&OP is the catalyst for reaching consensus. It significantly reduces people's ability to play games."* Ken Reiff, Vice President, Product Planning

Go to Chapter 4 to read more about **Benefits**

Lessons Learned

➤ *"S&OP is a great process to help people learn the roles of other functions: what they do and what they're responsible for. This leads to better decisions made more quickly, because people know who to talk to."* Marilee Cameron, Director of Planning, Ortho/RoundUp Business Unit

➤ In hindsight, they would apply more effort initially in educating top management to get their buy-in. This process was especially difficult at Scotts due to many new executives coming on board.

➤ Demand planning collaboration with key customers is vital, especially in a mass merchandisers marketplace

➤ S&OP helps aggregate and integrate information from separate business units, especially those recently acquired

Go to Chapter 5 to read more about **Lessons Learned**

Consultant's Summary

At Scotts, S&OP has survived - and prospered - over the last ten years in an environment of substantial change: major acquisitions, high growth, and many new people in the executive ranks including the chief executive officer.

Today they're much better able to cope with the challenges posed by their extreme seasonality. They collectively decide how early to start producing product in advance of the selling season. When things start to drift away from plan, they can respond much more quickly now because they're all on the same page. Before S&OP, they state, they couldn't do these things well at all.

The conclusions one can draw from this are, first, that S&OP works in highly seasonal businesses. Second, it works for companies selling to mass merchandisers, and supports their efforts to establish and maintain intimate relationships with them. Third, it can survive major changes to its operating environment: new acquisitions, high growth, and executive level changes." Tom Wallace, Consultant

Chapter 25

Unicorn Medical Company (UMC)[33]

Milwaukee, Wisconsin, USA

Medical Devices and Supplies

How well does S&OP work in a heavily matrixed organization? Why would a company successful with lean manufacturing use S&OP?

What's Unique?

Unicorn Medical Company (UMC) was formed over six years ago, as a combination of five different, smaller companies with similar product lines. Some of these companies were divisions of larger corporations that already had well-established business processes, including S&OP.

The major challenge then was to merge these separate businesses into one cohesive, effective, modern manufacturing and distribution company. Creating a single S&OP process for the businesses was an important first step in this integration. Then lean manufacturing was one of the key factors in achieving improvements such as shorter lead times to support more flexible schedules with smaller inventories. Its progress was monitored via the S&OP process.

See Figure 25-1:

---

[33] Unicorn Medical Products is a real corporation, but this is not their real name. They were a full participant in this project, provided us with all the necessary data, and were kind enough to review and verify the information being published about them. But some of the descriptive data about the company - annual sales dollars, number of employees, number of plants and locations - has been changed somewhat to disguise their identity. None of the information about their basic business processes has been modified. However, they have asked that their real name not be used in the book.

Figure 25-1

Major Events in Unicorn Medical Company's Journey From Five
Smaller Companies to a Standalone Publicly Traded Corporation

1994 - Company #1 implemented sales and operations planning
1998 - Company #1 acquired by Company #2
1999 - Company #2 merged with Company #3 (which had recently
        acquired Company #4 and Company #5)
2000 - Became Unicorn Medical Company
2001 - Began implementation of lean manufacturing
2002 - Began use of postponement
2003 - Initial public offering (IPO)
2005 - Stock price reaches 3 times IPO price

Over all these years, sales and operations planning has helped the company's management through all these changes.

Company Characteristics

Size:

➤ 2004 revenues of over $750 million

➤ over 4000 employees

➤ over 26,700 medical devices being used at customer sites

➤ one of the world's largest companies in its segment of medical products

Products: The two major categories of products are:

1. Medical devices - about fifty SKU's

2. Consumable supplies used by these devices - approximately 1,000 SKU's

The Demand Side

Through one hundred sales offices globally, Unicorn Medical Company sales representatives call directly on their customers, primarily hospitals and laboratories, with the key sales objective to place the medical devices at the customer site.

The sale and distribution of supplies and consumables is handled primarily by a network of distributors across the globe, which stock UMC's products and process the individual customer orders. Customers demand short lead times and a very high fill rate. Orders are shipped 98% on time from small finished goods inventories held in Unicorn Medical Company plants and distribution warehouses (two in the US, one in Europe, and one in Asia).

The Supply Side

While the production of some devices is outsourced to Asia and Europe, a majority are assembled in a Unicorn Medical Company plant in Iowa, which has:

➢ assembly lead time of two weeks (thanks to lean manufacturing) - typically shorter than the customer order lead time

➢ supplier lead times of between one and six weeks

➢ finished inventories replenished based on the "pull" of customer orders

Supplies and consumables are made in two plants in Europe and three in the US. They are moving towards cellular manufacturing, and away from functional plant arrangement. The basic steps include: mix, blend and package, with manufacturing lead times at four weeks, down from eight, thanks also to lean manufacturing.

Other Tools Employed

➢ Lean manufacturing

➢ Manufacturing resource planning (MRPII or ERP)

➢ A quality improvement program similar to 6 Sigma

The S&OP Process

"*S&OP establishes base plans for production and sales to measure their performance. We put all of our energy into limiting problems, avoiding organizational disagreements, and achieving these plans.*" Glen Melanson, Vice President, Manufacturing

Thanks to lean manufacturing, S&OP is seen as "*easier*" and less linked to short term decision-making. On the other hand, key managers at the company feel that Lean is somewhat "shortsighted" as regards future demand and capacity shifts. S&OP provides the basis for:

➤ manufacturing and supplier capacity planning

➤ a monthly comparison of dollarized sales and production plans to budgets and business plans

➤ quarterly updates to the business plan

➤ supplier raw material contracts and their future planning

➤ annual financial plans

Demand Planning

➤ forecasts are maintained at the SKU level, twelve to eighteen months into the future

➤ statistical tools are used for supplies and consumables

➤ based on customer inquiries, sales and marketing develop the device forecasts by product

➤ middle management reviews forecast accuracy variations, but by exception only

➤ executive management now rarely reviews forecast accuracy, but monitors only aggregate sales versus revenue targets - this to identify any dramatic changes in sales patterns

➤ sales and marketing are held accountable to meet aggregate revenue targets over the year

➤ maintaining the accuracy of the monthly, detailed forecasts is seen only as a means to give better planning information to manufacturing and the suppliers, so they can adjust their plans and schedules to easily accommodate customer orders when they are received

Supply Planning

➤ production plans maintain small finished goods inventory levels to accommodate some very short lead time repeat business from existing customers

➤ plans are smoothed, taking into account seasonal demands, cyclical demand surges, as well as quarterly and year-end demand surges

➤ assembly orders for equipment are released based on the receipt of customer orders, reflecting the very short final assembly time

➤ the monthly production plan directly drives requirements for key component suppliers, via a technique known as rough cut material planning

➤ the weekly Master Schedule, derived from the monthly production plan, is used to drive requirements planning on all other required parts

➤ for supplies and consumables, reasonable changes to the product mix in the monthly production plan can be made up to fifteen days into the current month

➤ Rough cut capacity planning is vigorously utilized to validate the monthly production plans and weekly master schedules. It is the major tool used for managing manpower levels.

Partnership Meetings

There are ten individual product line meetings, which review all the supply, demand and inventory data covering twenty-seven product lines or categories. Many of the meetings are held consecutively on the same day. They last three to six hours and have director level participants.

➤ Standard S&OP spreadsheets and KPI's are reviewed in detail

➤ The KPI's reviewed include customer service performance, manufacturing performance, bill of material accuracy, master schedule performance and schedule stability

➤ Forecast accuracy is reviewed only by exception, with root cause analysis for inaccurate items, to help focus future improvement efforts

> ➤ Standardized processes across all product lines and locations make it easier for everyone to focus on performance to target and opportunities for improvement

> ➤ Compared to five or ten years ago, more decision-making is now done at the middle management level, in the partnership meeting. This reflects senior management's confidence in the process, the data, and in each participant's understanding and commitment to analyze problems and make decisions in a structured manner.

The Executive Meetings: Five Teams - No Bosses!

The management of the business is done by five product teams, one for each of the five business lines, encompassing the twenty-seven individual product lines of both consumables and supplies, and devices.

> ➤ There are no business unit or product team general managers.

> ➤ Each team is comprised of a cross-functional group of vice presidents, who operate in a matrix or consensus style.

> ➤ There is a designated facilitator for each team (sometimes a marketing person, sometimes an operations person) who guides the process.

> ➤ Generally the teams reach consensus on all decisions that need to be made. In those rare cases where this doesn't happen, the issues are forwarded to corporate headquarters for final resolution.

> ➤ Though difficult, this management approach works. It works because the participants are fully committed to team principles, values and standards of behavior, and because there are well defined processes within S&OP to guide the teams' communications and decision-making.

Every month, there are two full days of meetings for each product team, with extensive use of video and teleconferencing for these meetings. One full-day is devoted to new product development. The other day is devoted to quality, marketing and sales, finance, HR and S&OP.

The S&OP portion of the meeting typically takes three hours, where it used to take up to ten hours. One of the ways they accomplished this was to apply lean manufacturing principles to their S&OP process.

Today, within UMC, sales and operations planning looks like this:

➢ There is a focus on getting at the root causes of problems, thus eliminating arguments and finger-pointing

➢ There is minimal debate about future projections and estimates.

➢ The meeting is highly collaborative and non-adversarial.

➢ The focus is on aggregate totals and performance vs. business targets by business line.

➢ The KPI's reviewed are linked and interconnected, following the approach of the "balanced scorecard"

➢ *Red Means Stop and Look*

   o Specific product detail is reviewed only by exception, when performance to target is lagging.

   o Each KPI and each issue is color-coded in the meeting agenda to facilitate the "by exception" approach:

   Red where there are severe problems, targets not being met, etc.
   Yellow if progress is being made, but not at the desired rate
   Green if things are tracking according to plans and expectations
   Only the red and yellow items are discussed in the meeting

An important part of their S&OP process is the ability to perform real-time analyses of different scenarios within the meetings. The financial consequences of every alternative, and of all the latest plans and variances, are validated within the meeting.

Planning in general, and S&OP specifically, has been simplified due to the decreased variability, shorter lead times and improved confidence in the data that has come with Unicorn Medical Company's lean manufacturing efforts. As we said back in Chapter 7, as the operating environment becomes simpler, the need for highly complex planning tools decreases accordingly.

Hard Benefits

➢ improved customer service (98%+) and delivery reliability

➢ increased flexibility

➢ major cost reductions

➢ inventory reduced by $100 million over the last three years

The inventory reduction was critical in supporting the cash needs for a corporate restructuring, and for taking the company public in 2003.

Soft Benefits

As Glen Melanson, UMC's Vice President of Manufacturing, said: *"Without such a good S&OP process, we would have still pursued the same business improvements. But I don't think we would've achieved the same level of results."*

S&OP provides them with:

➢ a clearer view of business issues

➢ a better connection between operational execution and business results

➢ a greater focus on the future

➢ more effective and collaborative decision-making, following a consistent method

➢ a well-defined forum to focus on supply chain responsiveness

➢ a reasonable ability to predict business performance, because underlying data is sufficiently valid

Go to Chapter 4 to read more about **Benefits**

Lessons Learned

➢ Because stability, predictability and control best enable continuous improvement, lean manufacturing works best when implemented in an environment managed via sales and operations planning and its related resource planning tools

➢ On the other hand, lean manufacturing changes and streamlines processes, including the mechanics and focus of S&OP

➢ So S&OP enables lean manufacturing, <u>and</u> lean manufacturing streamlines S&OP

➢ S&OP is vital for effective matrix management in a global environment, because it provides a consistent, structured approach to data analysis and decision-making

➤ S&OP can serve as a management tool to monitor progress in key initiatives like lean manufacturing, and also quality improvement programs such as 6 Sigma

Go to Chapter 5 to read more about **Lessons Learned**

Consultant's Summary

"Prior to the creation of the Unicorn Medical Company, the individual divisions had implemented S&OP with varying levels of success. After the merger, these processes were enhanced, integrated and extended to all parts of the business. A corporate supply chain management department was created to facilitate and guide improvements in the S&OP process.

Today the focus is on "what needs to be done to support the forecast and the customers." Each participant in the process, regardless of their job function, now thinks more like a "General Manager", seeking to optimize customer service and bottom line business results, not just departmental objectives.

In fact, the S&OP process has grown to become a key management communication framework, which monitors progress in every major business initiative - lean manufacturing, the quality improvement initiative, and others - to ensure that objectives are met." John Dougherty, Consultant

Appendix A

Biographies of the Consultants for the Model Companies

BILL BELT

(Client: ***Danfoss Commercial Compressors***)

President - Bill Belt Excellence
40, rue des Vignobles
Chatou, France F-78400
+33 (0)1.30.09.87.60

bbx@billbelt.com
www.billbelt.com

Bill BELT is the Founder and President of BILL BELT EXCELLENCE (BBX), functional integrators for lean production and supply chain management, assisting companies in audit, education, consulting, implementation and cost-effective usage of modern production and logistic systems. Bill holds a B.A. from Princeton, an MBA from Columbia (U.S.) and is certified CFPIM for life (Certified Fellow in Production and Inventory Management), by APICS.

Bill has worked for thirty years in industry, both in the U.S. and in France, including fourteen years in various management positions, with Westvaco, IBM, Honeywell Bull and Essilor, a French multinational optics manufacturer He has helped many companies to reduce inventories, shorten lead times, reduce costs, raise customer service and increase productivity, including Coca-Cola, Laboratoire Vetoquinol, Messier Bugatti, Alstom, Legrand, SNR Bearings, FCI Connectors, Merck, Techspace Aero, Danfoss, Bombardier, Norton and Novartis.

BILL BELT EXCELLENCE comprises a network of experienced industry and logistics specialists, all of whom have management and operational experience in various industry sectors. BBX runs thirty public classes a year in French and in English in lean supply chain management, high velocity manufacturing, advanced planning systems, sales and operations planning and demand driven supply networks. Many customized in-house classes are run as well. BBX also performs about twenty industrial and logistic audits of individual companies and of supply chains every year.

The BBX Technical Newsletter, a one-page monthly publication on a subject of topical interest, is available free of charge in French and English to anyone who requests it. Information on all BBX services is available on www.billbelt.com.

JOHN J. CIVEROLO

(Clients: *Interbake Foods* and *Norse Dairy Systems*)

Senior Partner - Partners for Excellence
3016 San Patricia, NW
Albuquerque, NM 87107
505-341-0845

CiveroloJJ@aol.com
www.partnersforexcellence.com

John Civerolo is president of **J. J. Civerolo, Inc.** and is a Senior Partner at **Partners for Excellence**, a firm specializing in consulting and education for manufacturing excellence and value/supply chain management and logistics implementations while integrating the lean manufacturing, visual factory, and people involvement and empowerment philosophies. John has helped a variety of manufacturing companies throughout the United States, Europe, North America, Asia, and South America. He has been an active user, educator, and consultant for over thirty years.

John was Director of Management Information Services, Internal Mfg. Consultant, and Materials Manager at Sunbell Corporation in Albuquerque, New Mexico. John holds a Bachelors degree in mathematics from the University of New Mexico. He is a frequent speaker at professional society dinner meetings, APICS conferences, and universities. He has been V. P. of Education for the Albuquerque APICS chapter, and was a committee member for the APICS Basic Supply Chain CPIM module.

John is the author of many widely read articles including:
- "Sales & Operations Planning Handbook" - coauthor
- "Does Your Company Need a Sales & Operations Planning Tune Up?"
- "Unloading the Overloaded Master Production Schedule"
- "Finite or Infinite Capacity Planning - Who Cares?"
- "Agile Manufacturing - Is It Just Another Buzzword?"
- "Are You Ready for Lean Manufacturing?"
- "Demand Pull: What are the Prerequisites for Success?"
- "People Empowerment - How to Guarantee Success"

John has helped many companies achieve supply chain management, manufacturing excellence, world class, and lean manufacturing success. John is known as an industry leader in his field working with companies from entrepreneurial start-ups to Fortune 500 companies.

JOHN R. DOUGHERTY

(Clients: *AGFA US Healthcare, Pyosa* and *Unicorn Medical Company*)

Senior Partner - Partners for Excellence
100 Fox Hill Road
Belmont, New Hampshire, 03220-3816
603-528-0840

jrd1@partnersforexcellence.com
www.partnersforexcellence.com

John is a highly effective counselor to senior management, while providing education and detailed guidance to middle management of manufacturers seeking to improve their management controls and productivity levels. John instructs company-focused education sessions on many topics, including: sales and operations planning (S&OP); sales planning, forecasting and demand management; and master production scheduling (MPS).

John has guided many companies to startling improvements in their business processes. His experience spans the capital goods, chemical, consumer goods, construction equipment, electronics, food, medical products, and pharmaceutical industries.

John has twenty-eight years of consulting experience and nine years of operational experience, including MRPII Project Manager, Materials Manager, Production and Inventory Control Manager and Corporate Planner/Master Scheduler. He was a Senior Industry Consultant for five years for two software firms. He was a Principal Consultant and Educator for The Oliver Wight Companies for nine years. Finally, John was co-founder of Partners for Excellence, and has been a Senior Partner for fourteen years.

John holds an MBA (Summa Cum Laude) from the Rochester (NY) Institute of Technology and a BS in Business Management from the University of Dayton (OH).

John is certified at the fellow level (CFPIM) by the American Production and Inventory Control Society (APICS). He has published numerous papers and articles concerning Management Improvement and Control. John is the co-author of "Sales and Operations Planning - Best Practices". He was co-editor of the Sixth Edition of the APICS Dictionary, and a six-year member of the Master Planning Committee of the APICS Curricula and Certification Council.

JACK GIPS

(Client: *Eli Lilly & Company*)

President, Jack Gips Inc.
57 East Washington Street
Chagrin Falls, Ohio 40022
440-247-2830

jgipsinc@aol.com
www.jackgipsinc.com

Jack Gips is President of Jack Gips, Inc., a firm that has provided high quality consulting and education to manufacturing companies since 1980.

Jack has spent 38 years in Manufacturing, both as a practitioner and as a consultant. Prior to his role as a consultant, Jack served as Production and Inventory Control Manager, Materials Manager, and Manufacturing Operations Manager for a large capital goods manufacturer. During this time, he was responsible for the design, implementation, and operation of a successful manufacturing system.

Jack has provided consulting support on manufacturing processes and systems to companies in many diverse industries.

Jack has also instructed hundreds of public and on-site private seminars for manufacturing companies. In addition, he has made presentations at many professional society conferences and meetings, industry associations, software users' group meetings, and corporate management meetings.

He has authored numerous articles and was Editor of the "Capacity Planning" chapter in The Production and Inventory Control Handbook.

Jack also served for a number of years as a member of the Board of Advisors of the Prentke Romich Company, a manufacturer of augmentative communication technology for people with disabilities.

EDUCATION AND PROFESSIONAL AFFILIATIONS
B.S., Case Institute of Technology
M.B.A., Case Western Reserve University

American Production and Inventory Control Society
Member Production Activity Control Certification Subcommittee (1980-86)
Member Curricula and Certification Council (1986)
Member JIT Certification Subcommittee (1987-92)
Chairman, APICS International Conference (1977)

CHRISTOPHER D. GRAY

(Client: *Coca-Cola Midi*)

Gray Research
181 Bunker Hill Avenue
Stratham NH 03885
USA
1 603 778-9211

cgray@grayresearch.com
www.grayresearch.com

Chris Gray has been at the forefront of applying proven manufacturing management methods and concepts for over three decades. His ideas about resource planning software (MRPII and ERP) have influenced the design of nearly every major ERP software supplier, and his concepts of how lean manufacturing can be supported by software have been used by the leading supplier of enterprise software to the automotive sector to develop a comprehensive lean manufacturing system.

Besides being a recognized authority on software for manufacturing and distribution applications, he provides seminars and workshops as well as consulting to teams implementing resource planning and Lean execution methods. His international consulting practice includes a number of Class A companies.

He has authored three books in addition to this one. In 1987, he authored his first book: *The Right Choice, A Complete Guide to Evaluating, Selecting, and Installing MRPII Software*, the definitive work on evaluating and selecting MRPII software. His books, *The MRPII Standard System, A Handbook for Manufacturing Software Survival* and *The MRPII Standard System Workbook*, both co-authored with Darryl Landvater, were published in 1989 and are generally accepted as defining the standards for MRPII software. He authored over thirty detailed analyses of MRPII and ERP software.

Chris is President of Gray Research and one of the founders of Partners For Excellence. Besides being a past president of the North Shore chapter of APICS and certified by APICS as a Fellow (CFPIM), he is listed in six different volumes of Who's Who: Who's Who in America, Who's Who in the East, Who's Who in America's Emerging Leaders, Who's Who in Finance and Industry, Who's Who in Science and Engineering, and Who's Who in the World.

PHILLIPE J. HEENAN

(Client: *Amcor Flexibles*)

Managing Director - Phil Heenan Consulting
PO Box 7032, Upper Ferntree Gully
Victoria, Australia 3156
61 3 9752 5355

pheenan@bigpond.com
www.heenan.com.au

Phil Heenan, CFPIM, has various supply chain, operations, and logistics qualifications and has served APICS in many positions since joining in 1978. He is in great demand for his practical education and consulting services throughout the Asia Pacific region where he pioneered "Class A" during the 1980s.

His early career was in front line supervision where two of the companies adopted the Lean approach to manufacturing which was totally against standard practice within Australia. He was Group Logistics Manager for Red Tulip and eventually The Beatrice Confectionery Group. As the full time MRPII/DRP Project Manager he was the first to achieve the internationally awarded "Class A" MRPII/DRP by Oliver Wight USA. He was also the first to achieve "Class A" in sales and operations planning in a multi-site environment.

He started his consulting firm in 1988 and was a founding director of Oliver Wight Australia and an Oliver Wight Education Associate from 1988-1993. He has been involved directly in over 35 "Class A" Accreditations, and indirectly a further 20, assisting companies or educating managers in Australia, Korea, China, The Philippines, Hong Kong, Malaysia, Thailand, Singapore and New Zealand. His client list includes an enviable list of Best Practice, Australasian Manufacturers and Distributors.

In 1990 he wrote the chapter on how to implement "Class A" projects based on his experience at Beatrice in the Gower Handbook of Logistics Management edited by John Gattorna, recently republished. Phil speaks at many conferences, including the APICS 2004 Conference held in San Diego, and the 2005 Symposium held in Melbourne Australia.

BILL KERBER

(Client: *EMS*)

Principal, Future State Solutions
P.O. Box 650 Moorestown, NJ 08057
856-220-7257

Bill.Kerber@FutureStateSolutions.com
www.FutureStateSolutions.com

Bill Kerber is a principal and the Vice President of Consulting for Future State Solutions, a firm providing both Lean Transformation software and consulting. He is currently helping several large multinational companies on their Lean journeys. Bill is a member of the faculty of the Lean Enterprise Institute, and has taught for the University of Michigan's Lean Certification Program.

Bill has a very strong manufacturing background, having worked in industry for over twenty-five years. Bill has worked as a manufacturer's representative, for two productivity-consulting firms, for a manufacturer of lawn mowers and bicycles, for two ERP consulting firms, and for several Lean consulting firms. He has specialized in material management systems, as both a practitioner and as a consultant. He is a Dale Carnegie graduate and has spoken to numerous groups including the APICS International Conference in New Orleans, Seattle, and San Diego, the QAD user conference, the Bull Users Society, the Computer Associates Applications Conference, and many APICS chapter meetings. Bill received his APICS Fellow level certification in 1991.

After dabbling in lean manufacturing for many years, Bill has now been working exclusively in that arena for over four years, providing guidance and training for more than twenty companies, including companies in the following industries: aircraft and aerospace, industrial metals, commercial and industrial pumps, hydraulic equipment, electronics, and automotive and industrial bearings. He brings a unique perspective to the Lean world and is currently working to capture some of his thoughts for posterity.

ROBERT A. STAHL

(Client: *Eclipse, Inc.)*

President, R. A. Stahl Company
6 Marlise Drive
Attleboro, MA 02703

RStahlSr@aol.com
www.tfwallace.com

Bob is an educator, author, and consultant, specializing in helping manufacturing companies improve their supply-chain performance. He is President of the R. A. STAHL COMPANY in Attleboro, Massachusetts.

While working in manufacturing management himself, Bob's efforts contributed to an improved ROI from 8% to 48%. Since leaving line management in 1981, Bob's consulting and teaching have helped many companies in varied environments enjoy similar improvements in their performance.

He provides counsel and education at both the management and executive levels of an organization. Bob has worked with organizations in North and South America, Europe and the Far East. His client list includes organizations such as: Angus Chemical, Baker Hughes, Dow Chemical, Eclipse Inc., Film Tec, Henkel, ICI, Jostens, Newell Rubbermaid, Polaroid, Sara Lee, and Tiffany, among many others.

Bob holds a BS degree from Villanova University, was certified (CPIM) by the American Production and Inventory Control Society (APICS) in 1981, and is listed in *Who's Who in America*. He has co-authored four books: "Sales Forecasting: *A New Approach*", "Master Scheduling in the 21st Century", "Building to Customer Demand", and "Sales & Operations Planning: Self Audit Workbook". Bob is working on his fifth book on "Managing Variance on both the Demand & Supply Side." He is a frequent speaker at professional corporate meetings, conferences, seminars, and chapter meetings; being recently distinguished as the *'Best Speaker'* at an International Conference attended by over five-thousand people.

THOMAS F. WALLACE

(Clients: *Cast-Fab Technologies* and *The Scotts Company)*

T. F. WALLACE & COMPANY
P.O. Box 43576
Cincinnati, OH 45243

(513)281-0500
tomwallace@fuse.net
tfwallace.com

Tom Wallace is a writer and teacher - specializing in S&OP, and supply chain management. He is a Distinguished Fellow at Ohio State's Center for Excellence in Manufacturing Management.

Writing

Tom has written or co-authored eleven books, including:

Building to Customer Demand (2005)
Sales & Operations Planning: The How-To Handbook, (2nd Edition, 2004).
Master Scheduling in the 21st Century (2003)
Sales Forecasting - A New Approach (2002)
ERP: Making It Happen - The Implementers' Guide to Success with Enterprise Resource Planning (2000)

Teaching

In his thirty plus years of experience, Tom has developed and taught a variety of seminars to over 10,000 executives, managers and specialists in the United States, Canada, the United Kingdom, and Australia. He has also created the video course, *Sales & Operations Planning - A Visual Introduction* (2003) for the Distance Learning Center at Ohio State.

Other

During his career as a consultant, he worked with companies in a wide variety of industries: consumer packaged goods, clothing, electronics, plastics, industrial equipment, pharmaceuticals, aerospace and defense, furniture, medical equipment, and others.

A native Ohioan, Tom holds an undergraduate degree in liberal arts and an MBA. He served as the editor of the 4th, 5th, and 6th editions of the APICS Dictionary of Production and Inventory Control Terminology.

Index

6 Sigma ..... vi, x, xx, 14, 39, 47, 56, 57, 86, 99, 100, 106, 107, 108, 109, 110, 113, 114, 228, 240, 282, 291, 297

ABCD checklist..85, 86

Accountability.. 231, 234, 262, 277

Accurate information 51, 52, 277

Acquisition 143, 176, 194, 262

Advanced planning systems - APS .... vi, x, 53, 95, 96, 97, 113, 228, 232, 299

AGFA ... iii, viii, xiv, xv, 1, 4, 6, 19, 21, 24, 29, 38, 39, 41, 42, 44, 46, 51, 55, 56, 57, 58, 75, 78, 79, 83, 88, 94, 99, 117, 122, 131, 133, 139, 141, 142, 143, 144, 154, 155, 157, 159, 167, 168, 169, 172, 173, 174, 175, 176, 177, 301

Alignment..47, 50, 215, 230, 256

Amcor ..... iii, viii, xiv, xv, 1, 17, 21, 24, 29, 38, 39, 40, 41, 42, 46, 68, 69, 82, 83, 86, 88, 94, 116, 121, 122, 128, 155, 179, 180, 181, 182, 183, 184, 185, 186, 187, 304

Annual ..... xx, 3, 12, 22, 46, 84, 128, 137, 148, 149, 155, 156, 157, 158, 175, 190, 221, 222, 223, 229, 230, 247, 261, 280, 289, 292

Assam, Emilio 31, 272

Assemble-to-order - ATO 74, 75, 77, 209, 218, 260

Assembly 6, 61, 71, 75, 76, 104, 133, 138, 189, 211, 217, 219, 238, 281, 291, 293

Attendees..... 24, 25, 29, 30, 32, 128, 173, 183, 195, 205, 206, 213, 214, 233, 243, 252, 253, 254, 262, 264, 265, 275

Backlog... 17, 18, 21, 24, 25, 52, 63, 69, 70, 71, 73, 75, 78, 80, 84, 87, 88, 93, 152, 171, 173, 191, 212, 241, 243, 251

Bancel, Stephan 234

Baxter, Ray .... xiii, 18, 257

Belt, Bill..xiii, 2, 216, 299

Best practice companies...... xviii, xxi, 3, 14, 19, 23, 58, 61, 64, 99, 128, 129, 134, 139, 154, 155, 162, 164

Best practices ...... 1, iii, xi, xviii, xix, xx, xxi, 3, 14, 19, 23, 58, 61, 64, 88, 99, 108, 128, 129, 134, 139, 141, 154, 155, 162, 164, 301, 322

Bill of material 92, 93, 94, 213, 251, 263, 293

Blanchard, Michel xiii

Blend-to-Order.. 75

Bohl, Ron .... xiii, 36, 40, 137, 235

Bookings..63, 69, 71, 75, 78, 84

Brinkman, Gunther... 51

Budget preparation vii

Budgeting 45, 149, 156, 157, 158, 162, 175

Build-to-order -- BTO... 75

Bullock, Denise ....xiii, 45

Bushman, Jim 143, 189, 192

Bushman, Ross .... xiii, 22, 43, 45, 106, 192
Business improvements 9, 37, 47, 255, 296
Business plan 12, 18, 22, 27, 30, 46, 53, 94, 120, 137, 150, 152, 155, 157, 162, 172, 212, 221, 222, 223, 229, 230, 231, 243, 245, 256, 257, 265, 268, 272, 292, 321
Business units 34, 35, 118, 210, 249, 284, 287
By exception 57, 172, 176, 254, 292, 293, 295
Cameron, Marilee .... xiii, 43, 286
Capacity ... 9, 11, 14, 19, 20, 24, 25, 26, 28, 32, 40, 45, 46, 47, 51, 52, 63, 64, 66, 67, 68, 77, 78, 79, 82, 91, 92, 93, 94, 97, 100, 102, 105, 106, 108, 113, 114, 115, 117, 121, 122, 124, 125, 136, 140, 143, 157, 159, 172, 173, 175, 182, 183, 187, 193, 194, 196, 202, 204, 205, 208, 213, 215, 220, 223, 225, 228, 231, 232, 233, 234, 235, 242, 245, 250, 251, 252, 253, 254, 255, 256, 261, 262, 263, 264, 265, 266, 267, 268, 271, 274, 275, 276, 283, 284, 285, 292, 293, 300, 302
Capacity requirements planning - CRP 92, 252
Capacity utilization 32, 106, 136, 172, 232, 250, 261
Capital needs .... vii, 157, 266
Capital planning 13, 157, 158
Cash flow ... vii, 9, 10, 38, 39, 65, 68, 144, 149, 159, 170, 174, 195, 237, 244, 273, 274, 278
Cast-Fab Technologies, Inc. .....iii, viii, xiii, 1, 19, 21, 22, 29, 38, 40, 41, 43, 45, 64, 69, 71, 72, 73, 78, 106, 116, 121, 122, 128, 129, 130, 141, 143, 154, 189, 191, 194, 195, 196, 197, 307
Cerminati, Claudio 152
Chemical manufacturing 6
Civerolo, John .... xiii, 2, 94, 257, 268, 300
Class A 38, 86, 93, 94, 109, 174, 181, 202, 249, 261, 272, 303, 304, 321, 322, 323
Clausen, Mads 209
Coca-Cola ...iii, viii, xiii, xiv, xv, 1, 6, 7, 21, 24, 25, 29, 38, 39, 41, 42, 55, 56, 58, 83, 84, 86, 94, 110, 116, 117, 121, 123, 131, 139, 152, 154, 155, 199, 200, 201, 202, 203, 204, 207, 208, 299, 303
Coca-Cola Midi ..... iii, viii, xiii, xiv, xv, 1, 6, 21, 25, 29, 38, 39, 41, 42, 83, 86, 94, 110, 116, 121, 123, 131, 139, 152, 154, 155, 199, 201, 202, 207, 303
Collaborative planning 117, 119, 183, 242
Communication ....x, xvii, 4, 9, 10, 14, 17, 28, 44, 49, 50, 58, 63, 96, 110, 116, 118, 120, 124, 127, 128, 130, 132, 133, 139, 140, 163, 173, 182, 184, 186, 187, 196, 203, 222, 224, 250, 255, 256, 264, 277, 297, 302
Company profiles .... viii, ix, 165
Compromise meeting 28
Computer hardware and software 54
Conformance 107, 259
Consumer products 6, 266
Continuous improvement... 14, 39, 46, 47, 50, 55, 57, 58, 99, 106, 109, 110, 168, 175, 176, 207, 208, 245, 255, 256, 261, 277, 296
Contract manufacturing 247, 248, 256
Cost reduction 4, 40, 152, 170, 175, 234, 295
Cross-functional .... xvii, 4, 13, 28, 44, 50, 127, 128, 130, 134, 139, 140, 156, 173, 181, 186,

202, 238, 249, 257, 261, 264, 272, 278, 283, 294

Customer order management.....................................12, 14, 43, 52, 53, 87, 94, 108, 114, 175

Customer retention...38, 68, 186

Customer service...3, 9, 10, 11, 30, 31, 37, 38, 39, 40, 41, 43, 44, 46, 52, 55, 65, 68, 76, 83, 84, 88, 89, 101, 102, 105, 106, 109, 116, 120, 130, 132, 136, 137, 139, 141, 143, 144, 154, 169, 173, 174, 175, 176, 184, 185, 203, 204, 205, 206, 207, 212, 213, 214, 216, 225, 229, 232, 234, 244, 245, 253, 256, 264, 265, 267, 275, 276, 285, 293, 295, 297, 299

Cycle time reduction...41, 104, 211

Cyclical..47, 63, 71, 197, 293

Danfoss Commercial Compressors..iii, viii, xv, 2, 3, 4, 6, 29, 38, 41, 45, 53, 69, 75, 76, 78, 84, 88, 94, 103, 104, 116, 122, 129, 130, 131, 138, 139, 141, 143, 155, 157, 209, 210, 216, 299

Data accuracy...4, 109, 187, 205, 272

Data gathering and review...v, 20, 26, 34, 35, 87, 137, 229

Decision-making....x, xvii, xviii, 4, 10, 14, 17, 19, 28, 32, 44, 45, 46, 50, 52, 53, 56, 58, 63, 93, 94, 96, 100, 104, 106, 110, 115, 120, 121, 123, 125, 127, 128, 129, 130, 133, 134, 137, 139, 140, 141, 142, 145, 156, 159, 163, 175, 177, 187, 196, 215, 222, 224, 229, 231, 234, 236, 257, 261, 277, 292, 294, 296

Defect...107, 205, 206

Deininger, John F. 157, 267

Delivered in full on time - DIFOT 68, 185

Dell...75, 133, 170

Demand .....v, vii, x, xvii, xx, 9, 10, 11, 12, 13, 14, 18, 20, 21, 22, 23, 25, 26, 27, 30, 31, 32, 33, 35, 36, 39, 40, 41, 43, 46, 47, 49, 50, 51, 52, 53, 54, 63, 65, 66, 68, 70, 71, 72, 73, 74, 75, 76, 77, 78, 80, 81, 83, 85, 86, 87, 88, 89, 90, 91, 92, 93, 95, 96, 97, 100, 101, 102, 103, 104, 105, 106, 108, 109, 113, 114, 115, 116, 117, 118, 119, 120, 121, 122, 125, 130, 133, 134, 135, 136, 137, 142, 143, 144, 147, 148, 152, 154, 156, 157, 158, 159, 161, 162, 163, 167, 169, 172, 179, 180, 182, 183, 184, 185, 186, 187, 189, 191, 193, 194, 195, 196, 197, 199, 201, 203, 204, 206, 207, 209, 210, 211, 212, 213, 214, 215, 216, 218, 219, 220, 221, 222, 223, 224, 226, 228, 229, 230, 231, 232, 233, 234, 235, 236, 237, 239, 240, 241, 242, 243, 244, 248, 250, 251, 252, 253, 254, 260, 262, 263, 264, 265, 266, 270, 272, 273, 274, 275, 276, 281, 282, 283, 284, 286, 291, 292, 293, 299, 300, 301, 304, 306, 307, 321

Demand chain 88, 90, 114, 115, 117, 119, 120

Demand driven supply network (DDSN)...114, 299

Demand management......14, 54, 87, 183, 201, 206, 214, 216, 226, 233, 240, 282, 301, 321

Demand plan, demand planning.......v, x, 22, 23, 25, 27, 35, 46, 65, 80, 87, 89, 90, 91, 101, 116, 118, 120, 121, 122, 137, 162, 172, 182, 193, 194, 195, 203, 204, 212, 213, 219, 226, 229, 232, 235, 241, 250, 262, 264, 272, 273, 274, 283, 284, 286, 292

Demand pull...92, 103, 104

Demand shaping 117

Demand shifting..117

Deming, W. E..107, 219

Design and development..50, 61, 81, 138, 162, 322

Design-to-order - DTO ....vi, xx, 25, 62, 74, 77, 78, 79, 80, 88, 91, 116

Diaz Trillo, Guillermo..38

Distribution cost 68, 185

Distribution resource planning - DRP vi, 52, 87, 89, 90, 115, 118, 228, 230, 272, 278, 304, 321

Dougherty, John ....iii, iv, xxi, 1, 3, 177, 278, 297, 319, 320

Downtime 40, 102, 250, 255, 266

Duchêne, Philippe 53

Eclipse, Inc. .....iii, viii, xiv, xv, 2, 6, 24, 29, 38, 43, 46, 53, 57, 69, 74, 75, 78, 105, 116, 122, 128, 129, 130, 131, 133, 137, 217, 219, 221, 222, 224, 306

Education.... 51, 106, 132, 208, 214, 228, 235, 268, 278, 299, 300, 301, 302, 304, 306, 321, 322, 323

Efficiency 39, 40, 41, 42, 58, 79, 106, 110, 115, 119, 171, 176, 185, 192, 240, 266, 285

Egido, Antonio..116

Eli Lilly & Company.....iii, viii, xiii, 2, 4, 6, 21, 22, 24, 35, 36, 40, 46, 51, 53, 56, 57, 58, 82, 86, 88, 90, 94, 96, 97, 106, 116, 122, 124, 131, 135, 137, 139, 143, 154, 155, 158, 225, 234, 302

Empowerment...44, 45, 261, 300

Engineered Materials Solutions, Inc. (EMS) .... iii, viii, xiv, xv, 2, 6, 21, 24, 29, 38, 39, 41, 57, 69, 75, 77, 78, 88, 101, 103, 105, 110, 116, 122, 128, 129, 130, 131, 133, 139, 141, 144, 157, 237, 238, 239, 240, 242, 243, 244, 305

Engineering......xx, 17, 31, 41, 47, 50, 74, 77, 78, 79, 90, 109, 162, 220, 223, 233, 254, 260, 262, 263, 264, 265, 266, 267, 268, 303, 323

Engineer-to-order - ETO 47, 77, 218, 260, 266, 267

Enterprise resource planning - ERP ...... vi, x, 13, 14, 37, 39, 51, 54, 56, 85, 86, 90, 96, 97, 127, 128, 150, 167, 181, 187, 211, 219, 227, 228, 231, 273, 278, 291, 303, 305, 307, 321, 322

Executive meeting ....v, 18, 19, 21, 23, 26, 27, 28, 29, 30, 31, 35, 58, 79, 88, 93, 128, 132, 133, 134, 173, 174, 184, 185, 203, 204, 221, 242, 275

Executive participation ....x, 31

Fabrication 61, 75, 138, 143, 181, 189, 191, 192, 194, 211, 217, 219, 281

Family ..12, 17, 19, 21, 24, 25, 26, 27, 30, 41, 52, 57, 63, 85, 87, 88, 89, 91, 92, 93, 94, 103, 116, 118, 122, 128, 129, 130, 131, 132, 136, 148, 154, 171, 172, 183, 184, 204, 206, 207, 209, 211, 212, 213, 217, 219, 220, 222, 229, 230, 231, 240, 241, 242, 243, 251, 252, 263, 269, 273, 278

Fernandez, Alberto..57, 278

Fernandez, Jose 44, 276

Finance ...... xiv, xx, 17, 23, 27, 31, 50, 52, 55, 115, 138, 140, 152, 162, 169, 173, 175, 187, 214, 221, 244, 267, 276, 277, 278, 285, 294, 303, 323

Financial impact..27, 64, 129, 152, 155, 172

Financial planning.........................vii, x, 45, 147, 148, 149, 152, 155, 156, 157, 158

Financial plans.................33, 41, 46, 53, 147, 148, 149, 150, 152, 154, 157, 159, 267, 292

Finished goods inventory 61, 63, 64, 65, 68, 69, 70, 76, 77, 89, 90, 101, 152, 170, 226, 239, 249, 293

Finish-to-order - FTO..vi, 24, 25, 62, 63, 74, 75, 76, 77, 78, 79, 87, 91, 113, 116, 209, 224, 239

Flexibility.... 47, 62, 68, 77, 102, 104, 106, 139, 193, 205, 211, 218, 239, 244, 245, 252, 295

Food and beverage.. 61

Forecast error 41, 77, 88, 244, 251, 262

Forecasting....... xvii, xx, 12, 14, 21, 22, 26, 42, 43, 49, 52, 53, 87, 88, 91, 94, 96, 103, 108, 114, 116, 117, 118, 119, 136, 170, 172, 175, 182, 183, 187, 194, 203, 212, 215, 220, 226, 230, 238, 241, 245, 250, 283, 285, 301, 306, 307, 321

Forecasts....... 17, 21, 23, 24, 46, 47, 52, 53, 63, 81, 82, 85, 87, 88, 89, 90, 91, 93, 108, 113, 115, 116, 117, 119, 127, 136, 158, 172, 174, 183, 193, 203, 204, 205, 212, 213, 219, 230, 231, 232, 234, 241, 242, 244, 251, 263, 265, 272, 273, 278, 284, 285, 292

Forecasts, statistical 20, 22, 23, 172, 183, 212, 220, 230, 242, 262

Four fundamentals 10, 12

Frequency...53, 91, 235

Fullbright, Scott...xiv, 256, 268

Future of S&OP .... vii, x

Future visibility...80, 102

Gehring, Dan...40, 234

Gil, Hector .... xiv, 52, 55, 277, 278

Gips, Jack.. xiv, 2, 95, 236, 302

Global .... v, vii, xi, xiii, xv, xx, 4, 9, 28, 29, 32, 33, 34, 35, 36, 38, 40, 45, 46, 56, 86, 90, 97, 124, 127, 130, 131, 132, 133, 134, 135, 136, 137, 138, 141, 145, 155, 157, 158, 159, 163, 164, 167, 169, 172, 173, 174, 176, 209, 213, 214, 226, 227, 228, 229, 230, 231, 232, 233, 234, 235, 236, 241, 244, 278, 296

Global S&OP ......v, 4, 33, 124, 132, 133, 134, 135, 136, 137, 155, 157, 159, 172, 174, 214, 229, 236

Graphical representations 52

Gray, Chris..iii, iv, xxi, 1, 208, 303, 321

Growth 7, 9, 40, 43, 80, 82, 84, 130, 137, 139, 156, 157, 209, 216, 219, 222, 223, 225, 234, 261, 279, 287

Hard benefits ...... vi, x, 37, 42, 174, 185, 195, 207, 214, 222, 234, 244, 255, 265, 276, 285, 295

Hazeldine, Graeme .... xiv, 17, 39, 182, 185

Heenan, Phil..xiv, 1, 187, 304

High growth..84, 287

Horizon 22, 23, 24, 26, 45, 53, 64, 69, 71, 81, 89, 92, 100, 105, 123, 125, 136, 137, 156, 158, 159, 171, 183, 190, 193, 194, 212, 229, 231, 232, 241, 245, 278, 282

Initial public offering - IPO 7, 141

Integration..12, 105, 141, 152, 157, 162, 163, 172, 175, 265, 289

Interbake Foods ... iii, viii, xiii, 2, 4, 18, 26, 29, 31, 39, 40, 41, 44, 45, 55, 57, 68, 84, 86, 88, 93, 108, 116, 117, 119, 122, 139, 141, 142, 144, 152, 154, 155, 247, 252, 259, 262, 300

Inventory .... xviii, 4, 14, 17, 18, 20, 24, 27, 32, 38, 39, 40, 41, 42, 44, 46, 47, 51, 52, 55, 61, 63, 64, 65, 66, 67, 68, 69, 70, 71, 75, 76, 77, 84, 88, 89, 90, 92, 100, 101, 102, 103, 104, 105, 106, 108, 114, 115, 116, 117, 118, 119, 120, 121, 122, 123, 124, 125, 130, 132, 133, 134, 135, 139, 141, 144, 145, 148, 152, 154, 155, 156, 158, 159, 169, 170, 171, 172, 173, 174, 175, 176, 179, 181, 182, 184, 185, 191, 195, 200, 205, 206, 207, 211, 212, 214, 215, 225, 226, 227, 229, 230, 231, 232, 234, 235, 239, 240, 242, 243, 244, 245, 249, 253, 256, 261, 264, 265, 266, 273, 275, 283, 284, 285, 293, 296, 299, 301, 302, 306, 307, 321, 322

Inventory accuracy... 56
Inventory reduction...4, 159, 175, 234, 266, 296
Inventory target.......................... 65, 66, 130, 154, 159, 232, 243
Investment decisions...149, 186
Jaggard, Malcolm .... xiv, 51, 57, 99, 141, 143, 171, 176
Kanban...92, 103, 104, 211
Kerber, Bill.. xiv, 2, 101, 245, 305
Key performance indicator - KPI......18, 20, 22, 30, 37, 43, 46, 55, 56, 84, 88, 121, 131, 134, 154, 155, 171, 174, 180, 205, 206, 230, 274, 276, 293, 295
Lafon, Rémi xiv
Lean manufacturing.......vi, x, xi, xx, 9, 14, 24, 37, 41, 47, 56, 57, 75, 76, 77, 86, 91, 92, 99, 100, 101, 102, 103, 104, 105, 106, 108, 110, 113, 114, 142, 144, 163, 192, 209, 211, 213, 214, 215, 216, 217, 219, 223, 228, 237, 240, 241, 242, 244, 245, 261, 267, 282, 289, 291, 292, 294, 295, 296, 297, 300, 303, 304, 305, 321, 322
Length of meetings..29, 32
Lessons learned ..... iii, vi, x, xi, xviii, 30, 32, 48, 49, 162, 176, 187, 196, 197, 208, 215, 223, 224, 235, 245, 256, 267, 268, 277, 278, 286, 287, 296, 297
Level of detail..24, 25
Leveraged Buy Out - LBO 7, 39, 141, 144, 237, 244
Ling, Richard ....xiv, 13
Linking....................vi, vii, 12, 13, 40, 85, 88, 89, 94, 116, 119, 121, 126, 272
Logistics........................ xx, 31, 114, 169, 199, 201, 207, 213, 214, 299, 300, 304, 321
Make-to-order - MTO....... vi, xi, xx, 25, 27, 52, 62, 69, 70, 71, 74, 75, 78, 87, 91, 116, 180, 197, 259, 266, 278
Make-to-stock - MTS .....vi, xx, 24, 26, 27, 62, 63, 64, 66, 67, 68, 70, 74, 76, 77, 78, 87, 88, 91, 115, 116, 180, 202, 218, 226, 239, 278, 281, 286
Manufacturing .... xvii, xx, 6, 9, 12, 13, 18, 20, 21, 22, 24, 25, 29, 31, 32, 34, 35, 41, 42, 45, 47, 49, 50, 51, 52, 62, 71, 75, 77, 78, 80, 81, 85, 86, 89, 90, 91, 92, 93, 94, 95, 96, 97, 99, 100, 102, 104, 105, 106, 108, 109, 110, 113, 114, 116, 117, 119, 120, 121, 122, 124, 127, 131, 134, 136, 137, 138, 139, 140, 149, 156, 157, 159, 161, 162, 163, 164, 169, 171, 175, 176, 179, 181, 182, 185, 192, 193, 199, 200, 201, 202, 203, 204, 205, 207, 208, 209, 218, 219, 220, 223, 225, 226, 227, 228, 229, 230, 231, 232, 234, 235, 237, 238, 239, 240, 245, 247, 248, 249, 250, 256, 257, 259, 261, 262, 266, 267, 271, 272, 274, 275, 277, 285, 289, 291, 292, 293, 296, 299, 300, 302, 303, 304, 305, 306, 321, 322, 323
Manufacturing resource planning - MRP II vi, x, 13, 14, 51, 85, 86, 90, 93, 94, 96, 97, 109, 152, 181, 185, 187, 192, 202, 203, 205, 211, 214, 219, 227, 228, 249, 255, 261, 272, 282, 291, 301, 303, 304, 321, 322, 323
Market channel...76, 116, 119, 256
Market share 3, 38, 73, 108, 176, 214, 247, 276, 281
Marketing .....xx, 12, 14, 20, 21, 22, 23, 27, 30, 31, 33, 38, 43, 50, 51, 53, 56, 77, 81, 83, 88, 93, 95, 105, 109, 118, 119, 120, 136, 137, 138, 140, 144, 149, 158, 159, 162, 172, 173, 175, 183, 185, 204, 216, 219, 220, 221, 226, 230, 231, 243, 244, 245, 250, 251, 252, 254, 255, 256, 262, 263, 264, 265, 266, 267, 276, 277, 283, 285, 292, 294
Martin, Andre 89
Mass merchandisers................................ xi, 68, 117, 118, 119, 279, 283, 286, 287

Master production scheduling, master scheduling - MPS. xx, 14, 21, 26, 43, 52, 53, 91, 93, 94, 113, 175, 183, 192, 204, 205, 219, 220, 266, 301, 306, 307, 321

Material requirements planning - MRP.... 12, 85, 89, 92, 103, 173, 184, 185, 187, 192, 194, 202, 203, 205, 211, 274, 282

Materials .... xx, 17, 31, 42, 61, 76, 79, 80, 81, 90, 92, 94, 104, 106, 117, 122, 125, 133, 162, 170, 181, 200, 201, 202, 205, 231, 237, 238, 252, 266, 269, 271, 274, 282

Matrix organizations .... vii, xx, 138, 139, 145

Melanson, Glen 28, 37, 56, 106, 292, 296

Merger 7, 297

Mix .... v, vi, 10, 11, 12, 13, 14, 15, 19, 21, 24, 26, 52, 53, 77, 85, 92, 93, 94, 101, 104, 135, 148, 172, 183, 199, 213, 220, 237, 240, 245, 251, 291, 293

Model companies ..... xi, xviii, xix, xx, xxiii, 15, 19, 20, 23, 25, 29, 31, 36, 37, 47, 48, 53, 55, 62, 69, 78, 86, 96, 103, 106, 108, 113, 116, 121, 122, 128, 129, 142, 162, 299

Monthly ...... v, xvii, 17, 19, 22, 24, 25, 30, 34, 44, 46, 52, 54, 81, 84, 87, 88, 89, 91, 93, 94, 116, 121, 132, 136, 149, 152, 154, 155, 156, 157, 158, 171, 174, 182, 184, 187, 193, 203, 206, 212, 213, 223, 229, 230, 231, 241, 251, 254, 263, 273, 274, 276, 282, 292, 293, 299

New product development ...... vi, xx, 13, 23, 25, 37, 40, 42, 47, 61, 80, 82, 83, 84, 86, 102, 113, 114, 140, 164, 187, 200, 228, 232, 234, 254, 267, 294

Norse Dairy Systems . iii, viii, xiv, 2, 6, 21, 25, 26, 29, 39, 40, 41, 42, 44, 46, 47, 50, 55, 69, 75, 78, 79, 80, 84, 86, 88, 90, 106, 109, 116, 117, 122, 139, 141, 142, 144, 152, 154, 155, 157, 247, 251, 252, 253, 254, 256, 259, 260, 261, 262, 263, 264, 265, 267, 268, 300

Number of meetings: 29, 32

Obsolescence 39, 67, 68, 76, 99, 180, 186

Offshore 6, 121, 161

Olson, Eric J. xiv

On-time 38, 39, 41, 42, 74, 79, 106, 171, 180, 205, 222, 230, 231, 244, 263, 265

Operational takt time 101, 102, 103, 213

Order fill 38, 68, 285

Order fulfillment 61, 62, 63, 64, 75, 84, 201, 209, 226, 249, 281

Order fulfillment strategy 62, 63, 75, 84, 281

Original equipment manufacturer - OEM 9, 76, 133, 189, 210, 212, 237

Outsource 27, 121

Outsourcing .... vii, 27, 121

Overtime 10, 26, 39, 40, 45, 46, 66, 79, 81, 101, 121, 148, 182, 185, 186, 264, 265, 267

Ownership .... vii, x, 4, 44, 47, 49, 57, 83, 90, 127, 129, 130, 141, 142, 143, 144, 145, 176, 208, 244, 255, 268

Participation .... x, xx, 31, 49, 50, 51, 56, 57, 110, 116, 117, 122, 125, 131, 140, 142, 145, 162, 163, 176, 182, 216, 219, 252, 255, 277

Partners .... iii, iv, xiii, xxi, 18, 88, 89, 90, 102, 113, 114, 115, 116, 119, 120, 121, 122, 123, 124, 125, 126, 135, 137, 163, 226, 229, 240, 300, 301, 303, 321, 322

Partnership meeting.... v, 25, 26, 27, 28, 29, 30, 35, 44, 45, 52, 79, 122, 128, 133, 144, 145, 172, 173, 176, 184, 195, 204, 205, 206, 221, 232, 242, 252, 254, 256, 264, 265, 268, 275, 284, 285, 293, 294

Performance review 52, 154, 193

Performance to plan 4

Perks, Doug 219
Perks, Lach.. xiv, 43, 137, 219, 223
Planning horizon:.. 22
Plant schedules 92
Point of sale - POS 117, 118, 163, 283, 284
Postponement 47, 74, 75, 76, 77, 209, 211, 223, 224
Pradeilles, Didier.. xv, 45
Pre-build... 67, 68
Predictable.. 42, 47, 49, 51, 66, 108, 110, 203
Pre-production services 78
Pre-S&OP meeting...28, 221
Privately held 197
Privately-held.................................... vii, 127, 129, 130, 145, 189, 197, 277
Process design 50, 51, 54, 55, 56, 81, 114, 131, 132, 133, 134, 278
Product variety 75, 76
Production planning.............................. 14, 52, 85, 162, 183, 193, 219, 231
Profit... 10, 37, 52, 63, 130, 139, 149, 150, 154, 223
Profitability 9, 17, 23, 42, 43, 66, 100, 108, 137, 144, 222, 223, 237, 277
Pryor, Bob... xv, 38, 142, 174
Purchase costs 40
Pyosa .... viii, 6, 21, 29, 31, 38, 39, 41, 42, 44, 45, 52, 55, 57, 58, 86, 90, 94, 109, 116, 121, 125, 128, 129, 131, 133, 154, 155, 158, 269, 270, 271, 272, 278, 301
Rabhi, Michel.. xv
Reconciliation meeting... 28
Regional. 33, 34, 46, 82, 89, 90, 116, 122, 131, 132, 133, 134, 135, 138, 145, 159, 172, 174, 204, 212, 213, 214, 215, 226, 230, 231, 250, 272, 322
Reiff, Ken.. xv, 42, 44, 119, 285, 286
Resource planning ... vi, 13, 14, 51, 68, 85, 86, 87, 89, 90, 92, 93, 94, 95, 97, 100, 107, 109, 110, 114, 115, 125, 128, 142, 163, 167, 181, 192, 202, 228, 249, 255, 261, 272, 278, 282, 291, 296, 303, 307, 321, 322
Retail sales data 117
Revenue..... 23, 40, 63, 64, 66, 71, 81, 82, 120, 139, 149, 150, 152, 154, 158, 168, 174, 210, 234, 273, 285, 292
Revenue shortfall 71, 120
Rough cut capacity planning - RCCP .. 52, 78, 91, 92, 93, 94, 102, 105, 122, 173, 183, 194, 204, 208, 242, 245, 252, 263, 274, 275, 284, 293
Rough cut material planning - RCMP 92, 94, 220, 293
Sales . 1, iii, v, ix, xi, xvii, xx, xxi, 25, 1, 3, 7, 9, 10, 12, 13, 14, 15, 17, 18, 20, 21, 22, 23, 24, 26, 27, 28, 30, 31, 33, 34, 38, 40, 43, 46, 49, 50, 51, 52, 53, 54, 55, 56, 57, 63, 64, 65, 67, 69, 71, 74, 77, 78, 80, 81, 82, 84, 85, 87, 88, 89, 90, 93, 95, 96, 97, 99, 100, 101, 105, 109, 113, 114, 116, 117, 118, 119, 124, 131, 133, 134, 135, 137, 138, 139, 140, 142, 144, 147, 148, 149, 150, 152, 154, 155, 158, 159, 161, 162, 163, 168, 169, 171, 172, 174, 175, 179, 180, 182, 183, 185, 189, 190, 191, 193, 194, 195, 203, 205, 209, 210, 212, 213, 214, 215, 216, 217, 218, 219, 220, 221, 222, 223, 224, 226, 228, 229, 230, 231, 232, 233, 234, 236, 238, 239, 241, 243, 244, 245, 247, 248, 250, 251, 252, 253, 254, 255, 256, 259, 260,

261, 262, 263, 264, 265, 266, 267, 269, 270, 271, 273, 274, 275, 276, 277, 279, 280, 283, 289, 290, 291, 292, 294, 296, 299, 300, 301, 304, 306, 307, 321, 322

Sales plans 17, 152

Scrap 17, 40, 108, 109, 250, 266

Seasonal .... xi, 47, 63, 67, 68, 77, 237, 239, 247, 251, 256, 279, 286, 287, 293

Seasonality .... vi, 66, 67, 105

Semi-finished inventory 75, 84

Shewhart 107

Shewhart, Walter 107

Shipments 63, 64, 68, 70, 71, 78, 191, 207, 230, 231, 239, 249

Simulation 66, 96, 97, 154

Single company game plan 50, 94, 256, 257

Small companies .... vii, 127, 128, 129, 145

Soft benefits .... x, 36, 42

Soft Benefits ...... vi, 42, 49, 175, 186, 196, 207, 215, 222, 234, 244, 255, 266, 277, 286, 296

Software .... xi, xvii, xviii, 13, 22, 54, 79, 85, 95, 96, 97, 118, 128, 170, 220, 230, 231, 232, 283, 301, 302, 303, 305, 321, 322, 323

SPC 107, 109, 243, 249

Stahl, Bob .... xv, 2, 75, 224, 306

State of the art xviii

Statistical process control - SPC 107, 108, 109, 243, 247, 249

Stevick, Kevin .... xv, 24, 241

Stocking policies 205

Subsidiary 80, 131, 133, 247, 251, 252

Success factors 223

Supplier schedules 92

Supply .. v, vii, x, xi, xiii, xiv, xv, xvii, xx, 9, 10, 11, 12, 13, 14, 17, 18, 20, 21, 22, 23, 24, 25, 26, 27, 30, 31, 32, 33, 35, 36, 37, 39, 40, 41, 42, 43, 47, 49, 50, 51, 52, 53, 56, 57, 62, 63, 64, 65, 66, 69, 70, 71, 75, 76, 77, 78, 81, 82, 83, 85, 86, 87, 88, 89, 90, 91, 93, 95, 97, 99, 100, 101, 102, 103, 106, 108, 113, 114, 115, 118, 119, 120, 121, 122, 123, 124, 125, 126, 130, 133, 134, 135, 136, 137, 142, 143, 144, 147, 148, 149, 152, 154, 156, 157, 158, 159, 161, 162, 163, 169, 171, 172, 173, 174, 175, 176, 181, 182, 183, 184, 185, 186, 189, 191, 194, 195, 197, 199, 200, 201, 202, 203, 204, 205, 207, 208, 209, 211, 213, 214, 215, 216, 218, 220, 221, 222, 223, 224, 225, 227, 228, 229, 230, 231, 232, 233, 234, 235, 236, 239, 240, 242, 244, 245, 248, 250, 251, 252, 253, 254, 260, 263, 264, 265, 268, 271, 274, 276, 281, 282, 283, 284, 285, 286, 291, 293, 296, 297, 299, 300, 304, 306, 307, 321

Supply chain. x, xi, 14, 20, 24, 25, 31, 42, 47, 50, 51, 53, 56, 62, 71, 76, 82, 89, 90, 97, 102, 113, 114, 115, 118, 119, 120, 121, 122, 123, 124, 125, 126, 130, 133, 136, 143, 144, 147, 159, 161, 162, 163, 169, 172, 175, 182, 186, 189, 197, 200, 201, 202, 207, 208, 209, 215, 216, 225, 227, 229, 230, 231, 232, 233, 234, 235, 236, 240, 244, 245, 282, 283, 285, 286, 296, 297, 299, 300, 304, 307, 321

Supply chain management vii, xi, xiv, 14, 24, 31, 47, 50, 51, 56, 57, 99, 114, 115, 123, 124, 125, 126, 136, 143, 159, 161, 169, 171, 172, 173, 175, 176, 182, 201, 202, 209, 215, 216, 227, 229, 230, 231, 232, 235, 236, 244, 245, 282, 297, 299, 300, 307, 321

Supply plan .... x, 35, 205

Supply plan, supply planning . v, x, 17, 18, 20, 21, 22, 24, 25, 26, 27, 30, 31, 35, 63, 64, 65, 66, 69, 70, 75, 77, 81, 83, 85, 86, 87, 88, 90, 91, 93, 95, 102, 103, 113, 115, 121, 122, 123, 124, 125, 133, 147, 148, 149, 154, 157, 158, 163, 172, 183, 194, 204, 205, 207, 213, 220, 231, 235, 242, 245, 251, 252, 263, 268, 274, 284, 293

Supply planning...x, 35

Tabular display 52

Takt time 101, 103, 240

Teamwork..........................4, 10, 28, 44, 49, 50, 58, 140, 143, 175, 186, 236, 244, 255, 286

The Danfoss Group ....iii, 2, 209

The Scotts Company ..iii, viii, xiii, xv, 3, 6, 21, 24, 29, 38, 39, 40, 42, 43, 44, 53, 67, 68, 88, 106, 110, 116, 117, 118, 119, 122, 131, 141, 143, 144, 155, 279, 281, 283, 284, 285, 286, 287, 307

Third party manufacturers.... 41, 46, 120, 121, 122, 124, 136, 159, 208, 227, 231, 233, 236, 266

Third party manufacturing vii

Thomas, Kenneth 51

Top management.. 18, 19, 25, 44, 49, 51, 54, 56, 58, 84, 128, 134, 137, 145, 154, 155, 162, 176, 215, 236, 256, 282, 286

Total quality management -- TQM . vi, xx, 14, 37, 39, 47, 51, 56, 57, 86, 99, 107, 108, 110, 114, 203, 240, 243, 249, 255, 272, 277, 278

Townsend, Jeff...xv, 219

Trillo, Guillermo Diaz..38

Two-level master scheduling...91, 113

UMC ..... iii, 3, 55, 56, 57, 58, 75, 76, 84, 86, 88, 94, 104, 105, 106, 110, 131, 139, 140, 141, 142, 143, 144, 154, 155, 159, 289, 291, 294, 296

Unicorn Medical Company .. iii, viii, xx, 3, 4, 6, 21, 22, 28, 29, 31, 32, 37, 39, 41, 117, 122, 289, 291, 295, 297, 301

Value-stream mapping 102, 103, 104, 211, 240

Variability......................................87, 105, 106, 108, 109, 110, 189, 203, 255, 295

Variation..54, 106, 107, 108, 243, 272

Vendor managed inventory - VMI..119

Visibility..... 9, 12, 41, 42, 45, 63, 74, 78, 80, 84, 85, 102, 119, 120, 125, 137, 159, 176, 196, 215, 222, 223, 229, 234, 235, 250, 256, 267

VMI...119

Volume v, vi, 10, 11, 12, 13, 14, 19, 21, 25, 26, 29, 64, 66, 67, 74, 77, 81, 83, 85, 88, 93, 94, 101, 116, 118, 121, 124, 125, 149, 157, 158, 163, 169, 170, 172, 180, 195, 196, 199, 200, 201, 202, 203, 206, 211, 212, 218, 220, 222, 225, 230, 237, 239, 240, 245, 251, 252, 259, 266, 279, 283

Wallace, Tom ....xv, xvii, 1, 3, 43, 75, 197, 224, 282, 287, 307

Waste 47, 100, 102, 106, 161, 181, 245, 261, 267, 272

Were, Peter ....xv, 183

Weston Foods ....iii, 2, 141, 155, 247

What-if...96, 154, 163, 231

Wight, Oliver...85, 118, 301, 304, 321, 323

About the Authors

John Dougherty:

John has, since 1977, provided direction for manufacturers and distributors seeking to improve their management controls and productivity levels. John instructs private, company-focused education sessions on many topics, including: logistics, value/supply chain management, lean manufacturing, ERP and manufacturing resource planning (MRPII) for senior, functional and project management; sales and operations planning (S&OP); sales planning, forecasting and demand management; distribution resource planning (DRP); master production scheduling (MPS); supplier management; plant scheduling; and inventory record accuracy.

John has guided companies to successful improvements in their logistics, lean manufacturing, resource management and planning and control processes and systems through a process management approach, utilizing state-of-the-art software tools, including ERP systems. Many of them have reached the coveted "Class A" or "World Class" level of achievement. His experience spans the electronics, consumer goods, food, medical products, capital goods, construction equipment, pharmaceutical and chemical industries.

Areas of expertise and emphasis include:

o   Logistics, lean manufacturing, value/ supply chain, ERP and MRPII implementation projects
o   Cross-functional business plan reconciliation and management through sales and operations planning (S&OP)
o   Sales planning, forecasting and demand management
o   Master production scheduling (MPS) policies and approaches
o   Distribution resource planning (DRP)
o   Supplier management
o   Plant scheduling
o   Inventory record accuracy in all environments
o   Issues specific to flow/process and repetitive industries
o   Techniques for planning and scheduling, inventory control and analysis, and purchasing
o   System effectiveness audits leading to "remedial" and "fine-tuning" approaches to maximize system benefits

John was co-founder of Partners for Excellence, and has been a senior partner for fourteen years. For nine years he was a Principal of The Oliver Wight Associates. For five years he provided and managed consulting for two major software vendors. Prior to that, the positions he held included: MRPII Project Manager, Materials Manager, Production and Inventory Control Manager and Corporate Planner/Master Scheduler.

John holds an MBA (Summa Cum Laude) from the Rochester (NY) Institute of Technology and a BS in Business Management from the University of Dayton (OH).

John is certified at the fellow level (CFPIM) by the American Production and Inventory Control Society (APICS). He is a frequent speaker at international, regional and chapter meetings of many professional and industrial groups and has published numerous papers and articles concerning Management Improvement and Control. John is the co-author, with Chris Gray, of the book "Sales and Operations Planning – Best Practices". He was co-editor of the Sixth Edition of the APICS Dictionary, and a six-year member of the Master Planning Committee of the APICS Curricula and Certification Council.

Christopher Gray:
Chris Gray has been at the forefront of applying proven manufacturing management methods and concepts for three decades. Since 1979, he has helped more manufacturing and distribution companies resolve resource planning software issues than anyone else in the field. He has been involved in the design and development of both resource planning and lean manufacturing software. His ideas about resource planning software (MRPII and ERP) have influenced the design of nearly every major supplier in the field, and his concepts of how lean manufacturing can be supported by software have been used by the leading supplier of enterprise software to the automotive sector to develop a comprehensive lean manufacturing system.

He has authored four books, over thirty in-depth software evaluations, and thirty published articles on ERP, enterprise software, and computers in manufacturing. He is also designed the "e-Sales and Operations Planner", a comprehensive stand-alone sales and operations planning system that has been downloaded from his internet site by hundreds of companies. Besides being a recognized authority on the software available for manufacturing and distribution applications, he provides seminars and workshops as well as consulting to teams implementing resource planning and Lean execution methods. His international consulting practice includes a number of Class A companies.

In 1987, he authored his first book: *The Right Choice, A Complete Guide to Evaluating, Selecting, and Installing MRPII Software*, the definitive work on evaluating and selecting MRPII software. His books, *The MRPII Standard System, A Handbook for Manufacturing Software Survival* and *The MRPII Standard System Workbook*, co-authored with Darryl Landvater were published in 1989 and are generally accepted as defining the standards for MRPII software. His most recent book, *Sales and Operations Planning - Best Practices,* co-authored with John Dougherty was published in 2006.

Chris is President of Gray Research and one of the founders of Partners For Excellence. Gray Research offers consulting and education on the concepts and methods of world class performance. Partners For Excellence offers counseling and public and private seminars and workshops for executives and managers trying to make the changes needed for improved performance.

Chris was president of Oliver Wight Software Research, Inc. and one of the Oliver Wight Education Associates. He also developed and taught the "MRPII Software Survival Course", a class covering software evaluation and selection, software trends, and the role of systems people in implementing effective systems. Earlier, he held consulting and teaching positions with Software International Corporation, working with companies implementing MRPII. Prior to that, he was Manufacturing Systems Analyst at Ohaus Scale Corporation, a Class A company. During his consulting career, he has been associated with both R. D. Garwood, Inc. and The Oliver Wight Companies.

Chris has a BA in mathematics from Washington and Jefferson College and a MS in mathematics from Carnegie Mellon University. He is a past president of the North Shore chapter of APICS and is certified by APICS as a Fellow. He has spoken at numerous international conferences on manufacturing systems and methods. He is listed in six different volumes of Who's Who: Who's Who in America, Who's Who in the East, Who's Who in America's Emerging Leaders, Who's Who in Finance and Industry, Who's Who in Science and Engineering, and Who's Who in the World.

ISBN 141208210-2